Remaking Ourselves, Enterprise and Society

Transformation and Innovation Series

Series Editors:
Ronnie Lessem, University of Buckingham, UK
Alexander Schieffer, University of St. Gallen, Switzerland

This series on enterprise transformation and social innovation comprises a range of books informing practitioners, consultants, organization developers, development agents and academics how businesses and other organizations, as well as the discipline of economics itself, can and will have to be transformed. The series prepares the ground for viable twenty-first century enterprises and a sustainable macroeconomic system. A new kind of R & D, involving social, as well as technological innovation, needs to be supported by integrated and participative action research in the social sciences. Focusing on new, emerging kinds of public, social and sustainable entrepreneurship originating from all corners of the world and from different cultures, books in this series will help those operating at the interface between enterprise and society to mediate between the two and will help schools teaching management and economics to re-engage with their founding principles.

Current titles in this series

Spiritual Capital:
A Moral Core for Social and Economic Justice
Samuel D. Rima
ISBN 978-1-4094-0484-2

Integral Community:
Political Economy to Social Commons
Ronnie Lessem, Paul Chidara Muchineripi and Steve Kada
ISBN 978-1-4094-4679-8

Islam and Sustainable Development:
New Worldviews
Odeh Rashed Al-Jayyousi
ISBN 978-1-4094-2901-2

Remaking Ourselves, Enterprise and Society

An Indian Approach to Human Values in Management

G.P. RAO

GOWER

Gower Applied Business Research
Our programme provides leaders, practitioners, scholars and researchers with thought provoking, cutting edge books that combine conceptual insights, interdisciplinary rigour and practical relevance in key areas of business and management.

Published by
Gower Publishing Limited
Wey Court East
Union Road
Farnham
Surrey, GU9 7PT
England

Gower Publishing Company
110 Cherry Street
Suite 3-1
Burlington, VT 05401-3818
USA

www.gowerpublishing.com

British Library Cataloguing in Publication Data.
A catalogue record for this book is available from the British Library.

The Library of Congress has cataloged the printed edition as follows:
Rao, G. P.
  Remaking ourselves, enterprise and society : an Indian approach to human values in management / by G.P. Rao.
     pages cm. – (Transformation and innovation)
  Includes bibliographical references and index.
  ISBN 978-1-4094-4884-6 (hardback) – ISBN 978-1-4094-4885-3 (ebook) – ISBN 978-1-4094-7356-5 (epub)
  1. Management–Moral and ethical aspects–India. 2. Business ethics–India. I. Title.

  HF5387.5.I4R363 2013
  174'.4–dc23

                                                                    2013023798

  ISBN: 9781409448846 (hbk)
  ISBN: 9781409448853 (ebk – PDF)
  ISBN: 9781409473565 (ebk – ePUB)

Printed in the United Kingdom by Henry Ling Limited, at the Dorset Press, Dorchester, DT1 1HD

Contents

List of Figures

List of Tables

Prologue:
Human Life, an Odyssey

Although I had planned to write a prologue to this book, the structure that emerged was not as I had initially envisioned. While considering how to begin, I randomly picked up an issue of *The Speaking Tree*, a weekly publication of The Times of India group, dated 4 March 2012. The issue contained six quotations, each printed at the top of six of its eight pages. I reproduce here those six quotations, each with a brief interpretation.

1. 'Let not the sands of time get in your lunch' (Tony Hendra).

    - Sands of time: deterrents, irritants, distractions in one's life in the form of prejudices and other human frailties.

    - Lunch: one's goal, objective.

    - Message: let not your (mostly) self-created mental blocks stand in the way of your life and its goal.

2. 'Everything has been figured out, except how to live' (Jean-Paul Sartre).

    - Human beings have successfully mastered numerous aspects of life, except perhaps the most the meaningful one of how to live.

3. 'Feelings are like a colour chart that God has given us' (Keith Miller).

    • Feelings and emotions – like affection, care and concern – are innate human qualities meant for promoting goodness (in ourselves and others).

4. 'It's better to light a small candle than to curse the darkness' (Confucius).

    • It is easy to blame and to criticize, but it is preferable, to work out a solution, to find a way out.

5. 'God could not be everywhere, so he created mothers' (Jewish proverb).

    • God is symbolic of divinity, goodness and compassion. Mothers are endowed with these qualities.

    • Message: love is related to the heart; love is innate in mothers. Imbibing the motherly (feminine) quality of affection is a means of remaking ourselves as human beings.

6. 'If you could only love enough, you could be the most powerful person in the world' (Emmet Fox).

    • Love, affection, care and concern towards others enables us to win them over and to influence them.

    • Message: let us all try to imbibe these qualities – to remake ourselves.

Remarkably, the above six quotations – although not ordered sequentially – appear to form a logical and coherent sequence: As a consequence of mental blocks (Hendra) human beings do not know how to live (Miller) and are therefore in need of finding a way out (Confucius), which the mother, as a symbol of divinity (Jewish Proverb) and of affection and love for others (Emmet Fox), provides by being a means for remaking ourselves as human beings.

Details regarding the sources or authors of the quotations, their professions and the times and the places in which they lived strengthens our insight on the subject:

1. Tony Hendra (1941–), English satirist and writer.

2. Jean-Paul Sartre (1905–1980), French existentialist philosopher, playwright, novelist etc.

3. Keith Miller (1909–2004), Australian Test cricketer and a Royal Australian Air Force pilot.

4. Confucius (traditionally 551–479 BCE), Chinese thinker and social philosopher of the Spring and Autumn period.

5. Jewish proverb (timeless).

6. Emmet Fox (1886–1951), US minister, author, teacher, healer and mystic.

The persons quoted represent a variety of professions, from different periods ranging from before the Common Era to the contemporary, and from both the West and the East. They defy categorization on the basis of time, profession and place. By the same token, however, they establish that the quest for self-development is universal and never-ending but always illuminating and enriching.

In further exploration I took time to peruse the literature available on the subject of human beings and their need to 'remake' themselves by realizing that they had forgotten their inherent worth. The literature available is, understandably, legendary. The wisdom accumulated, ethos developed and consciousness evolved by humankind through religions, philosophical and belief systems, saints and seers endorse and reiterate that a human being needs to know Self as a means for self-realization and growth.

The *Atharvaveda* is one of the four original scriptures of India, known collectively as the Vedas. These are the Rig, Sama, Atharva and Yajur Vedas. The *Atharvaveda* deals with knowledge of the physical world and spirituality. The *Atharvaveda* (8/12) states:

Anantham Vitatam Purutranata Bhantavacha Samante |

Te Nakparaghcharati Vichinvan Vidwanbhutamuta Bhavyamasta |

[The endless, limitless is omnipresent and the one who is limited is united with limitless ... The one and only eternal is omnipresent. The limited and limitless are fused in each other. Scholar! Think and contemplate on the past, present and future, and tread on the path of growth and self-development. This should be an ideal for all human beings.]

The pursuit of knowledge is endless. Life is indeed an odyssey.

PART I
Overview

1

The Context and the Issue

The Objective of the Book: Transformation through Human Values

This book aims to understand peoples' efforts to remake themselves as human beings through their adherence to human values in the different roles they assume at different levels in their lives. Specifically, the book examines the relative roles of the concept of Spandan – based on faith in a human being's innate divinity – and its 3D Process of Diagnosis, Discovery and Development in enabling an organization to achieve an optimal balance between and among Transformational, Transactional and Terminal Human Values such that human beings become more capable in dealing with themselves and the environment in which they operate. To capture the essence of human values as motivators of human existence and growth, a still-evolving instrument known as the Spandan Spectrum of Human Values has been developed. The Spandan (heartbeat) Approach emanating from the awareness and acceptance of the innate divinity of human beings, the Spandan Spectrum of Human Values that describes the ingredients of human growth at transformational, transactional and terminal levels, and the Spandan 3D Process as the carrier of such transformations thus constitute the crux of the Indian approach to human values in management being forwarded in the book. It is submitted that the outcome of the application of the approach, spectrum and process is the enhancement of humans' capabilities in balancing their knowledge, skills and attitudes and values, that is, balancing:

- head and heart at the individual level

- results and relations at the institutional/organizational level

- material comforts and happiness at the societal level

- economic growth and social justice at the national level

- peace and prosperity at the global level

- the identification of self with others and the environment at the cosmic level.

The Genesis of the Spandan (Heartbeat) Approach

The Spandan Approach originates from my experience as a teacher in management and related roles for more than four decades and the belief systems I have developed over a period of time.

From 1964 to 1966 I was one of the first batch of students at the Indian Institute of Management, Calcutta (IIMC). The IIM, Calcutta and its counterpart in Ahmedabad (IIM, Ahmedabad) ushered in management education at the national level as an instrument for economic growth in India. I later continued my career as a teacher in management. Following my retirement from teaching in management in 1997, I had the good fortune to continue my multi-faceted work in teaching, research, training and consultancy in the sphere of human values in management and management education, culminating in 2001 in my assuming the role of founder-chairman of *Spandan*,[1] a voluntary organization committed to the propagation and inculcation of human values in management and society. As a consequence, my career in management progressed concurrently with the country's growth in the sphere of management education.

The origin and evolution of the idea of human values as an integral part of management and management education in India is to be seen in the context of the Government of India's initiation of professionalism in management in the early 1960s when, as mentioned, it established its first two Institutes of Management at Ahmedabad and Calcutta. The period since then can be divided broadly into three phases:

1.   Early 1960s to early 1980s: Emphasis on managerial communication – with the assumption that communication effectiveness is equivalent to managerial effectiveness and organizational performance.

2.   Early 1980s to early 1990s: Emphasis on managerial interpersonal effectiveness – with the assumption that interpersonal effectiveness

---

1   *Spandan* (in italics) will throughout the book refer to the voluntary organization.

is equivalent to managerial effectiveness and organizational performance.

3.   Early 1990s onwards: Emphasis on values orientation at the organizational level – with the assumption that values-based organization is equivalent to managerial effectiveness and organizational performance.

The belief here is that all human beings are innately divine and that their innate divinity is manifested through their basic goodness. This basic goodness is reflected through human beings' desire to be of help to others; to do good without necessarily expecting any return or reward. Thus the innate divinity, basic goodness and intrinsic altruism of human beings are seen as the crux of human existence, growth and development. Human sentiments, interactions and activities based upon this belief are the essential ingredients for human harmony. These three values are accordingly considered as generic, foundational and transformational human values.

The emergence of such human harmony is in turn based upon the operation of a trinity of concepts related to human behaviour: the Mother (empathy of the highest order), Spandan (heartbeat) and Universal Consciousness (Oneness). The concept of Mother represents faith in others and empathy of the highest order. Spandan, a Sanskrit word, means heartbeat, vibration and pulsation. Spandan is thus symbolic of sensitivity to, and identification with, others. Universal Consciousness represents the ultimate Oneness in all elements of the universe including human beings. The odyssey undertaken by human beings of self-diagnosis, discovery and development thus reaches its ultimate point in the concept of Universal Consciousness. As stated by Jacquelyn Small (2007), the American spiritual psychologist, 'You are not a human being trying to be spiritual; you are a spiritual being learning to be human' (p. 3).

Key Concepts , Perspectives and Initiatives

The key concepts, perspectives and initiatives dealt with in this book are:

- the innate divinity, intrinsic altruism and basic goodness of human beings as determinants of human existence and growth

- Spandan (heartbeat, vibration, pulsation, echo), as the binding element of the entire universe and its living organisms

- the Mother, as a symbol of, among others, (a) nurturing, caring, sharing and compassion, (b) faith in the basic goodness of others, and (c) empathy of the highest order

- the Spandan Approach, with emphasis on a high degree of sensitivity (like a mother) towards the needs of others as a quality of a leader

- the Spandan Spectrum of Human Values 2011

- the Spandan 3D Process of Diagnosis, Discovery and Development of the inculcation of human values in an organization

- experiential learning

- the manager as a *karma yogi*

- the Functionally Humane Organization (FHO)

- Focal Person–Resource Persons Interactive Sessions (FP–RP ISs)

- the synergy of human values in management between India and the West

- Institutional Civic Responsibility to Community through Human Values (ICRC-HV)

- the infusion of family values in management

- humanizing globalization through spiritual democracy

- the Spandan 51:49 leadership philosophy

- Grace Light (Divine Energy): *Brahmn*, Oneness, Cosmic Consciousness

- Gross Divinity Propensity (GDP)

The Target Readership

This book addresses itself to decision makers at the institutional level interested in going beyond their own personal and professional interests and involving themselves in humanizing their organization, community and society. The primary target audience consists of entrepreneurs, institution builders, CEOs, policy makers and other related functionaries in government and other non-profit organizations. Decision makers from institutions playing complementary roles in humanizing management and organizations are equally welcome. Such institutions include management institutions, professional bodies, the training and development fraternity, civil society and nongovernmental organizations.

References

Cascio, Jamai. 2006. Remaking Ourselves. *Journal of Evolution and Technology*, 15(1) (February): 87–90.

Chakraborty, S.K. 2004. *The Management and Ethics, Omnibus*. New Delhi: Oxford University Press.

Loy, David R. 2003. *The Great Awakening: A Buddhist Social Theory*. Boston, MA: Wisdom Publications.

Maira, Arun M. 2008. It is Good for Business. *The Times of India*, July 4, 2008.

Rao, G.P. 2002. Spandan and the Integral Development of the Human Person: Indian Insides, Experiences and Experiments. *Journal of Human Values*, 8(1) (January–June): 67–70.

——2010. *Humanizing Management: Transformation through Human Values*. New Delhi: Ane Books.

Small, Jacquelyn. 2007. *The Sacred Purpose of Being Human: A Journey through the Twelve Principles of Wholeness*. Deerfield Beach, FL: Health Communications Inc.

Wolf, Susan. 2000. *Meaning in Life and Why it Matters?*, The Tanner Lectures on Human Values, Princeton University, 7–8 November 2007.

2

The Concept: Its Origin and Evolution

The Context and the Issue

The Spandan Approach, which draws on the idea of the heartbeat (the Sanskrit word *spandan* may also denote pulsation, vibration, echo, wavelength and, possibly, human chemistry) as the essential instrument of human existence and growth 'originated' in August 1981, following discussion I had engaged in with a gathering of faculty members and students of a management course, on the management style most suitable to Indian culture and ethos. The discussion had led to the idea that perhaps management could develop relations with people through care, love, compassion, trust and faith – like a mother, as a symbol of empathy of the highest order.

The following section reproduces my first article published after the discussion ('Maternalistic Management Needed', 1981). The section following that reproduces excerpts from my paper 'Work Ethics, Work Ethic and Indian Psycho-Philosophy' (1990), on psychosocial philosophy as related to maternalistic management, the style denoting a nurturing culture, or, as Douglas McGregor described in his celebrated work *The Human Side of Enterprise* (1960), an agricultural approach to leadership.

Maternalistic Management Needed[1]

'Which management style is most effective in India?' is a question which evokes numerous, highly-conflicting responses from academics, researchers, practitioners and the public alike. But while this question is being 'probed'

---

1   This section is based directly on G.P. Rao, Maternalistic Style of Management Needed, *The Hindu*, 4 August 1981.

intellectually by academics and researchers, the practitioners are trying 'the hard way'. The answer, however, still eludes us.

By management style we mean the manner in which a manager, an executive, an officer or an administrator deals with others while discharging his or her functions formally in the given organization. The literature on the several types of management styles obtainable in different countries is voluminous. Most of these styles can be found in India, a country of continental dimensions, but it is thought that four styles of management broadly cover the predominant manner in which managers in the country go about discharging their duties. These are authoritarian, paternalistic, constitutional (or legalistic) and democratic participative.

In the authoritarian style the manager feels and says that he is the sole rule maker, and that others are to comply with his directions.

In the paternalistic style the manager is again the sole rule maker, but because of his sympathy towards employees in lower positions in the organization, who may also be downtrodden in their lives outside work, he acts towards them in a fatherly way. In other words, he provides services which are not strictly required under law. He takes care of the familial needs of his employees. He also most likely knows the names of all the employees in the organization. But the basic underlying assumption in all this is that the employees require taking care of, thereby implying that they cannot take care of themselves and that they also cannot be allowed to take care of themselves. The manager, in other words, acts as the father of the organization and considers the employees his children and treats them as such.

In the constitutional style of management the manager has to share rule-making because of statutory requirements, trade union rules and so on, but he is not necessarily mentally attuned to the idea. He still believes that rule making is his managerial prerogative. As a consequence he will create a façade that suggests he is functioning democratically and that the organization is trying to be the model employer.

In the democratic participative style of management the manager is convinced that it is only by functioning democratically that his own effectiveness can be improved and that the organization as a whole will benefit the most.

Of these four styles of management prevalent in India, the first and third – authoritarian and constitutional (or legalistic) – are nowadays effective only in the short term. Moreover these styles are no longer considered worthy of adopting. This leaves the paternalistic and the democratic participative styles of management. There are still many people who believe the paternalistic style is the most effective style for India. They feel this is the arrangement in which the manager is most comfortable and in which the managed are able to work with him equally comfortably. True, this was once the most prevalent style in India, and continues to be so even today in certain regions of the country where it has still not lost its charm over the people.

There are, however, clear indications that the paternalistic style is no longer effective and in the future will be even less so. The basic reason for this lies in the treatment of employees as children. Parents know very well that children cannot be treated today as they themselves were treated by their elders. Today's children respect their fathers not simply because they are fathers but only if they deserve to be respected because of their greater knowledge, experience and maturity.

Employees' unwillingness to accept managers as fathers has emerged in many contexts and in many forms, two examples of which are cited here. In the early 1960s the All India Trade Union Congress (AITUC), in its memorandum to the committee on labour welfare (1965), constituted by the Government of India, took exception to the type of social work done by society's women *vis-à-vis* families living in *chawls*, *jhuggies* and *busties* (slums and shantytowns), for example distributing fireworks, sweets and clothes on the occasion of Diwali. While the downtrodden need all these and many more things, the AITUC maintained they should not be given out of philanthropy and sympathy but as a matter of right, as something that society owes them.

Another example I observed as a consultant. An owner-managed industrial organization in Uttar Pradesh had a long-standing unusual practice of distributing warm clothes to workers at the onset of winter. However, one year the workers, while thanking the management for the gesture, declined to accept the clothes on the grounds that these were being distributed out of sympathy and that they would rather have them as a matter of right.

WOOLLY NOTIONS

The democratic participative style is a concept that on paper looks good but is very difficult to translate into action. Of course some researchers advance arguments based on scientific knowledge that biologically human beings are not inclined to participation and sharing, while hard-headed practitioners dismiss things like worker participation in management as woolly notions. Even if we agree for the sake of argument that the democratic participative style of management is a desirable style at least in principle, the question still remains as to its applicability in India.

We do not say that Indians are not intelligent or competent enough to embrace the concept. Nor do we say that if as a nation we are not in a position to adopt democracy in its true sense we should feel ashamed. But the fact remains that the country is not ready to imbibe the values of democracy and act accordingly. This is in no way something to be ashamed of and therefore to be concealed.

We therefore find that while the authoritarian and constitutional (or legalistic) styles of management cannot be considered effective or desirable, and it is too late to continue practising the paternalistic style, it is also too early to start practising the democratic participative style. The question, therefore, is: what is the way out?

I for one am fond of saying that while we are engaged headlong in discussing the effectiveness or otherwise of the father as an ideal figure, it is the most obvious alternative that we miss: the mother. I believe that if at all there is any style of management that is most suited to Indian conditions, it is what I call the 'maternalistic' style of management.

ATTITUDINAL VARIABLES

The concept of Mother is highly respected in India, and we should therefore attempt to evolve a management style based on the primacy of the Mother. We can identify certain attitudinal variables as the basis of such a style. One such variable is interdependence, which refers to the awareness of the manager (or any superior for that matter) that his effectiveness is dependent equally upon the contribution made by his subordinates.

Another attitudinal variable is one of treating others as adults, thereby implying that others are responsible and responsive. The consequence of such an attitude will be that the manager will think twice before concluding that he was right and others were wrong.

The third and the most important attitudinal variable is empathy. This refers to the desire and the ability of the manager to place himself in the shoes of others before evaluating their behaviour.

I was once travelling in a bus and the two seats in front of mine were occupied by a couple along with a child of about five years. Somewhere along the way the child suddenly became quite boisterous. Despite the parents' efforts to calm her down, the child continued to be somewhat hysterical, disturbing other passengers. Immediately the father became angry and gave the child a tap on the head, while at the same time the mother gave the child a dummy.

Herein lies the difference between the paternalistic and the maternalistic styles of management. When a father becomes angry towards his undisciplined child he inflicts punishment as a means of correction. The mother, on the other hand, tries to find the reason behind the undisciplined behaviour by putting herself in the child's shoes and then thinks of the appropriate corrective action, in this case by offering the child a dummy to direct her in a less disturbing direction.

THE MOTHER–CHILD RELATIONSHIP CONCEPT

It is significant to note that the concept of the mother–child relationship – at least as perceived by the managed – is beginning to permeate the workplace in India. Some years back I was studying the industrial relations situation in major bank. As part of the fieldwork I was interviewing a clerk in one of its branch offices. In order to understand her loyalty to the bank I asked her the (usual) questions: If you were offered Rs 100/- per month less than what you are currently receiving, would you leave the bank? If you were offered the same salary as you are currently receiving would you leave the bank? If you were offered Rs 100/- per month more than what you are currently receiving would you leave the bank? To all the three questions she replied in the negative. I asked the reasons and her response was, 'The bank is my mother; how can I leave my mother?'

A little reflection reveals that the maternalistic style of management is more likely to be acceptable to managers in India because, unlike in the case of the democratic participative style, they need not abdicate their managerial prerogative.

Instead of struggling to rehabilitate a no longer workable paternalistic style of management or trying to invoke an as yet unworkable democratic participative management style, why not apply some method that is rooted in that which is most respected by the society, which is likely to be most effective and which is acceptable to the managers? This method, based on the primacy of the mother as an ideal figure, we call the maternalistic style of management.

Work Ethics and Indian Psycho-Philosophy[2]

THE CONTEXT AND THE ISSUE

Philosophy

Philosophy is defined, among other things, as the 'pursuit of wisdom and knowledge: Investigation of the nature of being: Knowledge of the causes and laws of all things' (*Chamber's Twentieth Century Dictionary* 1981, p. 1003).

It is agreed that defining philosophy as a discipline is a difficult task.[3] Discussing this issue in the context of the evolution of philosophy, Herbert Spencer feels that there is, however,

> *a real if unavowed agreement among them in signifying by this title a knowledge which transcends ordinary knowledge. That which remains as the common element in these conceptions of philosophy, after the elimination of their discordant elements, is – knowledge of the highest degree of generality. We see this tacitly asserted by the simultaneous inclusion of God, Nature and Man, within its scope; or still more distinctly by the division of Philosophy as a whole into Theological, Physical, Ethical, etc. For that which characterizes the genus of which these are species, must be something more general than that which distinguishes anyone species. (Spencer 1862, Pt II, Ch. 1, §37)*

In the Indian context, 'philosophy is knowledge that rises above creed and scripture, vision and ecstasy, art and science, its sole object being a complete realization of all that life implies'. This statement was made by Sri Sacchidananda Shivabhinava Narasimha Bharati Swami of Sringeri in Mysore, one of India's most distinguished philosophers of recent times (quoted in Subrahmanya Iyer 1966, p. 595).

A question, however, arises as to whether it is possible to define, describe or identify any particular sphere as 'Indian' philosophy. One can talk about

---

2   This section is based directly on edited excerpts from G.P. Rao, Work Ethics, Work Ethic and Indian Psycho-Philosophy: Some Ideas on a Maternalistic Model, in S.K. Chakraborty (ed.), *Human Response Development: Exploring Transformational Values* (New Delhi: Wiley Eastern, 1990), pp. 110–18.

3   Cf. 'Philosophy is not easy to define. It has no subject matter in the sense that a specialized discipline such as Chemistry or Geography does, for there is no restricted set of phenomena or object with which Philosophy is concerned' (Blackstone 1941).

'Hindu' philosophy, 'Muslim' philosophy and so on – but not a philosophy denoting the country as a whole.

Psycho-philosophy

A perusal of the literature, and discussion with academics involved in the field indicates that psycho-philosophy as an area of knowledge as such does not as yet exist. This is certainly the case with regards to India. The *Sadshastras* (Six *Shastras*), for instance, consist of *Tharka (dialectics, logic and reasoning)*, *Vyakarma (grammar)*, *Dharma (religious law)*, *Meemamsa (investigation and enquiry)*, *Vaidya (knowledge or science)* and *Jyothisah* (astronomy and astrology), but significantly, do not include psychology. One has, as a consequence, to create one's own interpretation as to what constitutes psycho-philosophy in the Indian context. A difficult job indeed!

Ethics

Ethics has been defined, among others, as 'the science of morals, that branch of philosophy which is concerned with human character, and conduct: A system of morals, rules of behavior' (*Chamber's Twentieth Century Dictionary* 1981, p. 448).

In the Indian context, quoting V. Subrahmanya Iyer (1966), we find:

> *In ethics the first rule of right conduct starts from the urge in the mother, to identify herself with her child in pain or pleasure and, to seek common good. It proceeds in ever widening circles of such identification, till it includes the whole of humanity. (p. 596)*

> *The various ethical ideals find their final explanation in the Hindu doctrine that another is non-different from one. The goal is to see one's self as all and all as one's self The all here comprehends even animals and plants. Hindu ethics enjoins not only the seeking of the common but also the scrupulous avoidance of injury to anyone because by inflicting injury one not only ignores non-different but also perpetuates the error of the conception that one's self or ego is a reality and that separate from the self the injured. The ideal in ethical conduct is to realize not merely the 'non-difference' of ego and non-ego, but the fact that the ego or the individual self, as 'idea', is unreal. The more one represses the ego till it is effaced as a separate entity*

the greater the virtue. This is not done by suicide or chloroform. For,
beginning with self-restraint, ethics leads one up to self-sacrifice in
life, which means the dissolution of the ego in others or in the all. And
this is the same as saying that the realization of the all as the ego is the
ideal or goal. (pp. 613–14)

Work ethics

Similarly to psycho-philosophy, it is difficult to define a concept like 'work ethics'. In view of the fact, however, that work is defined, among others, as effort directed to an end, or more specifically, employment, for the purpose of our discussion, we can define work ethics as 'that branch of philosophy which is concerned with human character and conduct in the context of employment' or 'a system of morals, rules of behaviour in the context of employment'.

To sum up the position so far: (1) by philosophy, we mean knowledge of the highest degree of generality; (2) by work ethics we mean that branch of philosophy which is concerned with human character and conduct in the context of employment; (3) by combining (1) and (2) we can say that the relationship of philosophy to work ethics is the identification or development of the knowledge of the highest degree of generality relating to the human character and conduct in the context of employment; but (4) with reference to 'Indian' philosophy and 'Indian' psycho-philosophy we are not on a sure footing; the former ('Indian' philosophy), because at yet no specific branch of knowledge, or sphere or activity, can be characterized as 'Indian philosophy'; and the latter ('psycho'-philosophy) because psycho-philosophy as a branch of knowledge is yet in its infancy – particularly with regards to India.

Given the complexities, ambiguities and uneven growth of the disciplines involved, one way to tackle the issue is to identify a concept, an idea, an image which (a) has been, and still is, sacred to all religions, (b) has been and still is, therefore, influencing the thinking and actions of Indians as a whole and, (c) has a bearing on work ethics in the present day. I submit that the concept of Mother satisfies all the conditions laid down. The subsequent part of this chapter, accordingly, shares my views, through an analytical framework, on the relevance of the concept of Mother to organizational functioning and its work ethics.

AN ANALYTICAL FRAMEWORK

The extra-organizational environment and the concept of Mother

The extra-organizational environment is taken as the input, and, following Farmer and Richman (1965), consists of the educational, socio-cultural, legal-political and economic environments. Of these, the socio-cultural environment has a relatively greater impact on the generation and growth of ideas and images, such as the Mother, in society, which have a bearing on the functioning of an organization and its ethics.

Table 2.1   The concept of Mother and its relevance to organizational functioning and work ethics

Extra-organizational environment	The concept of Mother	Intra-organizational environment (subsystems)	Impact upon organization and its work ethics
• Educational Sociological Cultural • Legal-political • Economic • Socio-cultural • (Philosophical stages) • Religions • Revelations • Ecstatic experience • Intuitions • Visions • Opinions • Hypotheses	• Identification with others • Seeking the common good • Avoidance of injury to others • Self-restraint • Self-sacrifice • Patience and tolerance • Expressing joy of creation • Compassion • Moral courage • Empathy • Trust • Forgivingness • Possessiveness	• Goals • Technical • Structural • Psycho-social • Managerial • Psycho-social subsystem • Knowledge • Skills • Attitudes towards organization, work, self, others etc. • Managerial subsystem • Assumptions about people • Styles of management • Motivation and leadership	• Organization • Survival • Growth • Groups • Performance • Cohesiveness • Morale • Individual • Productivity • Discipline • Satisfaction • Development

The generation of ideas and images in a society, following philosophical enquiry, takes place because of (a) religions, (b) revelations, (c) ecstatic experience, (d) intuitions, (e) visions, (f) opinions and (g) hypotheses.

The concept of Mother in India, as emanating from the above can be described by numerous attributes (see Table 2.1):

A)   It is significant – and perhaps not co-incidental – that ethics in the Indian context starts with the Mother, who has the following attributes:

   a)   self-identification with others

   b)   seeking the common good

   c)   as a corollary to (b), the scrupulous avoidance of injury to others

   d)   self-restraint

   e)   self-sacrifice

B)   The perusal of Indian scriptures, epics etc. reveals the following as other attributes of the Mother:

   f)   patience and tolerance

   g)   experiencing the joy of creation (for as a mother she is also the maker)

   h)   compassion

   i)   moral courage

   j)   empathy of the highest order. In a discourse on the empathy and nobility of the Mother, M.S. Rajagopala Sastrigal drew on one of the episodes from India's epic the *Mahabharata* that recounts the exemplary restraint shown by Draupadi when all her children were wiped out by Aswathama. Aswathama was caught and was due to be executed by the angered Arjuna, but Draupadi made him desist from resorting to this retributive act. An important plea she made to that end was: 'The greatest sorrow for a woman is to be robbed of her children by cruel fate. It is unfathomable. If Aswathama is removed, his mother's heart will collapse and I do not want this to happen.'

C)   For the last several years or so, I have been involved in understanding the concept of the Mother and its relevance to management in

India.[4] Based on such understanding, the following could be added as further attributes of the Mother:

k)   trust

l)   forgiving nature

m)   possessiveness

SUMMARY

This section of the chapter has aimed primarily at offering an analytical framework on the concept of Mother and its relevance to organizational functioning and work ethics. While certain parts of the framework, like the relevance of the concept of Mother to the managerial sub-system, have been put to the empirical test, much needs to be done in terms of strengthening and verifying such efforts. The extent to which such efforts help academics and practitioners to evolve indigenous models of management would be the true indicator of the success of the combined efforts of all concerned in India at looking meaningfully into our past and translating such meaning into effective action.

References

Blackstone, William T. (ed.). 1941. *Meaning and Existence: Introductory Readings in Philosophy*. New York: Holt Rinehart and Winston.

Farmer, Richard and Barry Richman. 1965. *Comparative Management and Economic Progress*. Homewood, IL: Richard D. Irwin.

McGregor, Douglas. 1960. *The Human Side of Enterprise*. New York: McGraw-Hill.

Rao, G.P. 1981. Maternalistic Style of Management Needed. *The Hindu*, 4 August.

——1982. Maternalistic Management. *Indian Management*, 21 (5 May): 17–19.

——1985–86. Maternalistic Management. UGC National Lecture, unpublished.

——1990, Work Ethics, Work Ethic and Indian Psycho-Philosophy: Some Ideas on a Maternalistic Model. In S.K. Chakraborty (ed.), *Human Response Development: Exploring Transformational Values*. New Delhi: Wiley Eastern, pp. 110–18.

---

4   See Rao (1981, 1982 and 1985–86).

Spencer, Herbert. 1862. *First Principles of a New System of Philosophy*. London: Williams and Norgate.

Subrahmanya Iyer, V. 1966. Man's Interest in Philosophy: An Indian View. In S. Radhakrishnan and J.H. Muirhead (ed.), *Contemporary Indian Philosophy*. New Delhi: S. Chand.

3

The Spandan Approach, 3D Process and Spectrum of Human Values

The Context and the Issue

The Price Waterhouse study *Straight from the CEO* (1998) captured the increasing need felt by CEOs the world over to be more people-oriented and humane in their dealings with others when it stated: 'CEOs of today wanted A, B and C: A, Awareness; B, Belief; and C, Conduct.'

- A = awareness and knowledge: of self, of self in others, and of one's self and of others at all levels, that is, at individual, group, institutional, national and global levels;

- B = beliefs and values of which human beings at different levels should be aware and accepting and to which they should adhere in their personal and professional life;

- C = the conduct and ethical behaviour that evolves at different levels as a result of adherence in their personal and professional life to the human values referred to in B.

What CEOs wanted more than a decade ago has become, in a way, 'the signature tune' for the current work on humanizing management.

The current author has had the opportunity to observe and come to understand human behaviour over a period of nearly five decades. This opportunity arose in his roles as a teacher, researcher, trainer, consultant and institution builder in management, and, finally, since 2001, as Founder/Chairman of *Spandan*, a voluntary organization committed to the propagation and inculcation of human values in management and society. As a consequence of the experiences and insights the author has gained, he has come to a rather unusual – one may even say 'quixotic' – insight regarding understanding and working with and through others.

Working *with* others denotes the one who is interacting (focal person) working with persons at the same or a similar level. These include colleagues, peers, friends, associates etc. These are lateral human interactions. Working *through* others denotes the focal person working with persons, who are usually at a lower level to the focal person, whose performance becomes the responsibility of the focal person. These are vertical human interactions.

The insight is that understanding and working with and through others is both extremely difficult and very easy. It is extremely difficult while one fails to develop an equation with others based upon mutual love, trust and respect. The equation could be functional, professional or personal, and the others within a given organization could include immediate superiors, colleagues and peers, and subordinates. Once the equation comprising, essentially, mutual love, trust and respect, is created, developed and maintained, working with and through others becomes very easy. The entire and only challenge facing all concerned in management and management education is thus: How is it possible to create, develop and maintain an equation, wavelength, chemistry, bond or vibration – integral to the work ethic and culture at the organizational level – such that a Functionally Humane Organization is created. (Point of view).

Going beyond the management of organizations, the challenge of developing the equation is similarly faced by all human beings at the levels of society, country, the world and the universe. (Viewing point).

The Spandan (Heartbeat) Way

Significantly, the answer to the challenges of developing an equation at the level of organizations for management, and at other levels for humankind in general, lies in one particular insight and phenomenon that can be described variously as Oneness, Cosmic Consciousness or *Brahmn* (a Sanskrit word denoting universal unity). Animate and inanimate beings, from the micro level of an individual organism like a human being to the macro of the entire universe are bound together. What binds these entities and levels is vibration, pulsation, echo, heartbeat or Spandan. This bond in turn emanates from the adherence of three fundamental values: innate divinity, basic goodness and intrinsic altruism.

The book *Humanising Management: Transformation through Human Values* (2010) accepted this postulate and attempted to translate the A, B and C in management described above through a 3D process of diagnosis, discovery and development to inculcate human values in the work ethic of an organization. These values are anchored to the mission statement of the given organization and integrated with its strategic management, with the assumption and experience that such integration enables management to achieve an optimal balance between results and relations, thereby developing a Functionally Humane Organization.

The Spandan 3D Process

A basic premise of the Spandan Approach is that human behaviour is a function of both individual and situation, and that primary responsibility for having correct and complete self-awareness, acceptance and action lies in the 'self', be it at the individual or any other broader level. The first message, therefore, is to 'start with self', and the first step, therefore, is self-diagnosis, self-discovery and self-development. This is the crux of the Spandan Approach: a 3D approach comprising diagnosis, discovery and development utilizing experiential learning consisting of introspection and feedback. The process begins with self at the individual level, and moves on to the levels of group, organization and society, and it is grounded in faith in the basic goodness of others. This faith becomes the credo for managers to humanize management, and it thus becomes the core human value in the process.

The manager in this process of humanizing management plays three roles. Since the manager first targets herself in the process, she becomes the object. And since she is part of the management system of authority that decides upon and initiates the change process, she also becomes the subject. Finally, since experiential learning, which provides the substance for change, in essence means 'self-learning'/'self-teaching', the manager also becomes the action. The manager thus is the subject, verb and object of the process of humanizing management.

This process of learning, with faith in the basic goodness of human beings as the pivotal credo, has been central to the author's five decades of experience at both personal and professional levels since he became initiated as a student into the field of management in the early 1960s. Furthermore, the author believes, it is a never-ending odyssey, always nerve breaking but ever enriching. As the Spandan 3D Process, the expected outcome of this transformation through human values, with faith in the human being as the ground, is the evolution of a Functionally Humane Organization with an on-going optimal balance between results and relations. The Spandan 3D Process of Diagnosis, Discovery and Development is thus a means of inculcating human values in an organization. The sequential salient features of the process can be described thus:

a)   Develop, or revisit, the mission statement as an anchor of the organization and …

b)   weave the values into the work fabric …

c)   through experiential learning and …

d)   by integrating the values with HRD and strategic management …

e)   to achieve an optimal balance between results and relations as a means …

f)   to evolve a Functionally Humane Organization with …

g)   top management support and an effective core group as its executive arm.

This process is outlined in Figure 3.1 in the form of a model based on the *systems* approach.

SPANDAN : INCULCATION OF HUMAN VALUES ANCHORED TO MISSION STATEMENTS
AND OBTAINING OPTIMAL BALANCE BETWEEN RESULTS AND RELATIONS

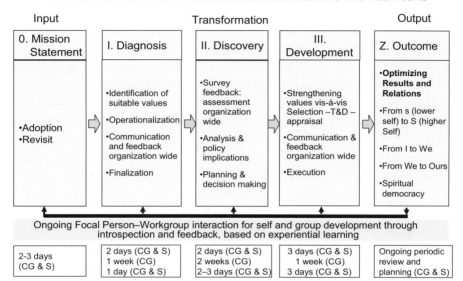

CG: Core group: Head of Institution, Chairman: 8–10 members, representing the different segments; and HRD/any other as Convenor
S: Spandan: Facilitator

Figure 3.1   **The Spandan 3D Process of Diagnosis, Discovery and Development**

MISSION STATEMENT – DIAGNOSIS – DISCOVERY – DEVELOPMENT – OUTCOME

- *Objective and duration*: Human values anchored to the mission statement of the given organization, enveloping selection, appraisal, training and development (T&D), work ethic and commitment. Seven to nine weeks involving 16 to 20 contact days with *Spandan* as the facilitator to complete one cycle of inculcation of human values.

- *Process*: 3D process consisting of diagnosis, discovery and development and based on experiential learning. The core group plays the role of executive arm, conductor of research, advisor to top management and as the change agent subsequent to the completion of the tasks of *Spandan* as the facilitator of the given cycle of inculcation.

- *On-going activity*: The core group with *Spandan* visiting periodically to continue the process, which is an ever-continuing activity.

MISSION STATEMENT AS THE ANCHOR

With human values the key to management achieving as best as possible the organization's objectives, the mission statement accordingly assumes a pivotal role in the process of inculcating those values. Furthermore, the mission statement becomes particularly important in determining the nature of and extent to which the values are woven into the work fabric, as, by taking this role, it assuages concerns and apprehensions that sometimes arise when it is thought that dealing with 'values' may involve preaching and/or renunciation. Such apprehension can easily lead to an organization going astray as it attempts to inculcate the values in the system. Whenever, therefore, an organization decides to adopt the Spandan 3D Process, the first step to take is adopting a new, or revisiting its current, mission statement. Hence, the first box in the analytical framework outlined in Figure 3.1 is the Mission Statement.

WEAVING THE VALUES INTO THE WORK FABRIC

Once the mission statement has been either adopted or revisited, the management or core group will assess the extent to which the objective of the organization has been achieved. Next, in order to improve upon accomplishment of the statement, the role of values will be examined. This process comprises three steps:

Step 1: Diagnosis

The management or core group assess the relevance of the 33 human values included in the Spandan Spectrum of Human Values 2011 (see following section), choosing those they consider relevant. There is no hard and fast rule on the number of values to be chosen. The purpose is to:

a)   maintain a balance between the values oriented to results and those oriented to relations

b)   choose an optimal number (normally between six and ten) and

c)   ensure that, to the members of the organization as a whole, the purpose is clear and focused.

Having identified the given number of values, three exercises are to be undertaken:

1. defining, describing or giving a meaning to each value

2. operationalizing each value in terms of behavioural manifestations and performance parameters

3. identifying the possibly undesirable consequences of improper, injudicious and inadequate or excess adherence to each of the values concerned.

A document delineating the values identified along with their relevant operationalization details and precautions will then be circulated and feedback solicited from all members of the organization. The core group will then finalize the diagnosis task, keeping in mind the feedback received.

Step 2: Discovery

This relates to assessing the nature and extent of adherence to the values thus identified, at the individual, workgroup and organization levels. Feedback is obtained and used to draw a picture of the extent of adherence at the different levels.

Step 3: Development

This refers to the steps to be undertaken to improve upon the level of adherence. Basic documents will be prepared by the core group and feedback will be sought. Thereafter, a plan of action will be prepared.

THE SELF AND EXPERIENTIAL LEARNING

The Spandan Approach and 3D Process of inculcating values has been – and still is – evolving. The bedrock of both the approach and the process is *self* – self-awareness, self-awakening and self-actualization at the individual, professional and organizational levels. This provides the rationale for experiential learning, which employs introspection and feedback. Experiential learning is basically the obverse of participant observation, wherein participants have the enviable task of participating in the discussions and deliberations 'intellectually' and animatedly and yet are required to observe and assess their own sentiments, interactions and activities as objectively as possible. In the Oriental tradition this is known as the 'witness approach'.

INTEGRATING THE VALUES WITH HUMAN RESOURCE DEVELOPMENT (HRD) AND STRATEGIC MANAGEMENT

Human resource development (HRD)

The inculcation of select values is necessary but not sufficient. The values and their adherence must be linked to other, related HRD functions.

The first such function is 'Selection'. When hiring – at senior levels and for certain critical positions in particular – care should be taken to select those candidates with the right mind-set and proper attitudes. As observed by Peter Drucker (1954), the damage done to an organization by a dishonest manager is more grievous than that caused by an incompetent manager.

The second HRD function is 'Training and Development' (T&D). In this regard the entire mechanism of the process should be made part of any induction programme. Workshops should be held on the 3D process as soon as the process is introduced, interactive sessions can be held with eminent persons in the related fields, and core group members and others can be sent for training and development at appropriate places and in appropriate areas.

The third HRD function is 'Performance Appraisal'. When select values have been incorporated as parameters in the appraisal system, the system becomes a powerful tool for motivation.

The fourth HRD function is 'Managerial Succession'. A well-planned managerial succession and career planning strategy will help greatly in attracting and retaining people of the right calibre and integrity interested in a long-term career with the organization.

The fifth sphere of activity relating to HRD is rather subtle but just as significant. The ambiance, social culture and informal atmosphere of an organization are important features of the organizational life.

For example, the Chairman and Managing Director (CMD) of a large organization, which he had built single-handedly, was respected – almost revered – by one and all. However, during interviews with senior functionaries of the organization, a very interesting set of responses emerged, stating that, although they respected the CMD, they did so only from a distance. Furthermore, they felt that his participation in family activities and social functions would go a long way to develop a closer relationship both to him and to the company.

At the final meeting, after a series of workshops on the inculcation of values had been completed, the CMD was apprised of these feelings and perception of him. His immediate and spontaneous response was, 'Professor, this is an eye opener for me.' Creating opportunities for informal get-togethers as part of the on-going process have been found to be effective in promoting *bonhomie* throughout the company.

Strategic management

Since the process of inculcation starts with the mission statement, its conclusion should be achieved through the strategic management of the company. In other words, all possible energy and resources should be geared towards completion of the process, keeping in view the company's long-term goals.

OPTIMAL BALANCE BETWEEN RESULTS AND RELATIONS

Balance between results and relations

The Spandan Spectrum of Human Values for the work situation contains 33 values, and these values can be categorized in terms of results and relations.

- Results relate to task orientation and are organization specific. Some examples of such values are profits, customer orientation and shareholders' claims.

- Relations refer to social, emotional functions and are people/individual specific. Some examples of such values are fairness, employee needs and compassion.

Some values are more difficult to categorize because they are more or less equally organization specific and individual specific. Some examples of such values are creativity, commitment and discipline.

In selecting the values, care needs to be taken to achieve an optimal balance between and among such values.

Balance with reference to the three broad categories of human values

The other way of achieving balance is with reference to the three broad categories of human values:

1. fundamental, transformational values

2. instrumental, transactional values

3. end-state, terminal values

The Spandan Spectrum of Human Values, 2011

As stated earlier, the Spandan Approach rests on belief in the innate divinity, intrinsic altruism and basic goodness of human beings, and the Spandan 3D Process aims to translate this belief into a reality in work situations. The process consists of (a) evolving a vision and mission statement for the organization, and (b) inculcating suitable human values in the work ethic through diagnosis, discovery and development, (c) as integral to HRD initiatives like selection, training and development and performance appraisal, and (d) linking them to its strategic management in the form of an on-going optimal balance between its results and relations.

A first attempt to identify human values considered suitable and important in work situations as a means to develop a values-oriented work ethic was made in 1995–96 (see Rao 1996). These values were subsequently modified in 1999–2000 (see Rao 2002) and 2010 (see Rao 2010). The most recent revisit, the Spandan Spectrum of Human Values 2011, attempts to simplify, rationalize, update and codify the human values. Experiences gained so far in the administration and application of the Spandan Spectrum of Human Values across the country to cross-sections of society, and recent and on-going developments of international importance such as globalization, cross-cultural management, economic meltdown and corporate arrogance, have all played an important role in the process.

Subsequent thought processes have been based on three assumptions which, in turn, lead to three categories of human values that act as pillars of human existence and growth.

The first assumption is that, starting with self as the smallest entity on the micro level and then moving on to group, institution, society, the world and the universe as a whole, *Oneness* (or *Cosmic Consciousness*) is the relevant fundamental human value. This belief and awareness is manifested at both the macro and the interpersonal levels. At the macro level, it manifests as *respecting nature and Mother Earth* and *sustainability*. At the interpersonal level, it manifests as *belief in the innate divinity, basic goodness and intrinsic altruism of human beings*. These five fundamental human values, I submit, enable human beings to transform themselves from the lower self to the higher Self and are thus here referred to as fundamental or Transformational Human Values.

The second assumption is that human beings aim, ultimately, at satisfaction at two levels. The first is the material level: material comforts, economic wellbeing and *prosperity*. The second is the psychic level: *happiness*, contentment and self-fulfilment. These two human values are considered end-state or Terminal Human Values.

The third assumption relates to the means and instruments required to obtain an optimal balance between *prosperity* and *happiness* based upon adherence to the five fundamental values. These are called instrumental or Transactional Human Values and can be classified into five categories: personal, professional, group-oriented, organizational/institutional and global. These five categories consist of a total of 26 human values, or clusters of human values.

Table 3.1 outlines the five Transformational, 26 Transactional and two Terminal Human Values – making a total of 33. As a whole, these represent the Spandan Spectrum of Human Values 2011. Figure 3.2 provides a pictorial representation of these groups of values as they relate to the concept of Gross Divinity Propensity (see Epilogue).

Table 3.1 Spandan Spectrum of Human Values 2011

Fundamental, Transformational Human Values	Instrumental, Transactional Human Values					End-state, Terminal Human Values
	Personal	Professional	Group	Organizational	Globalization-induced	
4. Belief in basic goodness of human beings	3. Behavioural flexibility	15. Emotional detachment	11. Cooperating attitude	1. Accountability	9. Competitive spirit	21. Happiness – contentment
5. Belief in innate divinity in human beings	10. Conviction	19. Equanimity	16. Empathy	2. Autonomy in decision making	12. Creativity – innovation	29. Prosperity – material comforts
6. Belief in intrinsic altruism of human beings	23. Humility	28. Professional attachment	25. Mutual understanding and respect	7. Commitment	13. Cultural adaptiveness	
26. Oneness	24. Integrity	32. Service orientation	33. Team spirit	8. Community interest	18. Entrepreneurship	
31. Respect for nature and Mother Earth				14. Customer satisfaction	22. Hospitable disposition	
				17. Employee orientation	27. Preparedness	
				20. Fairness		
				30. Respect for authority		

Note: numbers apply to values as listed alphabetically (see, for example, Spandan Spectrum Response Sheet – Chapter 4, Appendix)

SPIRITUALITY AND HUMAN BEINGS
Gross Divinity Propensity

TERMINAL HUMAN VALUES (2)
1: Prosperity, Material Comforts
2: Happiness, Contentment

TRANSACTIONAL HUMAN VALUES (26)
1: Personal (4)
2: Professional (4)
3: Group-oriented (4)
4: Organizational (8)
5: Globalization-induced (6)

TRANSFORMATIONAL HUMAN VALUES (5)
1: Basic goodness, Innate Divinity, Intrinsic Altruism (3)
2: Oneness, Respect for Nature (2)

Figure 3.2   The Spandan Spectrum of Human Values – Gross Divinity
              Propensity

References

Crum, Thomas. 1987. *The Magic of Conflict*. New York: Simon & Schuster.
Drucker, Peter. 1954. *The Practice of Management*. New York: Harper and Brothers.
Price Waterhouse. 1998. *Straight from the CEO*. New York: Simon & Schuster.
Rao, G.P. 1996. *Human Values in Industrial Organisations: Feminine Perspective* (IIMC-MCHV Research Monograph). New Delhi: Sage.
——2002. Self Control as a Managerial Value (AICTE Emeritus Fellowship Study, 1999–2002). Unpublished.
——2010. *Humanising Management: Transformation through Human Values*. New Delhi: Ane Books.

4

The Spandan Approach:
Further Insights

The Context and the Issue

This chapter – which offers an overview of the Spandan Approach – aims to add further insights into the approach. The following two sections present commentaries on the concepts of Mother and maternalistic management, and on the Spandan Approach as presented in the present work.

These are followed by a communication submitted, at my request, by Stephen Randall, who has developed a system he calls Management by Values (MBV), a system very similar to the Spandan Approach. His submission presents a brief comparative overview of the two.

The final section reviews certain well-established and ancient cultural milieus bearing similarities to the Spandan Approach. This section owes its origin to Ronnie Lessem of Buckingham University, UK. The concept of the Spandan Approach, Lessem suggested, might be comparable to the Japanese concept of *kaizen*, African *ubuntu* and Chinese *guanxi*.

Two Commentaries on Maternalistic Management

SWAMI YUKTANANDA, THE INSTITUTE OF VALUE ORIENTATION AND ENVIRONMENTAL EDUCATION, VIVEKANANDA NIDHI, CALCUTTA

> *I deeply appreciate the deep psychological insight of mother-concept and its multifaceted relatedness not only to work situations, but also to work life.*

I have gone through some of the puja rituals and can see that the whole approach is psychosomatic in quality improvement on the basis of holism-concept and at that almost anorganic view. If you and your team will go deeper into the psychological aspect of Patanjala's Yohadarshan, Bhagavat Gita and the common search for the identity of the self (individual), you will find assured methods to develop managerial attitudes by using the imaginations and images, faith and belief to the advantage. Just an illustration: Visada (depression) has been transformed into yoga in the very first chapter of Gita.

These few lines are just a reflection of my loud thinking and I became very informal while dictating the letter.

Calcutta, May 6, 1968.

H.R. KANORIA, A LEADING INDUSTRIALIST, CALCUTTA

The concept of mother in management is entirely innovative in these days of global economic crisis due to greed, greed and greed. The concept of mother is much more appealing than the concept of trusteeship of Gandhi and ethics in management. The concept of mother and spirituality through service in management will relieve the economy and the society of many ills and bring peace, harmony, service and growth in the corporate world.

Creation, sustenance, service, balance (destructive elements to balance new creation) are the eternal law of earth. Earth is sustained by dharma *(righteousness, welfare, equity and the magnetic force of love), scientists call them the law of gravitation.*

Look at the mother not only in human beings, but also animal mothers, bird mothers, plantation mothers, inanimate and animate mothers. How the mother gives unselfishly … for nurturing the child/offspring; even after the child becomes a man or woman, the mother continues to think of the welfare of children; mother treats all the children equally and fairly, but based on their individual nature and fair liking and so on mothers give their life for the sake of children.

How beautifully Adi Shri Shankaracharya said, 'the mother even takes care of children who hurt her'. Bhagawan Sri RamaKrishna told his disciples to see the relation with mother as with GOD. Be a child to GOD and affirm in GOD as we do to our mother.

The concept of Mother and Management will percolate:

1. *Unselfish love*

2. *Creative ideas*

3. *Innovation*

4. *Sustenance*

5. *Equity*

6. *Dealing differently with each human*

7. *Self-control and self-denial*

8. *Compassion*

9. *Harmony and peace*

10. *Justice for all*

11. *Faith in all.*

Two Student Commentaries on the Spandan Approach

BALASARASWATI BHARATHY, AN ENTREPRENEUR, CHENNAI

A. On altruism: Good/bad and altruism/selfishness co-exist in each of us. And to get in touch with the divinity in us, one has to transcend the dualities – both raga *(attachment) and* dvesa *(aversion).*

B. On balancing Head and Heart: One has to awaken the faculties of head, heart and hands. The head represents intelligence, wisdom, knowledge, understanding, awareness and observation. The heart represents feelings, emotions and sentiments. The hands represent the ability to act, to perform, to create. The ability to balance these three will make an individual complete. According to the yogic principle, the qualities of head, heart and hands are not balanced at present. There is a simple reason. Each personality, each nature, each person is governed by 3 attributes: sattwa, *the quality of purity and luminosity;* rajas, *the quality of activity, dynamism and aggressiveness; and* tamas, *the quality of lethargy and dullness. These three qualities condition the expression of head, heart and hands.*

FRANKLIN, A SENIOR SOFTWARE PROFESSIONAL

When I read your mail on 'vibration/sound' from the Indian Vedas, I was amazed at the striking similarity with the spoken 'Word' as in the Book of John Chapter 1 of the Israelite Vedanta. ... 'In the beginning was the Word, and the Word was with God, and the Word was God.'

The Spandan Approach and Stephen Randall's Management by Values (MBV) Approach: A Comparison by Stephen Randall, the Originator of the MBV Approach

In both academic and business worlds, by means of the Spandan Approach and its 3D Process, Dr Rao has helped business managers propagate and develop select human values that were integral to the mission, work ethics and culture in an organization. The goal has been to help achieve an optimal balance between results and relations in the organization. With its roots deep within Indian culture, the Spandan Approach and the 3D Process help managers develop sensitivity toward their work group and the organization in general.

The similarities between the primarily (?) Western 'managing by values' approach and that of Spandan are very striking. Managing by values is an approach to management that may have been named first by Kenneth Blanchard, who said, 'We believe that the essence of success in business lies in developing vision and values, and embodying them in planning, managing and decision making' (Humanising Management, p. 63). With this approach management creates a kind of 'playing field' where mission-relevant values selected by management and individual contributors are the ultimate boss. Then as employees pursue the organization's goals, efforts are made to embody and realize the values selected. This approach tends to foster an unprecedented level of trust that leads all toward peak productivity, self-actualization and deep-level realization.

Some organizational developers and peak performance researchers (including me) go even farther, and believe that the optimal *way to develop our organizations and societies, and to progress toward other typical material and bottom-line goals is to focus on developing and embodying performance values relevant for self-realization. In other words, focusing on inner values* optimally and most reliably *drives inner as well as outer forms of progress, including bottom-line goals. From this perspective, I believe that Dr Rao's work adds to the growing literature that is shifting the corporate world's emphasis on the bottom line toward a recognition of values not just as an end in themselves, but also as perhaps the best* means for producing results *in the workplace.*

Stephen Randall, PhD (steve@manage-time.com; stevrandal.wordpress.com; www.TSKassociation.org)

Similar, Ancient Living Cultural Milieus

KAIZEN, JAPAN

The Japanese word *kaizen* can be translated as 'Improvement' or 'Change for the better'. It refers to a philosophy or practice of continuous improvement that focuses upon improvement processes in manufacturing, engineering, development, business management and so on. It has been applied in health-care, psycho-therapy, life-coaching, government, banking and other industries. When used in the business sense and applied to the work place, *kaizen* refers to activities that continuously improve all functions and involve all employees from CEOs to assembly-line workers. The five main elements of *kaizen* are:

1.   teamwork

2.   personal discipline

3.   improved morale

4.   quality circles

5.   suggestions for improvement

As opposed to the Western philosophy of 'if it ain't broke, don't fix it', *kaizen* takes a more optimistic and proactive view: 'Everything can be made better, even if it ain't broke'.

UBUNTU, AFRICA

Ubuntu is an African ethic or human philosophy focusing on people's allegiances to and relations with each other. The word has its origin in the Bantu languages of southern Africa.

Archbishop Desmond Tutu defines *ubuntu* as the essence of being human: inter-connectedness. He also describes it as 'I am what I am because of who we all are'. Nelson Mandela (2006) comments: 'A traveller going through a country would stop at a village; and he would be offered food and water, even if he did not ask for them. The question therefore is: are you going to do so in order to enable the community around you to be able to improve?' This question is of particular relevance to the issue of management's contribution to society (see Chapter 16).

The philosophy of *ubuntu* is significantly related to the Indian saint Kabir's *Dohe* (reflections) and Gandhian philosophy.

GUANXI, CHINA

Interpersonal relationship, as defined by the term *guanxi*, is one of the major dynamics of Chinese society, and has been a pervasive part of the Chinese business world for the last few centuries (Luo 2007). Such interpersonal relations operate at three different but related levels:

1.   macro level – family, community and society

2.   semi-macro level – firm (managerial policy, business practices, marketing mix, organizational behaviour, human resources development, corporate culture and business strategy)

3.   micro level – individual (inter-personal relations, incentive structures, social status and family connections)

References

Banerjee, R.P. 2004. Beyond Human Values: Divine Values for New Era Corporations. In Ananda Das Gupta (ed.), *Human Values in Management*. Aldershot: Ashgate, pp. 112–26.

Byrne, Rhonda. 2007. *The Secret*. New York: Simon & Schuster.

Jayamani, C.V. 2008. *Business Ethics and Human Values*. [Online: 18 January 2008]. Available at: http://manomohanam-manomohanam.blogspot.in/2008/01/business-ethics-and-human-values.html [accessed: 14 July 2013].

Luo, Yadong. 2007. *Guanxi and Business*, 2nd edn. Singapore: World Scientific Publishing Company.

Mandela, Nelson. 2006. On Ubuntu Philosophy (Interview, conducted by Tim Modise, 24 May 2006). [Online]. Available at: http://en.wikipedia.org/wiki/Ubuntu_%28philosophy%29 [accessed: 14 July 2013].

Maslow, Abraham. 1971. *The Farther Reaches of Human Nature*. New York: Viking Press.

Randall, Stephen. Management by Values (MBV) approach. Communication with the author.

Rao, G.P. 1996, *Human Values in Industrial Organizations: Feminine Perspective* (MCHV, IIMC Research Monograph 2). New Delhi: Sage.

Shri Aurobindo Ashram, Auroville, Pondicherry. 1990. *Mother's Ministry of Management*. Pondicherry: Shri Aurobindo Ashram.

Wakhlu, Arun. 1999. *Managing from the Heart: Unfolding Spirit in People and Organizations*. New Delhi: Response Books/Sage.

5

'The Wonder that was India': An Indian Approach

The Context and the Issue

The title of this book is *Remaking Ourselves, Enterprise and Society: An Indian Approach to Human Values in Management*. The first part of the title indicates the book's broader perspective:

1. ourselves as human beings and our being remade

2. enterprise and its remaking – by human beings

3. society and its remaking – by human beings

The common factor in all three is ourselves as human beings. In the first case we need to understand (diagnose), assess (discover), and improve upon ourselves by remaking ourselves (develop). In the second case we aim to understand (diagnose), assess (discover) and improve upon, through remaking (develop), an enterprise/enterprises. In the third and final case focus is on making efforts to understand (diagnose), assess (discover) and improve upon, through remaking (develop), society. To approach these goals the question of a system comes into the frame.

Before considering systems though, another facet of the remaking process needs introduction because remaking ourselves, enterprise and society, while necessary, is not sufficient. The task will only be complete once the three entities – human beings, enterprises and society – have developed an optimal state of interaction, sharing sentiments and activities between and among themselves.

As preceding chapters have explained, the Spandan Approach – incorporating the Spandan 3D Process and the Spandan Spectrum of Human

Values 2011 – can play a crucial role in the process of remaking ourselves as human beings, our enterprises and our society.

The second part of the book's title refers to the *Indian* approach to remaking ourselves, with reference to the relevance and application of human values in management. Thus the two issues to be addressed are:

1.   human values in management *per se* – at the conceptual and operational levels;

2.   specific aspects of the Indian approach and contribution to the corpus of management knowledge and its practices.

In this chapter the relevance of Indian philosophy, culture and society to understanding India's contribution to the emerging and topical issue of humanizing management and mankind are addressed. A number of conceptual frameworks are considered in the process.

On Indian Philosophy, the Vedas and the Bhagavad Gita

INDIAN PHILOSOPHY – SALIENT FEATURES

Richard King's important work *Indian Philosophy: An Introduction to Hindu and Buddhist Thought* (1999) and the contribution on Indian philosophy to the *Encyclopaedia Britannica* made by Jitendra N. Mohanty offer a good introduction to Indian philosophy and its salient features.

Richard King states:

> *Philosophy refers to the world view or ideological position of a particular person or community. (p. 1)*

> *... in the modern era, [philosophy is viewed as] a meta discipline which can be applied to other intellectual disciplines ... (indeed) any branch of human activity. (p. 4)*

> *... philosophical thinking involves abstract reflection and the exercise of the faculty of reason in some kind of decontextualised and neutral regard, that is, 'pure argumentation', detached from particular concerns and agendas. (p. 4)*

> ... *philosophical movements and trends are representative of wider prevailing trends within cultures as a whole. (p. 7)*

As to *Indian* philosophy, King argues, 'there is no such thing as "Indian philosophy" if by that one means a particular way of looking at the world that is peculiar to and universally accepted by the people of India' (p. 1). He adds that by the same token there is no *Western* philosophy. The term most often used to denote a school of philosophy in India is *darsan* (*drs* – to see). *Darsan*, which accordingly can be translated as a point of view, thus denotes Indians' outlook on the world and their own role in it.

Encyclopaedia Britannica states that Indian philosophy consists of 'the systems of thought and reflection that were developed by the civilizations of the Indian subcontinent'. These systems of thought are nine in total: six orthodox (*astika*) and three unorthodox (*nastik*). The six orthodox systems are: Nyaya, Vaishesika, Sankhya, Yoga, Purva-Mimamsa (or Mimamsa) and Vedanta. The three unorthodox systems are: Buddhism, Jainism and Charvaca (Materialist).

The aim of Indian philosophy – like other contemporary systems of philosophy – is to study the material world to find the soul of existence. For example, Sankhya philosophy adopts an analytical approach and aims primarily at making the human being realize his/her true nature and glory. It tries to show that everything that exists in the world produces some kind of suffering and sorrow. The Sankhya system is so called because it enumerates (*sankhya*, in Sanskrit, means numbers) 25 categories or principles of the whole universe. Two important concepts in the system are *Purusha*, the intelligent conscious, and *Prakriti*, the unintelligent, inert *jada*, i.e. unconscious. The ultimate object of the process of evolution as described by the Sankhya system is to make the *Purusha* realize his/her true nature and glory and thus that *Purusha* is the real spirit and true nature of every individual.

Three basic concepts form the cornerstones of Indian philosophical thought:

1.   the self or soul (*atman*)

2.   works (*karma*)

3.   liberation (*mokhsa*)

THE VEDAS – ATHARVAVEDA[1]

The word *veda* means knowledge and the Vedas are considered the most sacred scriptures of Hinduism. They are considered *sruti*, meaning what was heard by or revealed to the *rishis* or seers. The most holy hymns and *mantras* were collated into four collections called the Rig, Sama, Yajur and Atharva Vedas. These collections are difficult to date because they were passed on orally for about a thousand years before they were written down. More recent categories of Vedas include the Brahmanas or manuals for ritual and prayer, the Aranyakas or forest texts for religious hermits, and the Upanishads or mystical discourses.

The *richas* of the *Rigveda* comprise prayers to and praise of the gods, the *Yajurveda* speaks of the different types of *yagya* (religious sacrifices), the *Samaveda* consists of many of the *richas* from the *Rigveda* but presented lyrically and musically, while the *Atharvaveda* abounds in knowledge of the physical world and spirituality.

Atharvaveda

The word atharv*a* (*a+tharva*), meaning devoid of movement, or concentration, comes from the word tharva, meaning fickleness or movement. Accordingly the word atharva means that which is unwavering, concentrated or unchanging.

The philosophy of Yoga states, 'Yogash Chitta Vritti Nirodhana' (Patanjali, *Yogadarshan*, Samadhi Pada, 2nd sutra), which means the state of union (*yoga*) arises through controlling the different impulses of the mind and senses. The *Bhagavad Gita* (see the following section) reiterates that when the mind is free from impulses and flaws, it becomes stable and the person becomes neutral. Moreover, only when the impulses of the mind and the other senses are brought under control is the mind made free from instability and perturbation. The word *atharva* therefore captures the essence of this neutrality of personality, if you will, and the *Atharvaveda* expounds more on Yoga, human physiology, different ailments, social structure, spirituality, appreciation of natural beauty, national religion and so on. The knowledge it sets out is both practical and worthwhile.

The substance of the *Atharvaveda* thus permeates this book, bringing the ancient wisdom and ethos of India to bear on the process elucidated here: how to remake ourselves as human beings and in relation to the enterprise and society.

---

1   This section is adapted from www.aryabhatt.com.

In particular it is of relevance to Chapter 8 'Transformational Human Values' and Chapter 19 'Spirituality and Management'.

THE MAHABHARTHA AND THE BHAGAVAD GITA

The great epic, the *Mahabhartha*, represents an attempt by vedic Brahmanism to adjust itself to new circumstances reflected in the process of the Sanskritization (the integration of vedic beliefs, practices and institutions) of the various non-vedic communities. Consequently the work synthesizes numerous diverse religious trends and philosophies.

The *Bhagavad Gita* ('Song of the Lord') forms part of the *Mahabhartha* and deserves attention by virtue of its great importance in the religious life and thought of Hindus. At a theoretical level, it brings together Sankhya metaphysics, Upanishadic monism, and the devotional theism of the Krishna-Vasudeva cult. In its practical teaching, it steers a middle course between the 'path of action' of vedic ritualism and the 'path of renunciation' of Upanishadic mysticism: furthermore it accommodates all three major 'paths' to *mokhsa*: the paths of action (*karma*), devotion (*bhakti*) and knowledge (*gnana*).

The most direct relevance of the *Mahabhartha* and the *Bhagavad Gita* to management theory and practice relates to the concept of *karma yoga* (doing one's best without craving recognition or reward), which is discussed in Chapter 10, on the manager as a professional.

On Indian Culture

B.L. Athreya's classic contribution for UNESCO, *Indian Culture: Its Spiritual, Moral and Social Aspects* (1949), forms the basis of this section.

> *From time immemorial Indians have been calling their culture by the name of Human Culture (*Manava Dharma *or* Manava Samskriti*). It has tried to be so comprehensive as to suit the needs of every human being, irrespective of age, sex, colour or race. As such it has a universal appeal. (p. 6)*

> *The most essential feature of Indian culture ... is [its] thorough-going understanding of the nature of Man and his relations with other beings in the universe and with the Universe as a whole. From time*

> *immemorial India has tried to build its civilization on the basis of this knowledge. Man being a part and product of Nature, India approached Nature through man, because it is in himself alone that man can be most aware of Reality. (p. 11)*

> *[The] Indian word for culture is* Samskriti *which comes from a root which means to purify, to transform, to sublimate, to mould and to perfect. A cultured man is a disciplined man, who has brought his natural propensities under control and has shaped himself in accordance with the ideal placed before him by his ethical consciousness. (p. 13)*

Other aspects of Indian culture will be referred to in subsequent chapters at the appropriate places.

On Indian Society

Family and caste are the two essential features of Indian society.

FAMILY

Marriage is considered a life-long bond carrying mutual obligations for the husband and the wife to each other and in their joint relations with other members of the family. Even today the joint family system is preferred as it is seen as providing a more nurturing environment for children, emotional and economic security, and, under the conditions of industrialization and globalization, a situation in which it is easier for the younger members of the family to be taken care of while their parents are away for work. The head of the family is the family's oldest member and is known as *karta*. All decisions are taken through discussion, but what the *karta* decides becomes final. Obedience is considered an essential feature of the family system in India.

Post industrialization and globalization, the institution of the joint family has undergone numerous challenges to its survival and has had to adjust to the changing circumstances. Nonetheless, in many parts of India the joint family system is still a popular and powerful institution. Research has shown (Shah 2008) that efforts are being made to revive the family system and to make it more functional in the context of globalization.

An valuable approach to integrate family with on-going industrialization and globalization, I submit, would be to infuse family values in management and business. Family-owned businesses are found to be dominant even in highly industrialized countries in the West and elsewhere. In the United States, for instance, 60 to 70 per cent of companies are estimated to be family owned and controlled.

The managing agency system was an institution through which business communities led and participated in the industrial development of India through finance, management and control. However, during mid-1950s, the managing agency system was abolished by law. Despite this, several prominent and influential families like the Birlas from the Marwari community in the western and eastern parts of India, the Tatas from the Parsi community in the west, and the Chettiars from business communities in the south have been playing a leadership role in the country.

The issue is to identify family values suitable to an industrial work culture and infuse them in management in business. *Spandan* has undertaken as one of its initiatives the Functionally Humane Organization, the objective being organizational transformation through faith in the basic goodness of others (see Chapter 3). Chapter 17 deals in greater detail with the *Spandan* initiative on infusing family values in management and business.

THE CASTE SYSTEM

Caste is another salient feature of Indian society. Traditionally, Indian society is stratified into castes consisting of people who are *born* into their particular caste. Thus birth, an ascribed – rather than achieved – status, determines one's caste. There are four broad categories of castes: *Brahmins, Kshatriyas, Vysyas* and *Shudras*. *Brahmins* are learned people, advising ruling or governing communities, conducting religious ceremonies and treated by and large as mentors, in rural India in particular. *Kshatriyas* constituted the warring community, providing law and order within the community and protecting the people from onslaughts from outside. *Vysyas* are the business community engaged in commerce and trade. They are rich and enterprising by nature and historically merchants travelled to countries far and wide and prospered. *Shudras* are people engaged in menial jobs and occupations as complementary to the rural economy led by *Brahmins, Kshatriyas* and *Vysyas*. These occupations include weaving, pottery, carpentry and house construction. The remaining large number of people were designated casteless – an situation that has been seen as a blot on Indian society. Over a period of time, and during the attacks and reign of Muslims, from the eleventh century to the mid-eighteenth century, and during colonial rule thereafter until the mid-twentieth century, the caste system degenerated into a rigid and exploitative tool in the hands of socially, economically and politically powerful people. The principle of the division of labour on which the caste system rests, as well as its flexibility, however, still enchants thinkers around the world. Gerald Heard (1941), a great American thinker and writer, for instance, has referred to the Indian social system as 'organic democracy', defined by him as

> the rule of the people who have organized themselves in a living and not a mechanical relationship; where instead of all men being said to be equal, which is a lie, all men are known to be of equal value, could we but find the position in which their potential contribution could be released and their essential growth so pursued. (p. 28)

The caste system in India has been closely associated with industrial growth and its structure in the country. In the mid-nineteenth century it was, unsurprisingly, the business community, the *Vysyas*, that took the initiative in investment, management and control in diverse areas like factories, mines, plantations, transport, trade and commerce. Furthermore the hierarchy in Indian society represented by the caste system reflected itself, at least in the initial stages, in the hierarchy in enterprises. Higher caste people usually occupied higher positions, in management and in supervisory roles, and members of the lower castes, lower positions. Over time, however, such compartmentalization has declined because of a variety of reasons including the spread of education, technology, government policies and increased self-awareness and self-dignity.

What is Expected of India?

In *The Wonder that was India*, possibly the most widely read book on India, noted historian and Indologist, A.L. Basham (1954) referred to the country as a land of contradictions. Endowed with rich natural resources, it is populated by one of the poorest countries in the world. A land of saints and seers, producing apostles of peace and spiritual leaders like Gautam Buddha, Emperor Ashoka, Swami Vivekananda and Mahatma Gandhi, Indians are now also known for their insensitivity towards their fellow human beings as well as Mother Earth, and the country has become notorious for its corruption and unethical practices. The question therefore is: What can India offer other countries? What is it that others can expect from her? In material terms, India is not rich; rather its spiritual heritage and ancient wisdom are its most valuable assets. In this context let us read what three notable personalities had to say on the matter.

Max Mueller (1823–1900), German philologist and Orientalist, in lectures delivered at the University of Cambridge on *India: What Can it Teach Us?* (1883) observed:

> *If I were asked under what sky the human mind has most fully developed some of its choicest gifts, has most deeply pondered on the greatest problems of life, and has found solutions of some of them which well deserve the attention even of those who have studied Plato and Kant, I should point to India. And if I were to ask myself from what literature we here in Europe – we who have been nurtured almost exclusively on the thoughts of the Greeks and Romans and of one Semetic race of the Jewish – may draw that corrective which is most wanted in order to make our inner life more perfect, more comprehensive, more universal, in fact more human, a life not for this life only, but a transfigured and eternal life, again I should point to India. (p. 6)*

F.S.C. Northrop (1893–1992), concludes his book *The Meeting of the East and the West: An Inquiry concerning World Understanding* (1946/1979), with the following suggestion and wish:

> *It should eventually be possible to achieve a society for mankind generally in which the higher standard of living of most scientifically advanced and the theoretically guided Western nations is combined with the compassion, the universal sensitivity to the beautiful and the abiding equanimity and the calm joy of the spirit which characterize the sages and the many of the humblest people in the Orient. (p. 496)*

Arnold Toynbee (1889–1975), the well-known English historian and historical philosopher, had perhaps the last word on the subject when he made comments to the effect that the problems created by Western civilization are to be solved by the wisdom of India:

> *It is already becoming clearer that a chapter which has a western beginning will have to have an Indian ending if it is not to end in the self destruction of the human race. At this supremely dangerous*

moment in history the only way of salvation for mankind is the Indian way. (1960, p. 54)

References

Athreya, B.L. 1949. *Indian Culture: Its Spiritual, Moral and Social Aspects*. Paris: UNESCO.

Basham, A.L. 1954. *The Wonder that was India*. London: Sidgwick and Jackson.

Heard, Gerald. 1941. *Man: The Master*. New York and London: Harper and Brothers.

King, Richard. 1999. *Indian Philosophy: An Introduction to Hindu and Buddhist Thought*. Edinburgh: Edinburgh University Press.

Mohanty, Jitendra N. no date. Indian Philosophy. *Encyclopaedia Britannica*. [Online]. Available at: http://www.britannica.com/EBchecked/topic/285905/Indian-philosophy [accessed: 5 August 2013].

Mueller, Max. 1883. *India: What Can it Teach Us? Lectures at the University of Cambridge*. New York: Funk and Waghalls.

Northrop, F.S.C. 1946/1979. *The Meeting of the East and the West: An Inquiry concerning World Understanding*. New York: Macmillan.

Shah, Grishma. 2008. The Impact of Economic Globalization on Work–Family and Family–Work Conflict in India. Paper presented at a conference of the Academy of International Business – North East, Atlanta City, NJ, October 2008.

Toynbee, Arnold. 1960. *One World and India*. Calcutta: Orient Longmans.

PART II

Remaking Ourselves as Human Beings: The Spandan Approach

6

Conceptual Framework

The Context and the Issue

In their pursuit of material comforts and happiness human beings assume different roles at different points in time. These roles emerge, more importantly, at individual, professional, group, institutional, national and global levels. Corresponding to these levels, suitable desirable norms and values evolve over a period of time to properly guide human living and human life. Human living refers to material comforts, prosperity and economic well-being, while human life relates to contentment, happiness and tranquillity. Proper human living and human life are all about the willingness and ability human beings have and develop to achieve and maintain an optimal balance between these cardinal cravings.

The issue therefore is one of remaking ourselves as human beings. This remaking is to be undertaken in different roles, beginning perhaps from the 'generic' level, that is, the human being as a human being, as an entity in and of itself. This remaking process can therefore be analysed at the level of a specific role, and at the generic level. Humanizing 'management' is an example of remaking at a specific role level, while humanizing self as a human being *per se* is remaking at the generic level. My 'awakening', so to speak, began with the specific role level of management – the reason being that this was my own sphere of activity, which was both a strength and, given its restrictions, a weakness. However the sequence of 'awakening' unfolds, the fact remains that remaking at both generic and specific levels, and their analysis, needs to take place if we are to remake ourselves as human beings in the real and total sense of whole and holy entities.

Thomas Crum (1987) once stated: 'Being willing to change allows you to move from a point of view to a viewing point – a higher, more expansive place, from which you can see both sides' (p. 166). Following his rationale, specific-role-level humanizing 'management' is our point of view, and generic- and whole-level humanizing is our viewing point. The conceptual framework as well as the sequence and plan of this book is based upon this rationale.

Systems Thinking

The conceptual framework of the book is based upon systems thinking. Also known as the systems approach and systems analysis, the purpose is to place understanding human behaviour in a new perspective. Its two cardinal principles are holism and interdependence. Holism refers to looking at an entity or issue in its entirety. Interdependence denotes the relationships between and among the different components and constituents of the given entity or issue. These concepts are also of relevance to supra-systems and subsystems. A supra-system is a larger entity that consists of smaller entities called subsystems. An organization, for example, is a supra-system and its departments are its subsystems. The organization, however, is in turn a subsystem of a society. When these subsystems are viewed as part of the given system, the concept of Oneness emerges. The human body provides a good analogy. Different limbs (subsystems) of a body (supra-system) have their own features and functions. Yet the common objective of all the limbs is the survival and growth of the human being.

The concept of input–transformation–output is the other component in systems thinking. An entity exists for a purpose, objective or aim (output). To achieve the given objective(s), the entity obtains the required resources (inputs) and uses them (transformation) as it sees fit. Feedback – that is knowledge of the results of the process – enables the constant review and planning needed for the survival and growth of the given entity.

When applied to humanizing management, the relevance of systems thinking can hardly be exaggerated in view of the fact that humanizing management by definition *is* the transformation of human beings from a particular state (lower self) to another desired state (higher Self) at individual, professional, organizational and societal levels.

- The context, the environment, the situation within which the transformation takes place constitute the input.

- The propagation and inculcation of values at the different levels constitutes Transformation.

- The intended/achieved end result of balance between results and relations is the output.

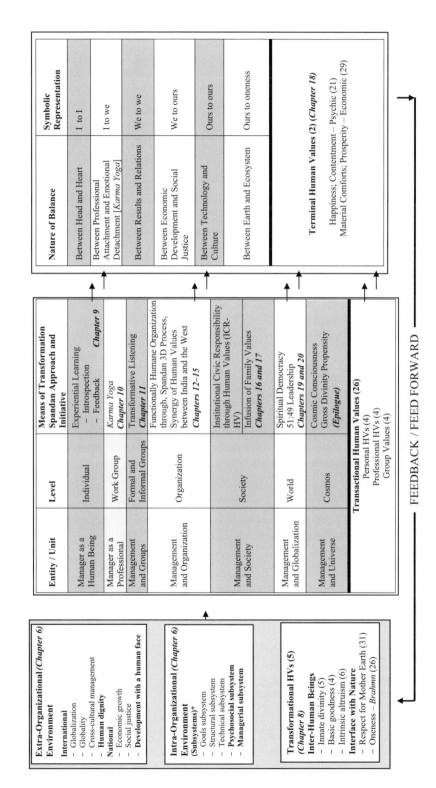

Figure 6.1 Remaking ourselves as human beings, enterprise and society: the Spandan Spectrum of Human Values 2011

Figure 6.1 presents systems thinking as applied to humanizing ourselves, enterprise and society.

INPUT – ENVIRONMENT (FIGURE 6.1)

By applying the system approach of input–transformation–output and feedback to the Spandan Spectrum of Human Values 2011, a conceptual framework for the current study has been developed. Environment for a manager and management functioning in an organization consists of two aspects: the extra-organizational and the intra-organizational.

Input: environment – external

The extra-organizational environment can be split into two levels:

- *National level*: Where society, government and economy become supra-systems of the given organization. Some select external factors influencing the management at the organizational level include: economic growth, social justice and development with a 'human' face.

- *International level*: Where the influences are globalization accompanied by globality (management of globalization), as well as cross-cultural management, requiring new sets of knowledge, skills and attitudes to deal with people located in units across the world in a variety of cultural milieus.

The impact of environment as an input on the functioning of management and its organization can hardly be exaggerated. Government and society cause or allow the creation of an organization, set its boundaries, lay down the rules, and act as the umpire and disciplinarian. The role and relevance of the national-level environment, in particular, permeates the entire functioning of the organization, and therefore the analysis of this work as a whole.

Input: environment – internal

The intra-organizational environment can be viewed as consisting of a number of subsystems. Kast and Rosenzweig, in their work *Organisation and Management: A Systems and Contingency Approach* (1970), enumerate five such subsystems (p. 16):

1.   *Goals subsystem(s)* – refers to the objective(s) with which an organization has been formed. Often specified in the mission statement, the objectives become the inspiration for its functioning.

2.   *Structural subsystem(s)* – involves the ways in which the tasks of the organization are divided (differentiation) and coordinated (integration).

3.   *Technical subsystem(s)* – refers to the knowledge required for the performance of tasks, including techniques used in the transformation of inputs into outputs.

4.   *Psychosocial subsystem(s)* – consists of individual behaviour and motivation, status and role relationships, group dynamics and influence systems.

5.   *Managerial subsystem(s)* – spans the entire organization by relating the organization to its environment, setting the goals, developing comprehensive strategic and operational plans, designing the structure and establishing control processes.

TRANSFORMATION–OUTPUT (FIGURE 6.1)

Towards self as a human being and as a professional

a)   *Manager as a human being*: Human behaviour is considered a function of the individual and the situation. Individual refers to the self, encompassing important concepts such as personality, learning, perception, motivation and attitudes. Situation refers to the environment surrounding and influencing the given individual, and, as mentioned, for the manager this comprises elements such as family, community, society, industry and the country. Further to this, transformation of the human being comes through experiential learning consisting of introspection and feedback. In other words, continuous interaction with all concerned helps the manager achieve the desired balance between head and heart. Symbolically this can be represented as an ascent from 'i' (lower self) to 'I' (higher Self).

b)   *Manager as a professional*: Relevant here are the knowledge, skills and attitudes required by the manager for performance at the individual and institutional levels. The manger has to work a) with and through a work group at the same time as b) with colleagues and seniors. Experiential learning sessions with the work group and others helps the manager to achieve the required balance between professional attachment while working and emotional detachment in not craving reward. This balance is called *karma yoga* (see Chapter 5: on the *Bhagavad Gita*). Symbolically, the progression is from 'I' (higher Self) to 'we' (group identity).

Towards organization: management as a group of professionals

Management, as a group of professionals, is responsible for the functioning of an organization. Managerial transformation through human values at the organizational level is achieved through the Spandan 3D Process of Diagnosis, Discovery and Development. The objective of the process is to integrate values with the work ethic as anchored to the mission statement of the organization. The intended outcome is a balance between results and relations. Symbolically, the transformation is from 'we' (small group) to 'We' (larger group).

Towards society

The immediate supra-system of an organization is the society with the government as that society's most important organ. The objective of a developing society such as India is to find a balance between economic development and social justice. The role of the management of an organization is that of an organizational citizen (in contradistinction to a *corporate* citizen) that can help the government achieve development with a human face. Symbolically the transformation is from 'We' (larger group) to 'ours' (identity with society).

The three preceding responsibilities towards self, organization and society relate to managers functioning in their professional capacity. This is the main subject of the present work, with the primary objective being to offer a process for transformation at the organizational level.

Moving beyond the management of organizations, we enter into dealing with a) the world and b) the universe. In this regard, management as an identity merges itself with humanity.

Management of the world

This assumes special significance in the context of on-going globalization, where managing people with diverse nationalities and cultures is a challenge calling for cross-cultural management. The two basic goals here are sustainable development and spiritual democracy.

The desired objective is a balance between technology and culture. Symbolically, the transformation is from 'ours' (national identity) to 'Ours' (global identity). The Sanskrit term for this is *Vasudhaiva Kutumbakam* (global identity).

Management of the universe

The frame of reference here is the cosmos and the goal is finding a balance between Mother Earth and ecology. The transformation occurs through universal consciousness. Symbolically the ascent is from 'Ours' (global identity) to the theory of Oneness. It is no wonder that these days physicists talk like vedic scholars. In Crum's terms (see above) this is the 'viewing point' and the inspiration for humankind to remake itself through its innate divinity.

FEEDBACK

The last component of the systems approach is feedback, which consists of constant monitoring and reviewing, and initiating timely corrective actions. Based upon the outcomes of humanizing management at the individual, professional, organizational and societal levels, suitable modifications and improvements are thus to be initiated in the transformation process.

The Application of Systems Thinking: A Case Study

As stated above, the conceptual framework of the book – and therefore of the Spandan Approach – is based upon systems thinking.

In one of the *Spandan* workshops initiated at an organization going through the 3D Process to inculcate human values, the issue of employee discipline arose. In discussion and debate based on experiential learning, it was concluded that the three Es of energy, empowerment and entrepreneurship play an important role in the nature and extent of the adherence of employee discipline.

In the process related to this case study the values-oriented organization is the input. Below are excerpts from the minutes and proceedings of the workshop together with the conceptual framework with employee discipline as a dependent variable (output). The three Es of energy, empowerment and entrepreneurship are independent variables (transformation).

Case Study: Delta Information Systems Ltd., Chandigarh, India

Spandan Workshop: Theme: Discipline and achievement of results, 16 July 2011

(Minutes, proceedings and model prepared by MD, and Convener, Core Group)

Attendees: Ravinder, Amitoz, Abha, Shweta, Harpreet Singh (IA), Rohit Sawhney, Ram K. Yadav, Vishal, Pathan, Renu

Round Zero: Review of progress

Round 1: Management communication and participant response

Round 2: Employee discipline

Round 3: Three Es and employee discipline in the company

Table 6.1   **Delta Information Systems, Chandigarh: assessment of three Es and employee discipline in the company**

Dimension	NOPs N=9			COO	MD
	Mean	Minimum	Maximum		
Energy	6.5	5(1)	8(1)	7	8
Empowerment	6.5	5(1)	8(1)	7	6
Entrepreneurship	6.9	4(1)	8(3)	6	5
Employee discipline	6.7	6(1)	7(2)	6	7

Observations:

- Assessment is sharper in the case of MD. Unique values used from 5 to 8.

- Assessment by COO should have been sharper. Being closer to the team makes this difficult.

- Correction factor of ± 5 is taken as statistically the same.

- MD's expectation is high on Entrepreneurship

- COO, MD's ratings on Entrepreneurship are lowest, whereas for the team, it is the highest.

Round 4: Question posed by Dr Rao and answered by MD

To be presented in terms of systems thinking and the Spandan 3D Process, with employee discipline as the dependent variable (output), and the three Es of empowerment, entrepreneurship and energy as the independent variables (transformation), and the company-values system as input.

References

Capra, Fritjof. 1973. *The Tao of Physics*. New York: Bantam Books.

Crum, Thomas. 1987. *The Magic of Conflict*. New York: Simon & Schuster.

Kak, Subhash. 2011. The Fifth Dimension. *The Speaking Tree (Times of India)*, 30 January 2011.

Kast, Fremont E. and James Irwin Rosenzwig. 1970. *Organization and Management: A Systems and Contingency Approach*. New York: McGraw-Hill.

Rokeach, M. 1973. *The Nature of Human Values*. New York: Free Press.

Table 6.2   Exhibit: Delta Information Systems, Chandigarh: company values, three Es and employee discipline

Input	Transformation	Output
Global scenario: Post-1980 (Millennial generation / Gen-Y) Virtual interaction e-DNA High risk takers Follow their heart Culturally liberal Peer oriented	A study in value orientation in the work situation Theme: 3 Es, employee discipline and value system in an educational organization 3 Es: *Empowerment* It is the duty of each one of us to align to the values and beliefs stated to deliver the best results to achieve our common objectives. We will have a positive regard for each other irrespective of the position we hold	Accountability and responsibility increases Peer pressure Reduction in time wasting Wants to form a company at the age of 21 … works in that direction Working smarter; tapping in to world information; travels globally Loves what he/she is doing, does not waste time; increased focus; improved results
Most of our front end is built with Gen-Y. They will over a period move into the middle management; this poses a challenge of keeping the fabric of the organization in tact Customer behaviour impacts customer relationship management (CRM) – customer relationships, customer satisfaction	*Entrepreneurship* We recognize the necessity of making mistakes and risk taking when it contributes to the purpose of the organization. We will be fair in all our dealings and promote business ethics. We will ensure profitability and growth through the best delivery execution. We firmly believe that our growth is the derivative of the growth of each one of us	Earlier integration of adoption of world's best practices (e.g. concalls, video conferencing) Flexibility; working from home; response time is improving
Post 2008, after the worldwide recession, the paradigm shifts from 'want' to 'need' at both company and consumer level. This has an impact on managers' key result areas (KRAs) and how the managers view the organization's top and bottom line, which means glocalization. (High savings). This will run for a decade before getting back on track	*Energy* Education gives us the fundamental purpose of changing someone's life forever. We will foster career building by creating opportunities that demand learning, thinking and innovation from each of us. This is the key enabler of our everlasting passion for what we are doing. This enthusiasm is further enhanced with opportunities to work with state-of-the-art technologies for the benefit of	Goes back to school; learning (sharpening the saw) Becomes a world class professional Globe trotting Organization's top line increases
Regulations: Emerging markets have taken attention away from developed markets because of the demographic advantages		Work on constant process improvement and imbibe new technology which causes reduction in cost / creates a non-linear business model

Needs of multi-lingual, multi-cultural teams

Indian context: India has maintained a sustainable growth rate, which remained insulated from the world economy. Due to the growth rates, a large middle class has emerged, with heavy consumerism

Indian government withdrew support to all subsidiaries. Huge exposure of mobile and internet space

Indian generation jumped a complete 'technology' set

Cultural impact:
Few dilution and some positives

Huge competition built up (peer to peer comparison); job hopping; low loyalty factor

Student–teacher relations; manager–supervisor relations changed

Education: college; institute
Pursue higher study after working for some time; start a career early

Social space; internet space

Student habits change before going into industry – they become future employees

Work from home culture

Shift from bricks and mortar to knowledge

humankind. India's young workforce is giving it a great demographic advantage over the West. We are powered by increasing consumerism in our country. We will channel our vigour to harness these two opportunities to the fullest. We will refill out energies with constant connection with our customers.

Employee discipline
We will balance the above 3 Es by promising to meet any and every commitment irrespective of any cost that we may have to incur. We will imbibe integrity at all levels of interface with self, operations, personal and society. We will align entrepreneurship, leadership and systems through a rigorous process. We will be sure to seek public victory only after achieving the private victory first.

We, in our education business, believe that it is our duty to espouse and give active effect to the values, motives and beliefs we state here. We will aim to experience innate divinity – being closer to God always.

Challenge:
Stickiness; organization's challenge is to retain him/her. Organization cannot catch up with ever-growing needs

7

The Spandan Spectrum of Human Values: Extent of the Adherence to Human Values: A Bird's-Eye View

The Context and the Issue

The Spandan Approach rests on belief in the innate divinity, intrinsic altruism and basic goodness of human beings. The Spandan 3D Process aims at translating this belief into a reality in work situations. The process consists of (a) developing a vision and mission statement for the organization and (b) inculcating suitable human values in the work ethic through diagnosis, discovery and development, (c) as integral to HRD initiatives like selection, training and development, and performance appraisal, and (d) linking them to its strategic management in the form of an on-going search for the optimal balance between its results and relations.

In Chapter 3 the evolution of the Spandan Spectrum of Human Values 2011 was presented. Soon after finalizing the 2011 version an attempt was made to examine the nature and extent of the human values in the spectrum at three levels: industry, one's own organization and one's own professional life.

Extent of Adherence: The Study of 2011

A response sheet (see Appendix to this chapter) was prepared and forwarded to around 200 select eminent persons from different walks of life involved in the propagation and inculcation of human values at one or more of the three levels. Each respondent was asked to assess adherence to the 31 human values included in the spectrum at the levels of their own professional life, their own organization, and Indian industry as a whole. Fifty-eight invitees responded.

RESPONDENT PROFILE

No. of respondents	Total: 58	From India: 51	From abroad: 7
Age (years)	Mean: 50	Min.: 26(1)	Max.: 82(1)
Work experience (years)	Mean: 24	Min.: 2(1)	Max.: 65(1)

Based on the responses, an effort was made to identify the human values perceived as important (diagnosis) and their adherence at the three levels mentioned (discovery). Finally, policy implications were focused upon (development) to strengthen and balance the different human values thus selected and assessed. The assumption and experience is that such strengthening would enable an organization to achieve an optimal balance between material comforts and happiness, the two end-state Terminal Human Values.

Tables 7.1 to 7.4 contain the relevant data, in terms of the three levels analysed, viz. Indian industry, one's own organization and one's own professional life.

Table 7.1 sets out the extent of adherence in terms of the top and bottom human values in Indian industry as a whole. Material comforts (29) ranks first, followed by competitive spirit (9) and respect for authority (30). Of the top five human values most adhered to in Indian industry, two – competitive spirit (9) and entrepreneurship (18) – are globalization-induced human values.

Emotional detachment towards recognition and reward (15) is ranked lowest (33rd) in Indian industry, followed by community interest (8) and oneness (26), preparedness (27) and respect for nature and Mother Earth (31), the last three bracketed together. It is significant that both the Transformational Human Values related to nature – oneness (26) and respect for nature and Mother Earth (31) – are among the five least adhered to human values in Indian industry.

Table 7.1   Extent of adherence to human values at the level of Indian industry [research study, 2011 (N-58)]

Rank	Value no.	Human value	Mean (N)	Category of human value
Top-Ranked Human Values				
I	29	Material comforts	7.2	Terminal Human Values
II	9	Competitive spirit	7.1	Transactional – Globalization-induced
III	30	Respect for authority	6.5	Transactional – Organizational
IV	18	Entrepreneurship	6.1	Transactional – Globalization-induced
V	10	Conviction	6.0	Transactional – Personal
Bottom-Ranked Human Values				
XXXIII	15	Emotional detachment towards enjoying the benefits of results	4.6	Transactional – Professional
XXXII	8	Community interest	4.7	Transactional – Organizational
XXXI	26	Oneness	4.8	Transformational II – Towards universe
XXXI	27	Preparedness	4.8	Transactional – Globalization-induced
XXXI	31	Respect for nature and Mother Earth	4.8	Transformational II – Towards Mother Earth

Table 7.2 sets out the extent of adherence in terms of the top and bottom human values in the category of one's own organization. Respect for authority (30) and service orientation (32) are bracketed together in first place; cultural adaptiveness (13) and customer orientation (14), bracketed together in third; and creativity and innovation (12) placed fifth. It is notable that the top five includes two organizational human values – respect for authority (30) and customer satisfaction (14) – and two globalization-induced human values – cultural adaptiveness (13) and creativity and innovation (12). Further, the two globalization-induced human values here and the two globalization-induced human values in the top five adhered to at the level of Indian industry – competitive spirit (9) and entrepreneurship (18) – make a total of four out of six such human values. This indicates a rather strong adherence to globalization-induced human values in India at the industrial and organizational levels.

Table 7.2   Extent of adherence to human values at the level of one's own organization [research study, 2011 (N-58)]

Rank	Value no.	Human value	Mean (N)	Category of human value
Top-Ranked Human Values				
I	30	Respect for authority	7.6	Transactional – Organizational
I	32	Service orientation	7.6	Transactional – Professional
III	13	Cultural adaptiveness	7.5	Transactional – Globalization-induced
III	14	Customer satisfaction	7.5	Transactional – Organizational
V	12	Creativity	7.2	Transactional – Globalization-induced
Bottom-Ranked Human Values				
XXXIII	15	Emotional detachment	6.1	Transactional – Professional
XXXII	26	Oneness	6.2	Transformational II – Towards Universe
XXXI	19	Equanimity	6.7	Transactional – Professional
XXX	23	Humility	6.8	Transactional – Personal

The bottom four human values in terms of adherence include, again, emotional detachment towards recognition and reward (15) and oneness (26). The other two are humility (23) and equanimity (19), ranked 30th and 31st respectively. Emotional detachment (15) and equanimity (19) are both professional values. As at the industry level (Table 7.1), emotional detachment (15) was the least adhered to human value, ranked lowest, in thirty-third place.

Table 7.3 contains corresponding data at the level of one's own professional life. Here, belief in the innate divinity in human beings (5) ranks first; commitment (7), second; and accountability (1), faith in the basic goodness of others (4), integrity (24), and professional attachment towards the completion of the task are all bracketed together in third. Of the five, two are Transformational Human Values, related to other human beings – belief in innate divinity (5) and faith in the basic goodness of others (4) – and two are organizational – commitment (7) and accountability (1). This indicates that managers in their own professional life are inclined to be strongly oriented to adhere to relations-oriented Transformational Human Values like belief in the innate divinity in human beings (5) and faith in the basic goodness of others (4). Neither of these two Transformational Human Values are rated among the top human values at the levels of industry or one's own organization. Does this indicate an unwillingness or inability, or both, on the part of managers to influence others to adhere to values in the organization to which they themselves adhere? This suggestion is strengthened when we discover that none of the other four top-ranked human values in this set are placed among the top ranks at either the industry or organizational level.

Table 7.3   **Extent of adherence to human values at the level of one's own professional life [research study, 2011 (N-58)]**

Rank	Value no.	Human value	Mean (N)	Category of human value
Top-Ranked Human Values				
I	5	Belief in the innate divinity in human beings	8.5	Transformational I – Relational
II	7	Commitment	8.4	Transactional – Organizational
III	1	Accountability	8.2	Transactional – Organizational
III	4	Faith in the basic goodness of others	8.2	Transformational I – Relational
III	24	Integrity	8.2	Transactional – Personal
III	28	Professional attachment towards completion of the task	8.2	Transactional – Professional
Bottom-Ranked Human Values				
XXXIII	15	Emotional detachment	6.9	Transactional – Professional
XXXII	9	Competitive spirit	7.1	Transactional – Globalization-induced
XXXII	29	Material comforts	7.1	Terminal Human Values
XXX	18	Entrepreneurship	7.4	Transactional – Globalization-induced
XXX	19	Equanimity	7.4	Transactional – Professional
XXX	22	Hospitable disposition (Marwar culture)	7.4	Transactional – Globalization-induced
XXX	26	Oneness	7.4	Transformational II – Towards universe

Emotional detachment towards recognition and reward (15) is again the lowest-ranked human value, and thus has the unique distinction of being ranked lowest at all the three levels of industry, organization and professional life. This, however, raises the issue: how can this happen in a country like India, known for its philosophical bent, simplicity, contentment and a certain degree of aloofness towards achievement and success? Oneness (26) is another that appears in the lowest-ranked values adhered to at all three levels.

Of the remaining five lowest-ranked human values at the level of one's own professional life, as many as three – competitive spirit (9), material comforts (29) and entrepreneurship – are ranked among the top five human values at the level of Indian industry. This reinforces the above-mentioned feeling of a 'disconnect' between the manager as professional on the one hand, and as part of an organization and industry on the other – in a *contrary* direction, however. Above it was suggested that managers may have an unwillingness and/or inability to influence others in the direction – adherence to Transformational Human Values – in which they perceive they are strong. The dichotomy though is that a weaker adherence at the individual professional level and stronger adherence at the industry level suggests an unwillingness and/or inability among managers to be influenced in a positive direction by what is happening in the larger context of industry.

Table 7.4 presents the human values that are common to two or more of the top and bottom ranks at the three levels. The table supports the idea that there is a need for a better 'connect' between managers, industry and the organization. All in all, this is a promising research proposal – worthy of probing through further investigation and analysis.

Table 7.5 offers a bird's-eye view of the responses category-wise – Transformational, Transactional and Terminal Human Values.

Table 7.6 aims to identify the top and bottom five human values category-wise – Transformational, Transactional and Terminal Human Values.

Table 7.4   Extent of adherence to human values at the levels of Indian industry, one's own organization and one's own professional life: human values common to two or more of the top and bottom ranks at the three levels [research study, 2011 (N=58)]

Value no.	Human value – Category	(a) Top human values – Indian industry		(b) Bottom human values – one's own professional life	
		Mean value	Rank	Mean value	Rank
29	Material comforts – Terminal	7.2	I	7.1	XXXII
9	Competitive spirit – Globalization-induced	7.1	II	7.1	XXXII
18	Entrepreneurship – Globalization-induced	6.1	IV	7.4	XXX

Table 7.5   Transformational, Transactional and Terminal Human Values: extent of adherence – a bird's-eye view [research study, 2011 (N=58)]

Human value	Indian industry as a whole	One's own organization	One's own professional life
Transformational HVs (5)			
Innate divinity – basic goodness – intrinsic altruism			
Overall average	5.1	7.3	8.2
Respect for nature and Mother Earth – Oneness			
Overall average	4.8	6.8	7.7
Transactional HVs (26)			
Personal HVs (4)			
Overall average	5.4	7.0	7.9
Professional HVs (4)			
Overall average	5.4	7.0	7.7
Group-oriented HVs (4)			
Overall average	5.4	7.2	8.0
Organizational HVs (8)			
Overall average	5.4	7.3	8.0
Globalization-induced HVs (6)			
Overall average	5.9	7.1	7.4
Terminal HVs (2)			
Overall average	6.3	7.1	7.4

Table 7.6   Extent of adherence to human values: strongest and weakest human values [research study, 2011 (N-58) (assessment on a ten-point scale ranging between one and ten)

Category of human values	Extent of adherence (on a ten-point scale) at the level of:		
	Indian industry	One's own organization	One's own professional life
Transformational HVs (5)			
Strongest	Belief in innate divinity in human beings (5)	Belief in innate divinity in human beings (5)	Belief in innate divinity in human beings (5)
	5.3	7.4	8.5
Weakest	Oneness (25)[+]	Oneness (25)	Oneness (25)
	4.8	6.2	7.4
Overall average	5.0	7.1	8.0
Transactional HVs (26)			
Personal HVs (4)			
Strongest	Conviction (10)	Integrity (24)	Integrity (24)
	6.0	7.3	8.2
Weakest	Integrity (24)	Humility (23)	Humility (23)
	5.1	6.7	7.6
Overall average	5.4	7.0	7.9
Professional HVs (4)			
Strongest	Professional attachment towards completion of the task (28)	Service orientation (32)	Professional attachment towards completion of the task (28)
	5.9	7.6	8.2
Weakest	Emotional detachment towards recognition and reward (14)	Emotional detachment towards recognition and reward (14)	Emotional detachment towards recognition and reward (14)
	4.6	6.1	6.9
Overall average	5.4	7.0	7.4
Group-oriented HVs (4)			
Strongest	Team spirit (33)	Cooperative attitude (11)[++]	Cooperative attitude (11)
	5.7	7.3	8.1
Weakest	Empathy (16)	Empathy (16)	Empathy (16)
	4.9	6.9	7.8
Overall average	5.4	7.2	8.0
Organizational HVs (8)			
Strongest	Respect for authority (30)	Respect for authority (30)	Commitment (7)
	6.5	7.6	8.4
Weakest	Community Interest (8)	Employee orientation (17)	Community interest (8)
	4.7	7.0	7.5
Overall average	5.4	7.3	8.0

Globalization-induced HVs (6)			
Strongest	Competitive spirit (9)	Cultural adaptiveness (13)	Cultural adaptiviness (13)
	7.1	7.5	7.7
Weakest	Hospitable disposition (22)	Competitive spirit (9)[+++]	Competitive spirit (9)
	5.5	6.9	7.1
Overall average	5.9	7.1	7.4
Terminal HVs (2)			
Stronger	Material comforts	Material comforts	Happiness
	7.2	7.3	7.7
Weaker	Happiness	Happiness	Material comforts
	5.4	6.9	7.1
Overall average	6.3		7.4

+ bracketed with respect for nature and Mother Earth
++ bracketed with mutual understanding
+++ bracketed with entrepreneurship, hospitable disposition and preparedness

A perusal of Tables 7.1 to 7.3 reveals that none of the human values ranked highest at the three levels was common to all three or even two levels. Three human values have, however, been found to be common among the bottom-ranked at two or more levels:

- Emotional detachment towards recognition and reward (15) (Transactional – Professional): Indian industry, one's own organization and one's own professional life

- Oneness (26) (Transformational): Indian industry, one's own organization and one's own professional life

- Equanimity (19) (Transactional – Professional): One's own organization and one's own professional life

Thus, of the three human values ranked among the lowest, two are professional – emotional detachment (15) and equanimity (19). Given that the four professional human values identified in the spectrum are symbolic of the concept of *karma yoga* (doing one's best, as an act of offering to the Supreme Power, and not craving for recognition and reward), and since the manager being *karma yogi* is recommended as organically related to the Spandan Approach and congenial to increasing human self-awareness, expectations and aspirations world over, the above finding is to be taken as a wakeup call that remaking ourselves as human beings does indeed deserve our attention.

Certain Responses to the Spandan Spectrum as an Instrument for Identifying and Developing a Suitable Inventory of Human Values in Work Situations

I find this tool a very good one to map what the different employees of the organization believe, particularly for in one's organizational context. It may help us to locate pockets of problem areas that need a focused intervention for correctness.

—Mukesh Gulati, Founder Director, Foundation for MSME Clusters,
New Delhi, 14 February 2011 – a respondent in the study,
Rekindling Innate Divinity in Human Beings.

Dear Professor,

My view on the 33 Human Value/Cluster of Human Value questionnaire is as under:

- *Human value has two factors, from the point of view of the respondent – Positive factors and Negative factors. All the 33 factors mentioned in the questionnaire were Positive factors.*

- *Positive factors by their 'presence' contribute to the bedrock for human existence and growth. Negative factors by their 'absence' [also] contribute to the bedrock for human existence and growth.*

- *A few of the Negative factors that come to mind are – apathy or indifference, insecurity, irresponsibility or lack of accountability, self-doubt, low self-esteem, lack of confidence, laziness, procrastination, destructive competitiveness, disbelief in social order, arrogance (intellectual, ego), hostility, belligerence, racial/social bias, an attitude to succeed at any cost, despotism, manipulative behaviour, politicking, an environment of constant anxiety, me-myself selfishness, I-alone-succeed-let-others-perish, habit of hoarding, compromising long-term good for short-term gain.*

- *It is the management's responsibility to pick [these] out, [and to] rectify the organization behaviour to ensure that the Negative factors are minimized/eliminated as a part of the culture. Weeding out the unwanted behaviour/traits is equally important to an organization's cultural agriculture, as too is growing the positive human values.*

- *The mythological representation of our Hindu Gods has always symbolized that while two of the hands bless the devotees, the other two carry weapons of war/punishment and destruction. The Korean Yin and Yang symbolizes the balance between good and bad.*

- *Hence, the study would have been even more complete if the absence of the Negative factors were also measured along with the presence/ adherence of Positive factors.*

—*R. Vishweswaran, Financial Software & Systems P Ltd (FSS), Chicago, USA, 27 January 2011*

Author's response:

Dear Mr. Vishweswaran,

Thanks for your prompt response.

Human Value(s), unless otherwise mentioned, denotes positive meaning. The negative, dysfunctional side of human value is designated as 'disvalue'. Disvalue to value can be viewed as a continuum – which is incidentally implied. To accommodate this enlarged viewpoint, the scale/range can be extended to 10 to 10, in place of 0 to 10.

Thanks once again for your insight and input.

Cordially

G.P. Rao

Appendix: Spandan Spectrum Response Sheet

Spandan Spectrum of Human Values in an Organization 2011 © G.P. Rao

Human value/cluster of human values	Extent to which the value/cluster is being adhered (10-point scale)		
	Indian industry (max 10)	My own org./ institution (max 10)	My own professional life (max 10)
1. *Accountability* – Owning responsibility			
2. *Autonomy in Decision Making* – Flexible work culture — Accepting diversity and divergence			
3. *Behavioural Flexibility* – Adaptiveness – Open mindedness			
4. *Belief in the basic goodness of human beings* – Faith in basic goodness of others – Trust			
5. *Belief in innate divinity in human beings* – Human dignity – Self-respect – Respect for others			
6. *Belief in intrinsic altruism in human beings* – Caring – Sharing – Compassion			
7. *Commitment*			
8. *Community Interest* – Social good – Sustainable development			
9. *Competitive spirit*			
10. *Conviction*			
11. *Cooperative attitude*			
12. *Creativity* – Innovation			
13. *Cultural adaptiveness* – Cross-cultural management			
14. *Customer satisfaction*			
15. *Emotional detachment towards recognition and reward*			
16. *Empathy* – Transformative listening – Sensitivity to others' feelings and needs – Social sensitivity			
17. *Employee orientation*			
18. *Entrepreneurship* – Risk-taking			
19. *Equanimity*			

20. *Fairness* – Equity – Justice			
21. *Happiness* – Contentment			
22. *Hospitable disposition* (Marwar Culture)			
23. *Humility* – Self-awareness			
24. *Integrity* – Consistency in saying and doing			
25. *Mutual understanding and respect* – Psychological contract			
26. *Oneness* – Cosmic consciousness – *Brahmn*			
27. *Preparedness* – Proactiveness – Environmental sensitivity			
28. *Professional attachment towards the work*			
29. *Prosperity* – Profits – Economic wellbeing – Material comforts			
30. *Respect for authority* – Managerial prerogative			
31. *Respect for nature and Mother Earth* – Sustainable development			
32. *Service orientation*			
33. *Team spirit*			

8

Transformational Human Values

The Context and the Issue

As has been submitted, the Spandan Approach rests on a belief in three essential qualities of human beings.

1. innate divinity

2. basic goodness

3. intrinsic altruism

These three qualities are symbolically represented by what could be referred to as heartbeat, pulsation, vibration or echo. This unseen but omnipresent feeling is the binding force of humankind.[1] These qualities are the essence of what we here refer to as Transformational Human Values – I, which, in the Spandan Spectrum of Human Values 2011, appear as:

- 4: Belief in the basic goodness of human beings – Faith in the basic goodness of others – Trust

- 5: Belief in innate divinity in human beings – Human dignity – Self-respect – Respect for others

- 6: Belief in the intrinsic altruism in human beings – Caring – Sharing – Compassion

---

1   His Holiness the Dalai Lama, in his work, *Beyond Religion* (2011), states: 'What all of us – of all religions, and those of no religion – have in common is our humanity. We all belong to humankind. Or humankind, the kind part is what makes us human. This kind-ness of us humans – which we share with other mammals, with all creatures whose off-spring need maternal care and nurture – is based on compassion: the ability to feel empathy for one's fellow beings.'

Human beings also have to interact with nature, consisting of the five elements of Earth, Air, Water, Fire and Ether. Human beings are in fact constituted of these five elements through which they are bound, by which they are nourished and nurtured, and to which they return after death. This is the essence of Indian philosophy and its approach to humankind. Human values that describe normative behaviour with regards to nature are here referred to as Transformational Human Values – II and in the Spandan Spectrum of Human Values 2011 appear as:

- 26: Oneness – Cosmic consciousness – *Brahmn*

- 31: Respect for nature and Mother Earth – Sustainable development

Awareness and acceptance of and adherence to these five human values, which constitute the Transformational Human Values I and II, enables us to know our real self and worth. In doing so we remake ourselves accordingly, capable of interacting with other human beings and with nature in a manner beneficial to each and all. However, we also need different but related human values specific to the roles we play in our profession, group affiliation, institutional membership, societal citizenship and being an integral part of the world and cosmos as a whole. These we refer to as Transactional Human Values, which are dealt with in Chapters 9 to 14, constituting Part III of the book.

The present chapter aims at diagnosis of the Transformational Human Values, assessing the extent of adherence to them (discovery), and offering experiential learning as a possible means to continuously re-examine ourselves through introspection and through the feedback of others.

Diagnosis: Transformational Human Values

The Spandan Spectrum of Human Values 2011 identifies the five Transformational Human values as follows:

Transformational Human Values I – in relation to fellow humans:

- 4: Belief in the basic goodness of human beings – Faith in the basic goodness of others – Trust

- 5: Belief in the innate divinity in human beings – Human dignity – Self-respect – Respect for others

- 6: Belief in the intrinsic altruism in human beings – Caring – Sharing – Compassion

Transformation Human Values II – in relation to the environment and universe:

- 31: Respect for nature and Mother Earth – Sustainable development

- 26: Oneness – Cosmic consciousness – *Brahmn* (Supreme Power)

4: BELIEF IN THE BASIC GOODNESS OF HUMAN BEINGS – FAITH IN THE BASIC GOODNESS OF OTHERS – TRUST

Belief in the basic goodness of human beings is a generic human quality. Faith in the basic goodness of others is specific to the dyad, group and institutional contexts of human emotions, interactions and activities.

Belief in the basic goodness of human beings is rooted in Buddhist psychology and based upon the notion that all people are fundamentally good, their qualities being positive ones: openness, intelligence and compassion. This viewpoint is reflected in traditional concepts like *bodhicitta*, the awakened mind and *tathagatagarbha*, meaning birthplace of the enlightened, but used in the connotation of Buddha nature (Theophil 2012).

In formal enterprises, organizations and institutions in particular, such faith should be the credo of management and its organization. Trust is the logical corollary of such faith. It is impossible to visualize an organization coming into being without mutual trust – not to mention its survival and growth.

5: BELIEF IN THE INNATE DIVINITY IN HUMAN BEINGS – HUMAN DIGNITY – SELF-RESPECT – RESPECT FOR OTHERS

Thomas E. Hill Jr., in his Tanner Lectures on Respect for Humanity, delivered at Stanford University in 1994, observes:

> *History echoes with passionate pleas for justice and charity, but in our times, increasingly, what we hear are demands for respect …*

> *The respect that the people want is something more than material benefits, more even than such benefits offered in a charitable spirit, or from recognition that they are owed ... Every human being has a claim, namely, full recognition as a person, with the same basic moral worth as any other, co-membership in the community whose members share the authority to determine how things ought to be and the power to influence how they will be. (1994: 4)*

6: BELIEF IN THE INTRINSIC ALTRUISM IN HUMAN BEINGS – CARING – SHARING – COMPASSION

The genesis, existence and growth of human systems is dependent upon a sense of understanding and togetherness. Caring, sharing and compassion play an important role in this context, in particular in developing among members what Robert Tannenbaum (1957) has called 'social sensitivity'. This refers to the extent to which one empathizes and resonates with the pain and pleasure of others. The ability to respond through actions to this happiness or pain is called behavioural flexibility. The willingness and ability to empathize, resonate and respond through gestures, words and actions to the pain, unhappiness, suffering and unpleasantness of others constitutes the concept of compassion.

Compassion is essential in human interactions and activities in work situations, as elsewhere, irrespective of the hierarchy and the nature of one's responsibilities. Indeed, the humaneness that members of an organization possess toward one another becomes a critical factor in the organization's functioning and growth. Organizations, however, have their own characteristics which may not always synchronize with the willingness and ability of the given focal person to project his or her compassion in action. A formal organization's web of rules and regulations could be one such characteristic. A second could be the organization's concept of fairness and equity. One person's act of compassion towards another may actually be motivated by favouritism, thus disallowing compassion towards others. Achieving parity, that is, being consistent in one's actions, is the logical extension of fairness.

A relevant example in this context is provided by the AICTE Emeritus Fellowship study which appeared in the author's 'Self Control as a Human Value' (Rao 2002). As related by the Executive Director of a large textile mill located in the hill state of Himachal Pradesh in India, for some months the company could not provide transport facilities for its employees from home to the workplace. Being a hill station, public transport was somewhat inadequate, and commuting by foot was particularly onerous for women and elderly employees. The Executive Director therefore used to offer lifts to some of the employees on the way to work and in particularly from the factory gate at the end of the working day. This practice was not popular with other employees, who considered it an act of favouritism on the part of the Executive Director. As a result, he had to discontinue the practice.

26: ONENESS – COSMIC CONSCIOUSNESS – BRAHMN (SUPREME POWER)

B.L. Athreya, in his scholarly treatise on Indian Culture for UNESCO (1949), underlines Indian understanding that 'Man at bottom is Spirit which is identical with the spirit in and behind the Universe'. He elaborates:

> The knowledge of man, and of the Universe, whose product and part he is, has gone too deep to be fathomed by the methods of modern science. By their yogic methods, Indian seers discovered that man was a microcosm in which the whole macrocosm is represented. (p. 14)

31: RESPECT FOR NATURE AND MOTHER EARTH – SUSTAINABLE DEVELOPMENT

> Earth, in which lie the sea, river and other waters, in which food and cornfields have come to be, in which live all that breathes and moves, may she confer on us the finest of her yield. Earth, my Mother! Set me securely with bliss in full accord with Heaven. (Atharvaveda, 12.1)

> You visit the earth, and water it. You greatly enrich it. The river of God is full of water. You provide them grain, for so You have ordained it. You drench its furrows. You level its ridges. You soften it with showers. You bless it with a crop. (Psalm, 65: 9–10)

Discovery: Extent of Adherence

Table 8.1 summarizes the perception of 58 select invitee respondents to a study on rekindling the innate divinity in human beings, 2011. As noted in an earlier chapter, these respondents were management professionals, academics, entrepreneurs, industrialists and administrators. Their perception of the extent to which the five Transformational Human Values are adhered – as also the

28 Transactional and Terminal Human Values constituting the Spandan Spectrum of Human Values 2011 – was solicited at the levels of Indian industry, one's own organization and one's own profession life.

The responses revealed that the overall mean value of adherence to Transformational Human Values was – on a ten-point scale – 5.0 in Indian industry as a whole, 7.1 in the respondents' own organization and 8.0 in their profession life. This indicates that they perceive and believe that adherence to the Transformational Human Values is highest in terms of their own actions, but less when it comes to their performance in their own organizations, and the lowest in the context of – a rather distant – Indian industry as whole. This is a very subtle but significant human tendency – to estimate one's self higher compared to one's colleagues in the context of an organization and much higher compared to the country as whole. This perhaps indicates a very subtle human tendency to 'own' success and 'disown' failure.[2]

This tendency, to assess one's own professional life above one's own organization followed by Indian industry as whole is a trend we find – with few exceptions – throughout the subsequent analysis.

Table 8.1 also shows that belief in innate divinity (5) has been ranked highest at 8.5 and 7.4 at the levels of one's own professional life and one's own organization, while faith in basic goodness (4) stands highest with 8.2 at the level of one's own professional life. It is heartening to know that these two values have been perceived as important in the Spandan initiative on remaking ourselves in the context of enterprise and society (see further Chapters 15 to 18).

With regards Oneness (26) and respect for nature and Mother Earth (31), the two values binding human beings with nature and the cosmos are ranked low at all three levels of Indian industry, one's own organization and one's own professional life. Perception of the extent of adherence to these two values is indeed very low, with both ranked equal 29th (out of a total of the 33 human values comprising the Spandan Spectrum of Human Values 2011). This trend, one would think, should be another wake-up call for us all.

---

2   The present author has had the opportunity of conducting around 2,000 workshops on interpersonal effectiveness over a 15-year period in different organizations with participants representing different hierarchies and functional areas. One of the objectives of the workshops was the assessment of self, and the assessment by others of the focal person, on select components of interpersonal effectiveness. With a few rare exceptions, the findings arrived at almost always revealed that the focal person's self-assessment was higher than his or her assessment by others.

Table 8.1   Transformational Human Values: adherence by managers at the levels of Indian industry, one's own organization and one's own profession [research study, 2011 (N=58)]

HHV no.	Category	Human value	Extent of adherence (N=58)					
			Indian industry		One's own organization		One's own professional life	
			Mean	Rank	Mean	Rank	Mean	Rank
		Transformational Human Values – I: in relation to other humans						
4	Transf. HVs-I	Belief in the basic goodness of human beings – faith in the basic goodness of others – trust	5.0	XXVI	7.3	IX	8.2	III
5	Transf. HVs-I	Belief in the innate divinity in human beings – human dignity – self-respect – respect for others	5.3	XVIII	7.4	V	8.5	I
6	Transf. HVs-I	Belief in the intrinsic altruism of human beings – caring – sharing – compassion	5.9	XVII	7.3	IX	8.0	XI
		Transformational Human Values –II: in relation to Mother Earth and the universe						
26	Transf. HVs-II	Oneness – cosmic consciousness – Brahmn	4.8	XXIX	6.2	XXXII	7.4	XXVII
31	Transf. HVs-II	Respect for nature and Mother Earth – sustainable development	4.8	XXIX	7.3	IX	7.9	XIV

Light grey boxes indicate highest-ranked human values.
Dark grey boxes indicate lowest-ranked human values.

Development: The Spandan Perspective: Experiential Learning

Efforts in the directions of self-awareness and action with regards to one's self in relation to others can, and does, vary from very simple acts to complex human endeavours. A very simple but effective instrument in this context is experiential learning – that is, self-analysis (introspection) and assessment by the others concerned and involved (feedback) being used continuously and informally to help improve upon interpersonal relations and understanding in various settings such as among friends, and in the family, neighbourhood, community, organizations and society. This, in other words, is dialogue and discussion. In the Indian context, the *panchayat* system from ancient times, that exists even now in many villages in the country, is a model worth consideration by all concerned. A *panchayat* consists of five (*panch*) members selected from the village, and considered to be five Gods. The *panchayat* deliberates on matters of mutual interest and resolves differences of opinion and misunderstandings through dialogue and discussion.

Arthur Kleinman, in his Tanner Lectures on Human Values on Experience, delivered at Stanford University (1998), states experience is 'the felt flow of interpersonal communication and engagement ... and is characterized by an orientation of overwhelming practicability' (pp. 358, 360). Kleinman observes that interaction in the 'local world' consisting of 'ethnographic wage, neighborhood networks, family and other institutions' would be useful. The Western version would be the big three of morality that are autonomy, community and divinity. The Chinese tradition, however, Kleinman observes, is to 'relate Xing (physical nature) with Qing (emotion) and the moral order'.

Chapter 12, on Management and Organizations, discusses experiential learning as applicable to the institutional context.

References

Athreya, B.L. 1949. *Indian Culture: Its Spiritual, Moral and Social Aspects*. Paris: UNESCO. Bhaumik, Mani. 2011. True Nature, *The Speaking Tree* (Times of India), 18 December.
Bookchin, Murray. 1990. *Remaking Society: Pathways to a Green Future*. Boston, MA: South End Press.
——2005. Social Ecology versus 'Deep' Ecology: A Challenge for the Ecology Movement. *Green Perspectives*, 4–5 (Summer): 1–23.

Bruteau, Beatrice. 2012. We are the World. *The Speaking Tree* (Times of India), 26 February.

Capitalism vs Altruism: SKS Rekindles the Micro Finance Debate. *India Knowledge @ Wharton*. [Online: 7 October 2010]. Available at: http://knowledge.wharton.upenn.edu/india/article.cfm?articleid=4533 [accessed: 17 July 2013].

Cohen, Andrew. 2012. Evolve with the Universe. *The Speaking Tree* (Times of India), 26 February.

Haught, John. 2012. A God Shaped Hole to Fill. *The Speaking Tree* (Times of India), 26 February.

Hill Jr, Thomas E. 1994. *Respect for Humanity*, The Tanner Lectures on Human Values, Stanford University, 26 and 28 April 1994.

His Holiness The Dali Lama. 2011. *Beyond Religion: Ethics for the Entire World*. New Delhi: HarperCollins.

Huxley, Thomas H. 1863. *Evidence as to Man's Place in Nature*. London: Williams and Norgate.

Kleinman, Arthur. 1998. *Experience and Its Moral Modes: Culture, Human Conditions, and Disorder*, The Tanner Lectures on Human Values, Stanford University, 13–16 April 1998.

Rao, G.P. 2002. Self Control as a Managerial Value (AICTE Emeritus Fellowship Study, 1999–2002). Unpublished.

Sagan, Carl. 1980. 'Who Speaks for Earth?' *Cosmos*, Episode 13.

Shri Shri Anand Murti. 2012. From Intellect to Intuition. *The Speaking Tree* (Times of India), 18 February.

Tannenbaum, Robert. 1957. Dealing with Ourselves before Dealing with Others. *Office Executive*, 32(8): 29–30, 35.

Thakar, Vimala. 2012. Revolution. *The Speaking Tree* (Times of India), 26 February.

Theophil, Marguerite. 2012. Attending to Basic Goodness. *The Speaking Tree* (Times of India), 7 June.

Yunker, James A. 2007. *Political Globalization: A New Vision of Federal World Government*. Lanham, MD: University Press of America.

PART III

Management Contribution in Remaking Enterprise through Human Values: Transactional Human Values

9

The Manager as a Human Being: Personal Human Values

The Context and the Issue

The *Times of India* article 'Groundhog Buddhism' (12 April) raises – among others – the issue 'Can the self guide itself (out of its self-created misery)?' The issue at hand is the survival, growth and transformation of self, though the transformation is not only of self, but by self, for self. To expand, this odyssey of transformation is to be of human beings at individual, professional, organizational and societal levels and to be initiated by self within the framework of the given society. It aims at propagating and inculcating the required knowledge, skills, attitudes and values to enable human beings to become 'humane'. The human being is thus the subject, predicate and object of the process of self-transformation, and the pivot of growth, development and transformation is self. We can therefore say the aim is to move from lower self (pettiness) to higher Self (dignity) (Chakraborty 1993), or 'to remake ourselves', as Mahatma Gandhi famously said: 'As human beings our greatness lies not so much in being able to remake the world – which is the myth of the atomic age – as in being able to remake ourselves.'

However, the rather sad and surprising reality is that, more often than not, we forget that the biggest responsibility for guiding transformation lies with one's self, although as stated earlier, the transformation of self is to be initiated *within the framework of the society*, and thus society does have a stake in its citizens. So while socializing agents like family, education and culture do therefore have a role to play, as well as a right and responsibility in the process of transformation of each human being as their integral component, their stakes cannot override one's own and therefore one's own responsibility in realizing the need for self-development. In other words the buck stops at self; responsibility keeps coming back to self again and again. In fact, responsibility has never left self, has always been with self and always will be with self. For the truth is that, as Jacquelyn Small (2007), the French psychologist, stated, 'You are not a human being trying to be spiritual; you are a spiritual being learning to be human' (p. 3).

How rich and, at the same time, how poor we are!

It is therefore appropriate that Jiddu Krishnamurti (2010), the renowned Indian religious thinker and philosopher stated:

> *There is a learning which begins with self knowledge ... awareness of your every-day activities .... If you are not aware of your response to every challenge in life, there is no self-knowledge. You can know yourself as you are only in relation to something, in relation to people, ideas, and things. If you assume anything about your self ... your mind is incapable of learning.*

Diagnosis: Personal Human Values

The personal human values identified and enumerated in the Spandan Spectrum of Human Values 2011 are:

- 3: Behavioural flexibility – Adaptiveness – Open-mindedness

- 10: Conviction

- 23: Humility – Self-awareness

- 24: Integrity – Consistency in saying (*vacha*) and doing (*karmana*)

Figure 9.1 presents the Spandan personal values within the conceptual framework of the book.

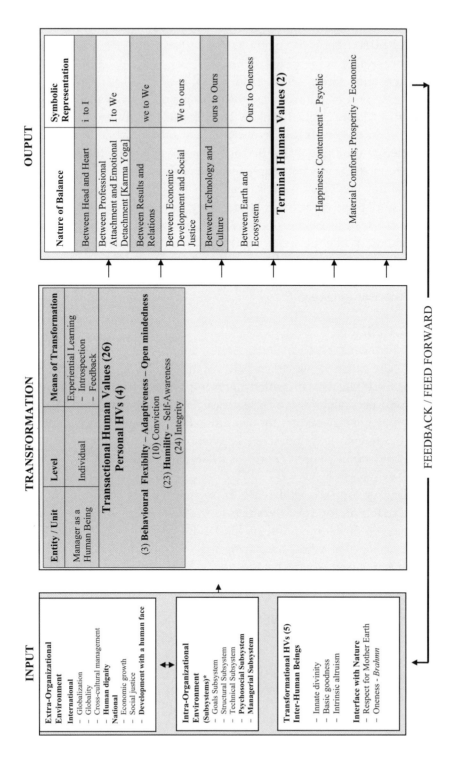

Figure 9.1   Remaking ourselves as human beings, enterprise and society: Transactional Human Values: personal human values

3: BEHAVIOURAL FLEXIBILITY – ADAPTIVENESS – OPEN-MINDEDNESS

Robert Tannenbaum, in his widely read paper, *Dealing with Ourselves before Dealing with Others* (1957), introduced the concepts of 'social sensitivity' and 'behavioural flexibility'. Social sensitivity refers to the ability of a person to be sensitive to the needs and expectations of others, while behavioural flexibility refers to the ability of the person to change or modify her behaviour dependent upon the understanding she obtains through social sensitivity. Such behavioural flexibility is closely associated with adaptiveness, open mindedness and positive attitude. The nature and extent of behavioural flexibility is a function of the organization and its formal structure and informal system. While behavioural flexibility is necessary, 'too much' of it may turn out to be undesirable and dysfunctional. When a person is too adaptable, it may be seen as her weakness and may result at times in inconsistent decision-making.

10: CONVICTION

Conviction is the extent to which one believes in what he or she is doing, the strength and the intensity with which a person pursues his or her objectives. Persistence and perseverance are closely associated with conviction. A high degree of conviction is necessary for institution building and for great things to happen. In my own way, I describe conviction as 'burning oneself to the given cast'. Conviction, in other words, is a hallmark of idealism.

'Too much' or excessive adherence to or projection of conviction is not especially desirable as, for example, a person with conviction in his profession or career may become unmindful of his family and his role therein. His ability to listen to what others are saying may become diminished and his impatience may increase when what the other person says contradicts his own view points.

23: HUMILITY – SELF-AWARENESS

Humility refers to an individual not always having to project in public what she knows. It denotes the person showing or revealing her abilities and competence to others only when she perceives they are needed. Self-awareness, being even more subtle than the projection of integrity through a consistency in saying (*vacha*) and doing (*karmana*), is a function of humility. Humility, therefore, is symbolized by saints and seers.

It is significant that management world over is realizing the need to be humble to be effective in their performance. It is also significant to note the recent increasing awareness and importance of humility as a desirable human value. Certain data and insights on humility are provided below:

> It's the age of honchos with a heart – opening lift doors and flying economy. For Tata and Murthy, influence comes from their personalities as much as from their wealth. (Indrani Rajkhowa Banerjee, CEO at your service, Sunday Times, 9 August 2009)

> Humility ... is marked by the willingness and preparedness to learn and learn all the time. (Sudhmahi Regunathan, A Lesson in Humility, The Speaking Tree (Times of India), 7 March 2010)

The above-stated growing emphasis on humility is perhaps indicative of the increasing realization of a need to be spiritual by the corporate sector in particular (see further Chapter 19).

Like other human values – and any human action for that matter – an excessive adherence to humility can become dysfunctional. Though a humble person may perceived as meek and mild-mannered, his leadership may turn out to be what is sometimes referred to as 'doormat' leadership.

24: INTEGRITY – CONSISTENCY IN SAYING AND DOING

As discussed earlier, the three planes of the human mind and human behaviour are thinking, communicating and doing. In Indian parlance, the thinking mind is referred to as '*manasa*', communicating as '*vacha*' and conduct or action as '*karmana*'. Human behaviour is, in other words, a function of what the individual thinks and says. Of course an individual's thoughts can only be inferred by what he or she says and does. Communication and conduct are thus the visible phenomena of a human being. Integrity can be equated with consistency in one's speech and action and is an important feature of, and therefore of value to, managerial effectiveness. Michel C. Jensen (2011), for instance, includes integrity as one of the three important human values for a great person, a great organization and great leadership.

Discovery: Extent of Adherence

Tables 9.1 and 9.2 contain the relevant data.

Table 9.1   Personal human values: extent of adherence [research study, 2011 (N=58)]

HHV no.	Category	Human value	Extent of adherence (N=58)					
			Indian industry		One's own organization		One's own professional life	
			Mean	Rank	Mean	Rank	Mean	Rank
3	Personal	Behavioural Flexibility – adaptiveness – open-mindedness	5.3	XVIII	6.9	XXIII	7.7	XX
10	Personal	Conviction	6.0	V	7.2	XVI	7.9	XIV
23	Personal	Humility – self-awareness	5.3	XVIII	6.7	XXXI	7.6	XXIII
24	Personal	Integrity – consistency in saying and doing	5.1	XXIV	7.3	IX	8.2	III
Overall average			5.4		7.0		7.9	

Table 9.1 reveals that the overall mean average for the four personal human values at the different levels are: Indian industry, 5.4; one's own organization, 7.0, and one's own professional life, 7.9. Conviction (10) is ranked highest at the level of Indian industry, while integrity (24) is ranked highest at the level of one's own organization, and at the level of one's own professional life.

Looking back to Chapter 7, Table 7.5 offers a bird's-eye view of the values at the three different levels. The overall average for personal human values is 5.4 at the level of Indian Industry, which is one of the four lowest ranked values among all the Transactional Human Values – the others being professional, group-based and organizational human values. At the level of one's own organization the overall average is 7.0, again one of the two lowest – the other being professional human values. The overall average of 7.9 at the level of one's own professional life is ranked third after group-based and organizational human values.

Table 9.2   Personal Human Values – extent of adherence – perceptual gaps

Individual – personal value	One's own professional life	One's own organization	Perceptual gap
3. Behavioural flexibility	7.7	6.9	-0.8
10. Conviction	7.9	7.2	-0.7
23. Humility	7.6	6.7	-0.9
24. Integrity	8.2	7.3	-0.9
Overall average	7.9	7.0	-0.9

Table 9.2 presents the perceptual gap between assessments at the levels of one's own professional life and one's own organization. The gaps with reference to humility (23) and integrity (24) are greatest, at -0.9. The perception of adherence to humility and integrity at the level of one's own profession life is higher than that at the level of one's own organization. This is a matter worthy of consideration.

Development: Indian Approach

GUNA THEORY AND ITS RELEVANCE

In Sanskrit the mental temperaments of human beings are known as *gunas*, which are of three types. Each has a distinct character.

- *Tamas* – inactive: inertia, lethargy, indolence and indifference. A person lives a dull, inactive life, with hardly any response to the world.

- *Rajas* – active: passionate, desirous and agitated. A person bristles with frenzied actions leading to involvement in the affairs of the world.

- *Satva* – trans-active: equanimity, serenity, objectivity. A person is poised, mature, contemplative, detached from worldly involvement and excitement.

Satva, rajas and *tamas*, in different proportions, account for the heterogeneous variety of human beings. Every individual possesses all three *gunas*. The role of a human in his or her lifetime is to rise gradually from *tamas* to *rajas* to *satva* and then to reach trans-*satva*, wherein lies the Supreme Self.

Malcolm Innes-Brown and Samir Chatterjee (1999) discuss the relevance of Guna theory:

> *In its essence, the Guna theory depicts values which constitute human personality into a 'sattwa–rajas' delineation of deepened understanding, giving direction to action and which, in turn, illustrates negative values ('tamas') likely to cause obstruction. For managers to appreciate this level of understanding while simultaneously sensing these values which inhibit purposeful action, may be regarded as containing strength in a more intuitive, subjective way than values of moral judgment adopted to guide managerial action in the West. As such, the Guna theory has deep relevance in the face of egoistical, contractual or legal values, so often defining the parameters of Western management.*

DEVELOPMENT: THE SPANDAN PERSPECTIVE: EXPERIENTIAL LEARNING

As stated in Chapter 8 the Spandan Approach of remaking ourselves as human beings in relation to others involves experiential learning, an important instrument in self-appraisal and development. Experiential learning consists of personal introspection and feedback from relevant others on any specific issue, so that proper insights may be obtained on the said issue (discovery) and suitable ways and means worked up to deal with it (development). The person doing the introspection is called the focal person. The person(s) offering feedback are the resource person(s). The resource persons could be parents, relatives, friends, community leaders or others. The conditions necessary for persons to be resource persons are: being in close contact and aware of the given situation and issue (awareness), having interest and involvement in the growth of the given focal person (willingness), and being able to be free and frank when needed in offering feedback (ability). Awareness, willingness and ability are thus the three critical components of an effective resource person.

Selection of the issue(s), resource person(s), timing and place is to be informal, spontaneous and open. It has been found that such interactions between and among the persons involved and interested in mutual growth go a long way to easing interpersonal relations and enhancing mutual understanding and respect.

Experiential learning is equally an integral part of – as discussed in Chapter 3 – the Spandan 3D Process of the inculcation of human values in an organization. Designated Focal Person–Resource Persons Interactive Sessions (FP-RP IS), are experiential learning sessions providing opportunities for the members of an organization to develop higher social sensitivity. The underlying assumption is the adage that an institution is only as good or as bad as its members.

References

Chakraborty, S.K. 1993. *Managerial Transformation by Values: A Corporate Pilgrimage*. New Delhi: Sage.

Enderle, Georges. 2007. The Ethics of Conviction of Responsibility: A False Antithesis for Business Ethics. *Journal of Human Values*, 13 (December 2007): 83–94.

Frankfurt, Harry. 2004. *Taking Our Selves Seriously*, The Tanner Lectures on Human Values, Stanford University, 14–16 April, 2004.

Innes-Brown, Malcolm and Samir Chatterjee. 1999. The Relevance of Guna Theory in the Congruence of Eastern Values and Western Management Practice. *Journal of Human Values*, 5 (October 1999): 93–102.

Jensen, Michael C. 2011. The Three Foundations of a Great Life, Great Leadership and a Great Organization. *HBS Working Knowledge*, 28 July.

Krishnamurti, J. 2010. The Creative Impulse. *The Speaking Tree*. [Online]. Available at: www.speakingtree.in/spiritual-articles/.../the-creative-impulse/comments [accessed: 6 August 2013].

Small, Jacquelyn. 2007. *The Sacred Purpose of Being Human: A Journey through the Twelve Principles of Wholeness*. Deerfield Beach, FL: Health Communications Inc.

Stroud, Barry. 1989. *The Study of Human Nature and the Subjectivity of Value*, The Tanner Lectures on Human Values, University of Buenos Aires, 7 June 1989.

Tannenbaum, Robert. 1957. Dealing with Ourselves before Dealing with Others. *Office Executive*, 32(8): 29–30, 35.

10

The Manager as a Professional: Professional Human Values

The Context and the Issue: The Manager as *Karma Yogi*

The concept of *karma yoga* denotes duty, *dharma*, being discharged diligently and wholeheartedly, without hankering for recognition and reward in return, as a means to achieve Self-realization. *Yoga* may be defined as 'spiritual discipline to link one's self with the Supreme', and *karma* as 'material activities, for which one incurs subsequent reactions'. *Karma yoga*, therefore, refers to 'the path to God realization through dedicating the fruits of one's work to God'.

Karma yoga constitutes an important part of the *Bhagavad Gita* ('Song of the Lord') (see Chapter 5), which is universally renowned as the jewel of India's spiritual wisdom. Spoken by Lord Sri Krishna, the Supreme Personality of Godhead, to his intimate devotee Arjuna, the *Gita's* 700 verses provide a definitive guide to the science of self-realization. If one's goal is freedom, self-realization, the best path is to perform one's duties with a spirit of nonattachment, without caring for the fruits of one's actions and without the thought of pleasure or pain, profit or loss, victory or failure, and with a sense of equanimity and equality. Jitendra Mohanty, the primary contributor on Indian Philosophy to *Encyclopaedia Britannica*, states that, at this stage,

> the Kantian ethic of 'duty for duty's sake' seems to be the nearest Western parallel to Krishna's teaching ... But Krishna went beyond it by pointing out that performance of action with complete nonattachment requires knowledge (jnana) of the true nature of self, its distinction from prakriti, or matter ... with its three component elements, sattva, rajas *and* tamas *and of the highest self,* Purushottama *or* Purusha.

This particular philosophical approach, as can be observed, is congruent with – rather integral to – the Spandan Approach, with faith in the innate divinity, basic goodness and intrinsic altruism of human beings as its credo. It is equally congruent with and integral to Spandan's 51:49 leadership philosophy, coextensive with its concept of the Functionally Humane Organization (see Chapter 20).

The four professional values included in the Spandan Spectrum of Human Values 2011, as listed below, aim to embed the concept of *karma yoga* as a professional ethic for any person entrusted with the task of working with and through others – managers, leaders, mentors, parents, teachers, bosses, friends and so on.

Diagnosis: Professional Human Values

The Spandan Spectrum of Human Values 2011 enumerates four professional human values:

- 15: Emotional detachment towards recognition and reward

- 19: Equanimity – Self-control

- 28: Professional attachment towards completion of the task

- 32: Service orientation

Figure 10.1 presents the Spandan professional human values within the conceptual framework of the book.

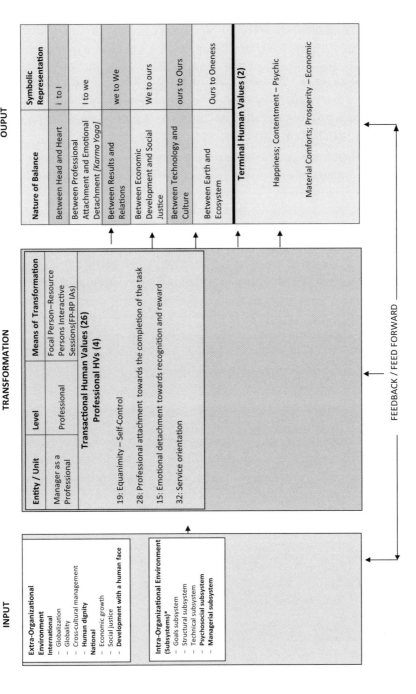

Figure 10.1 Remaking ourselves as human beings, enterprise and society: Transactional Human Values: professional human values

Discovery: Extent of Adherence

Tables 10.1 and 10.2 present the relevant data.

Table 10.1   **Manager as a professional: manager as a *karma yogi*: adherence to professional human values at the levels of Indian industry, one's own organization and one's own professional life [research study, 2011 (N=58)]**

HV no.	Category	Human value	Extent of adherence (N=58)					
			Indian industry		One's own organization		One's own professional life	
			Mean	Rank	Mean	Rank	Mean	Rank
15	Professional	Emotional detachment toward recognition and reward	4.6	XXXIII	6.1	XXXIII	6.9	XXXIII
19	Professional	Equanimity – self control	5.5	XXIX	6.8	XXX	7.4	XXVII
28	Professional	Professional attachment towards completion of task	5.9	V	7.4	V	8.2	III
32	Professional	Service orientation	5.4	XV	7.6	I	8.1	VII

Light grey boxes indicate highest-ranked human values.
Dark grey boxes indicate lowest-ranked human values.

Table 10.1 reveals an overall average of adherence to the four professional human values of 5.4 (out of a maximum of 10) in the case of Indian industry, 7.0 in the case of one's own organization and 7.7 with reference to one's professional life. This trend of the average at the industry level being the lowest and that at the personal professional level being highest is consistent with other values. One very subtle but unmistakable message, as noted, is the estimation that one's own adherence is higher as compared to one's organization and much higher as compared to industry as a whole. This disconnect between perception of self and the perception of others is, as noted earlier, an issue worthy of further probing and investigation.

Professional attachment (28) has been ranked as the most adhered to value in the case of Indian industry and at the level of one's own professional life, while service orientation (32) is rated highest with regards to one's own organization. Emotional detachment (15) has been rated lowest at all the three levels.

Table 10.1 also compares the extent of adherence to the professional human values as against the total 33 human values in the spectrum. Emotional detachment (15) is ranked lowest (33rd) in the case of all the three levels. Equanimity (19) is one of the bottom five human values at the level of one's own professional life, while service orientation (32) is ranked highest in one's own organization.

The perceptual gap between the assessment of adherence at the levels of one's own professional life and one's own organization is presented in Table 10.2. Such perceptual gap is highest in the case of professional attachment, at -0.8. This again confirms the over-valuation of one's self – as also the unwillingness or inability, or both, of senior professionals to improve upon the professional attachment in their organization.

Table 10.2   Manager as a professional: professional human values: extent of adherence – perceptual gaps

Professional value	One's own professional life	One's own organization	Perceptual gaps
15. Emotional detachment	6.9	6.1	-0.8
19. Equanimity	7.4	6.8	-0.6
28. Professional attachment	8.2	7.4	-0.8
32. Service Orientation	8.1	7.6	-0.5
Overall average	7.7	7.0	-0.7

Development: Management Philosophy: An Indian Perspective[1]

Management can be defined as 'getting things done'. A manager, accordingly, is expected to get desired results from and through people. For this purpose, he is expected to motivate, that is, 'induce' others such that they behave in the manner he wants. Thus management's and managers' focus is on results. While it is true that management and managers should be results oriented, it appears that almost exclusive attention is laid on results. Management education and training, for example, talks of 'management by results'. And numerous management techniques and methods have been developed with the aim of enabling managers to attain results without fail. This almost exclusive attention to results, however, has led to certain undesirable consequences.

---

1   This section is comprised of an edited and abridged version of G.P. Rao, Management Philosophy: An Indian Perspective, *Indian Management*, 31(1) (February 1992): 29–31.

A manager's attention to results has made the manager almost blind to the other aspects of task performance, like human relations, sentiments, concern for others and so on.

Secondly, in the pursuit for results, the manager is likely to ignore, or sacrifice knowingly or unknowingly, the means adopted in achieving the said results.

Thirdly, the organization's emphasis on measuring managerial performance through results has made the manager literally obsessed with results – thereby ignoring the long-term interests of the organization.

Fourthly, when the desired results are achieved, the manager is likely to attribute, in all sincerity perhaps, the success to him- or herself alone, whereas the fact is that no managerial success can be attributed to the manager alone. The manager's subordinates, colleagues and superiors, along with the organization as a system, play equally important roles in the success of the manager.

Fifthly, when the desired results are not achieved, the manager is likely to attribute the failure, in all sincerity again, to anything and everything other than him- or herself, whereas the fact is that no management failure can be attributed entirely to others. The manager's own limitations, weaknesses and frailties also play an equally important role in not being able to achieve the desired results.

Sixthly, the obsession of a manager with results can account for several executive health problems like high blood pressure, heart attacks, ulcers, insomnia, tension etc. Significantly, such executive health problems can arise whether the executive succeeds in getting the desired results or not. At times the desired results are obtained through exertion, strain, tension, stress etc., at others the results cannot be achieved, in which case, in addition to the problems of stress and so on, problems such as dejection, frustration, insomnia, which are essentially related to failure on the part of the persons involved in achieving the desired results, are added to the unhealthy mix.

The above analysis of the consequences of a rather exclusive emphasis on results is very real, and is germane to the problem, with catastrophic results – unless the whole issue is re-examined in its entirety. The very first step in such a re-examination is to understand the extent to which a manager can assume responsibility for achieving the results. The answer to this question can be sought through the following very simple but profound formula:

$B = f (I, S)$, where

B = Behaviour

I = Individual

S = Situation

The above formula states that behaviour (B) is a function of the individual (I) and the situation (S). This means that both the individual concerned and the environment within which he or she operates accounts for the given behaviour. When applied to a manager, it means that managerial success or otherwise depends to some extent on others and their contribution or the lack of it.

The above discussion and depiction of the managerial obsession with results and its undesirable consequences thus calls for newer insight, for which I turn to Indian tradition and ethos. I refer to the concepts of *karma yoga* and *sthitha pragnya* as propounded in the *Bhagavad Gita*. *Karma yoga* calls for action with indifference to the achievement or otherwise of the results, and *sthitha pragnya* denotes equanimity no matter whether the results are achieved or not. When applied to the management context, the concepts of *karma yoga* and *sthitha pragnya* ordain incessant action accompanied by a high degree of equanimity on the part of the manager. In other words, a manager should aim at professional commitment in relation to action, and emotional detachment in relation to results. The above management philosophy, based on the touchstones of *karma yoga* and *sthitha pragnya*, is, I believe, the only realistic approach because, as was outlined, any achievement, behaviour or result-getting is an outcome of the interface of the individual and his or her environment, and cannot be attributed solely to either. This approach is most suitable to the Indian context because the concepts of *karma yoga* and *sthitha pragnya* are already part of the Indian psyche.

The differences between and the consequences of the present approach of laying exclusive emphasis on results and the proposed approach based on professional commitment and emotional detachment are depicted in Table 10.3.

Table 10.3   Management philosophy: comparative analysis

Aspect	Existing approach (almost exclusive emphasis on results)	Suggested, Indian perspective (professional commitment and emotional detachment)
Manager's obsession with 'results-getting'	Neglect of human aspects	Due consideration to human relations
Manager's obsession to 'somehow' achieve the results	Ignoring sacrificing means, their ethicality in particular	Due importance to means; a better balance between ends and means
Organization's almost exclusive emphasis on results as the index of performance appraisal	Ignoring/neglecting the long-term perspective of the organization, in particular	Due importance to the long-term perspective of the organization and its members
Manager being able to achieve the results	Attributing the success to self; egotism; complacency	Greater balance in assessing one's own contribution
Manager failing to achieve the results	Attributing the failure to others; passing the buck	Greater balance in assessing others' limitations
Manager's failure *vis-à-vis* his health	Executive health – an important causality	Less executive stress

When I discussed the above ideas with a group of young, intelligent and prospective executives, the spontaneous reaction was: 'Yes, it is true that what you are saying is desirable. But the question is, to what extent is it practicable?' Significantly, the above question itself contains the answer – that is, while the concepts of *karma yoga* and *sthitha pragnya* are desirable, their application is difficult. When the desirability of something is accepted, its practicability should not really be difficult. It would, however, mean that greater and greater efforts of self-analysis and self-evaluation need to be made by managers to internalize the knowledge, skills and attitudes of *karma yoga* and *sthitha pragnya* while infusing that within their work situation.

Another word of caution: the sense of equanimity and detachment when over emphasized may result in inactivity, defeatism and fatalism – in that order. The manager, accordingly, needs to be ever vigilant in seeing that the very thin line between emotional detachment and inaction etc. is not obliterated.

References

Mohanty, Jitendra N. no date. Indian Philosophy. *Encyclopaedia Britannica*. [Online]. Available at: http://www.britannica.com/EBchecked/topic/285905/ Indian-philosophy [accessed: 5 August 2013].

Rao, G.P. 1992. Management Philosophy: An Indian Perspective. *Indian Management*, 31(1) (February): 29–31.

11

Management and Groups: Group-oriented Human Values

The Context and the Issue

Any human value, by its very nature, is an idea, concept, thought. But the concept in the mind of the person (*manasa*) needs to be translated into observable and measurable phenomena in order that it may be articulated, communicated and inculcated in the work ethic of the given organization. The extent to which the articulation takes place in terms of operational definition thus becomes a critical factor in the subsequent process of inculcation. To arrive at a clear, simple and comprehendible definition for any one of the 33 human values of the Spandan Spectrum requires special effort on the part of management and others. This is to be done, following the Spandan 3D Process (Chapter 3), through two stages: one, discussion and debate by the core group members, with experiential learning as the fulcrum; two, communicating the results of the discussion, and receiving and processing feedback from all the members of the given organization. Based upon the feedback thus received, the core group finalizes the operational definitions and communicates them throughout the organization.

It may at this point be reiterated that like any other human-related concept, either too much or too little adherence and application of any human value is not desirable. Overemphasis of a value may create an imbalance in the required equilibrium in the spectrum of human values as whole and its role in first, human development and then, statistic management. Scant or inadequate attention, on the other hand, will rob the utility of the given value.

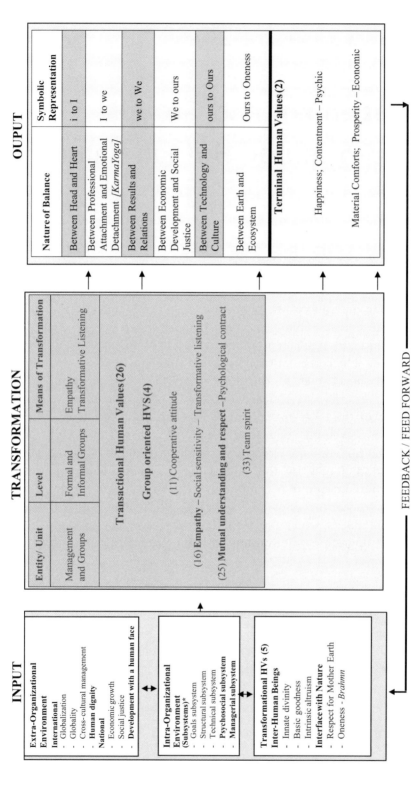

Figure 11.1   Remaking ourselves as human beings, enterprise and society: Transactional Human Values: group-oriented human values

Diagnosis: Group-oriented Human Values

The Spandan Spectrum of Human Values 2011 has identified the following four group-oriented human values:

- 11: Cooperative attitude

- 16: Empathy – Transformative listening – Sensitivity to others' feelings and needs – Social sensitivity

- 25: Mutual understanding and respect – Psychological contract

- 33: Team spirit

Figure 11.1 presents the Spandan group-oriented human values within the conceptual framework of the book.

11: COOPERATIVE ATTITUDE

The early days of humankind are viewed from two perspectives. The first claims that as survival and protection both from the elements and from other living creatures was paramount, the fight for survival manifested as competition and killing where ever needed. Violence thus became a corollary of human beings' struggle for existence. Darwin's theory of survival of the fittest and Marx's allegory of big fish eating the little ones are relevant in this context.

The second perspective holds that cooperation was the stronger element in human survival. This perspective is relatively new and increasingly being accepted by scientists. The example of bitter enemies putting aside their differences to come together with a view to protect themselves from a common enemy supports the theory. The principles of fraternity, shared genes and shared culture support the argument that it is the need to work together that is more natural to the human psyche.

16: EMPATHY – TRANSFORMATIVE LISTENING – SENSITIVITY TO OTHERS' FEELINGS AND NEEDS – SOCIAL SENSITIVITY

Empathy is the ability to put one's self into another's shoes, in order to understand a given issue from the point of view of the person affected. Unless I try to see the given problem from the perspective of the person concerned,

I cannot be of much help to him or her. Empathy is an essential characteristic of the Mother, and, as the concept of maternalistic management advocates, a requirement for management to develop the skills, attitude and ability to understand the needs of others *without even being asked*. Management need to develop empathic listening to be sensitive enough to deal with people and matters effectively. Transformative listening is the highest form of empathy and is practised by environmentalists and social activists.

25: MUTUAL UNDERSTANDING AND RESPECT – PSYCHOLOGICAL CONTRACT

Mutual understanding and respect emanates from the Transformational Human Value belief in the innate divinity in human beings (5). Edgar Schein, in his work *Organizational Psychology* (1980), introduced the concept of 'psychological contract', in which the mutual expectations of the management and the managed form the basis, over a period of time, of the contract. Such expectations are acknowledged, respected and integrated with the policies and practices of the organization, but unlike with a legal contract, the breach of a psychological contract cannot attract any legal remedy or redress.

33: TEAM SPIRIT

Team spirit is an important concept in group dynamics. Also referred to as *esprit de corps*, team spirit denotes the readiness with which members of a team come together and help each other beyond the prescribed requirements of the given job.

Human beings generally excel in their individual work, as they can apply their talent through individual thinking and performance. In the group context, however, a person often falters. Thinking together, coming to a particular understanding and solution together, and then working together towards the solution is more difficult than individual thinking, decision making and action. Interestingly, though, it appears that as one moves higher in status, so one's competence in a group context lessens. Ego could be the reason. It is therefore necessary that top management periodically take time away from their jobs and companies to spend more time as ordinary human beings. This helps them sensitize themselves to 'the common man' and his needs on the one hand and the relative decline in one's aura when out of one's own domain, on the other. J.N. Tata, the legendary visionary, industrialist and founder of the highly respected Tata group of companies in India, once conveyed his desire to Swami Vivekananda that company executives should be made to spend time in *ashrams* (places of worship and meditation and the abodes of saints and seers) periodically.

Discovery: Extent of Adherence

Tables 11.1 and 11.2 contain the relevant details.

Table 11.1 reveals that team spirit (33), with a mean average of 5.7, is perceived as the most adhered to group-oriented value at the level of Indian industry. Empathy (16) is lowest with at 4.9. At the level of one's own organization, cooperative attitude (11) and mutual understanding (25) are equal top with 7.3. Empathy (16), again, is lowest with 6.9. In one's own professional life, cooperative attitude (11) is rated highest with 8.1, with empathy (16) again lowest with 7.8.

Table 11.1   Group-oriented human values: extent of adherence [research study, 2011 (N=58)]

HV no.	Category	Human value	Extent of adherence (N=58)					
			Indian industry		One's own organization		One's own professional life	
			Mean	Rank	Mean	Rank	Mean	Rank
11.	Group-oriented	Cooperative attitude	5.6	XI	7.3	IX	8.1	VII
16.	Group-oriented	Empathy – Transformative listening – Sensitivity to others' feelings and needs – Social sensitivity	4.9	XXVII	6.9	XXIII	7.8	XVIII
25.	Group-oriented	Mutual understanding and respect – Psychological contract	5.2	XXI	7.3	IX	8.0	XI
33.	Group-oriented	Team spirit	5.7	X	7.1	XX	7.9	XIV
Overall average			5.4		7.2		8.0	

To sum up, cooperative attitude (11) is perceived as the most effectively adhered to group-oriented value at the levels of one's own organization and one's own professional life. Empathy (16), on the other hand, is lowest at all three levels. Higher cooperative attitude and lower empathy are therefore the issues to be tackled.

Table 11.2 depicts differences in the perception of the extent of adherence to group-oriented human values between the levels of one's own organization and one's own professional life. This hints at the extent to which professionals, which includes management in the given organization, are able to inculcate the given human values at the level of their own organization.

**Table 11.2   Group-oriented human values: extent of adherence –
            perceptual gaps**

Group-oriented human values	One's own professional life	One's own organization	Perceptual gap
11. Cooperating attitude	8.1	7.3	-0.8
16. Empathy	7.8	6.9	-0.9
25. Mutual understanding and respect	8.0	7.3	-0.7
33. Team spirit	7.9	7.1	-0.8
Overall average	8.0	7.2	-0.8

The table reveals the rather uncomfortable news that the perceptual gap is as high as -0.8 in the cases of cooperative attitude, mutual understanding and respect, and team spirit – with empathy leaving them behind with a gap of -0.9. This gap is an issue which – as stated in earlier chapters – deserves due attention from the captains of industry.

Table 7.5 shows that group-oriented human values stand highest (at 8.0) compared to other Transactional Human Values at the level of one's own professional life. This implies that the perceived group solidarity in the respondents' organizations is impacted greatly by their own professional competence. This is perhaps reflected in the corresponding data at the level of one's own organization. Group-oriented values are ranked second (at 7.2), between organizational human values and globalization-induced human values. At the level of Indian industry, they are rated lowest – with a mean average of 5.4 – along with personal, professional and organizational human values.

References

Gentry, William, et al. 2007. Empathy in the Work Place: A Tool for Effective Leadership. Paper presented at the Society of Industrial Organisational Psychology Conference, New York, April 2007.

Schein, Edgar. 1980. *Organisational Psychology*. New Delhi: Prentice-Hall.

12

Management and Organization: Organizational Human Values

The Context and the Issue

An organization represents a collectivity of persons engaged in achieving its given objective(s). Since, generally, the number of the members of an organization is large and the nature of the tasks involved is complex, the principle of division of labour is applied in its structuring, and a hierarchy and departmentalization follow, the former (hierarchy) being a vertical division in terms of authority, responsibility and status, the latter (departmentalization) being a horizontal division that is the result of classifying the organization's overall objective into distinct but related functional areas. Synthesizing the departmentalization and hierarchy, an organization as a system can be visualized as comprising five subsystems (Kast and Rosenzweig 1985). These, as described in more detail in Chapter 6, are: goals, structural, technical, psychosocial and managerial subsystems. These subsystems are incorporated in the conceptual framework of the present work (Chapter 6) as representing the intra-organizational environment.

The important task for management of striking an optimal balance between results and relations can be achieved only through the wholehearted cooperation of the members of its departments and hierarchy alike. Eliciting such cooperation, in turn, requires that management weave suitable human values into the work ethic and strategy fabric of the organization. The Spandan Spectrum of Human Values aims to develop an inventory of such human values, and the Spandan 3D Process aims to identify which values are suitable to the organization (diagnosis), to assess the extent of their adherence (discovery) and to inculcate them in the work ethic, integrate them with the strategic management and interface them with the environment (development).

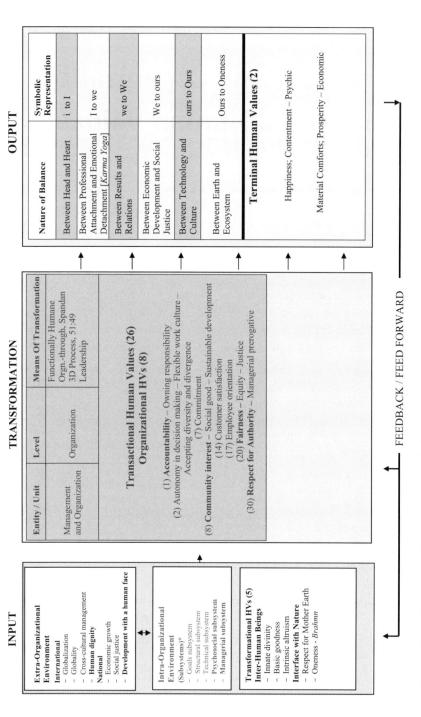

Figure 12.1   Remaking ourselves as human beings, enterprise and society: Transactional Human Values: organizational human values

An organization, while an independent and autonomous entity, is a product of society. The organization has to function within the boundaries laid down by the society and, preferably, to strive for its good – certainly not against the interests of the society. The human values identified by and inculcated in the organization are accordingly to be congruent with the norms, traditions, law and culture of the society.

Diagnosis: Organizational Human Values

The Spandan Spectrum of Human Values identifies eight Transactional Human Values that constitute the spectrum's organizational human values:

- 1: Accountability – Owning responsibility

- 2: Autonomy in decision making – Flexible work culture – Accepting diversity and divergence

- 7: Commitment

- 8: Community interest – Social good – Community service

- 14: Customer satisfaction/orientation

- 17: Employee orientation

- 20: Fairness – Equity – Justice

- 30: Respect for authority – Managerial prerogative

Figure 12.1 presents the Spandan organizational human values within the conceptual framework of the book.

1: ACCOUNTABILITY – OWNING RESPONSIBILITY

Accountability refers to the responsibility of the given position holder to complete the task and be able to explain deviations' or discrepancies, if any. When the given position holder volunteers to be accountable it is known as owning responsibility.

The idea that the one who is given a job should be accountable for its completion or otherwise appears axiomatic, but the reality is somewhat different. In organizations with multiple locations, diversified activities, highly-advanced technologies, and divergent and at times conflicting cultural milieus, visualizing a one-to-one relationship between and among the task assignment, its execution, completion and accountability is not straightforward. Therefore, while important, adhering effectively to the value of accountability is often difficult.

Furthermore, participative management, shared leadership and industrial democracies, while aimed at increasing productivity and satisfaction, have the built-in difficulty of isolating and ascribing task assignment execution and completion at the individual level. The concepts of matrix organizations and statistic business units (SBUs) are two of the initiatives taken to make enhanced accountability possible.

2: AUTONOMY IN DECISION MAKING – FLEXIBLE WORK CULTURE – ACCEPTING DIVERSITY AND DIVERGENCE

Autonomy in decision making is another important characteristic and human value emerging in the industrial scenario today. Interestingly, the difficulties in diagnosing and adhering to autonomy in decision making effectively are similar to those encountered in relation to accountability, yet it was possible to communicate the importance of and difficulty in adhering to these two values in a workshop held in a small organization involved in a traditional industry with a relatively uneducated workforce.

7: COMMITMENT

A concept taken from sociology, commitment relates to the extent to which an employee in an organization is 'prepared' to complete his or her task as effectively as possible, even going beyond working hours and prescribed work norms. It is estimated that normally in a work situation, an employee can complete a given task effectively using less than half her actual ability and competence. The remaining 50 per cent is unutilized potential, which can either be tapped by the management through incentive and other motivational efforts or offered voluntarily by the employee. When offered voluntarily, it becomes commitment.

Two experiences from *Spandan* initiatives may be quoted in this context. One relates to how commitment was diagnosed as an important human value in an industrial organization and its work ethic. The other illustrates how a very simple but powerful comment made by a relatively less educated person can capture the spirit of commitment.

a) *Identification/diagnosis*: The incident happened in late 1990 while I was conducting the AICTE Emeritus Fellowship study on Self Control as a Managerial Value. The Chairman/Managing Director (CMD) of the company was explaining the relative strengths and weaknesses of his people at the management level and among the rank and file. At one point he said: 'Professor, I have the best available scientists and engineers with me as my management team. However, the overall performance of the company is much below their potential. What do you think is the reason?' As a typical management consultant, I shot back, 'What do *you* think is the reason?' He thought aloud for some seconds, and exclaimed 'Commitment'. Commitment was then focused upon as the possible critical variable in the study in his company. Further, commitment was added to the Spandan Spectrum of Human Values 2011.

b) *'Operational definition' of commitment*: The second incident occurred during a workshop conducted at a medium-sized, industrialized organization. Around 40 members representing the management and supervisory staff participated in the workshop. They were discussing which of the human values from the Spandan spectrum could be useful for inculcation in their company. Commitment was mentioned as one such value. Immediately, discussion began on what the meaning of commitment could be. Several members offered their insights. An older person in the group hesitantly raised his hand indicating his desire to answer the question. When asked to speak, he struggled for a moment and then said that commitment is when an employee is determined to complete the task, 'come what may'. This, I felt, was a very simple but powerful expression of the complex concept of commitment, and an 'operational definition' of commitment I have communicated on numerous suitable occasions ever since.

8: COMMUNITY INTEREST – SOCIAL GOOD – COMMUNITY SERVICE

Community interest is a human value that relates to the interface of the organization with society, and the role and contribution of management to the community and society of which it is a part. Contribution to a society by its own organizations is not an act of philanthropy or a public relations exercise. Community service is a normal and natural act of a subsystem (organization) to its supra-system (community / society).

In ancient India – as elsewhere – amenities and facilities were provided to the subjects of monarchies, and to the citizens in other systems. Industrialization and perhaps the advent of globalization has, however, changed the concept of community and social service by the government. The recent and on-going efforts of 'The Giving Pledge' campaign by Bill Gates and Warren Buffet are to be seen in this context as possible amendments in the neglect of society by the corporate sector.

In *Spandan* workshops, the very low adherence to community interest has emerged repeatedly. A note on the possible reasons for such neglect in India is included later in the chapter.

14: CUSTOMER SATISFACTION/ORIENTATION

Customer is king and is treated as such by the industrial world. Customer satisfaction and its importance for an organization's very survival can therefore hardly be exaggerated.

Of late, customer orientation has become the be-all and end-all to such an extent that it is hardly worth mentioning as something specific to be perceived. Some recent workshops confirm this emerging trend. For example, an IT organization diagnosed customer orientation as one of the six values to be inculcated for about five years up until 2005. The Managing Director, based on his experience and discussions in the organization, then came out with a revised list of five human values. The list did not include customer orientation but contained values induced by globalization such as preparedness, continuous improvement and a commitment to change. When asked, the Managing Director replied that customer satisfaction is the very objective for which his organization was created. He therefore thought there was no need specifically to mention it in the list of the organization's values.

17: EMPLOYEE ORIENTATION

If an organization is the kingdom, the customer is its king, and an employee of the organization is a subject of the kingdom. Until recently, as the history of industrialization testifies, the employees of organizations have been treated as such. Moreover, employee discrimination has resulted in the mutilation of the concept of fairness, equity and justice, the next human value discussed here.

The concept of an employee as an internal customer and as a stakeholder are of recent origin.

An important consequence of globalization over the last few decades has been a sea-change in the profile of a typical employee and his/her world: increased skills; autonomy in functioning; a higher standard of living; the forceful proliferation of democracy as a political system; the reduced gap between the rich and the poor; the emergence of the middle class as a powerful force in society; an exposure to foreign work cultures in multi-cultural milieus; virtual organizations; and the concept of flexible working hours. As a consequence the employee has become a critical component. Recent HRD initiatives such as employee attraction, engagement and retention are to be viewed in this context.

20: FAIRNESS – EQUITY – JUSTICE

On several occasions I have had the opportunity of eliciting responses from and generating data on important desirable human values in organizations. Normally human values thus identified range between half a dozen and ten. Thus far I have not come across any list of organizational values that has not included fairness as one of its values. This clearly shows the basic human need and expectation to be treated fairly. Whether in a family, an educational institution, work place, community, political organization or any organized collectivity of human beings with a particular cause, the importance of being fair, and being perceived as fair can hardly be exaggerated. A parent, the father in particular, may not be close. A teacher may be strict. The boss may be severe. However, as long as they are consistent in their strictness and severity, and mean business, they are not only tolerated but are appreciated. They are preferred over the parents, teachers, bosses and other such leaders who are very pleasant but inconsistent in their treatment and assessment of children, students, subordinates and followers.

30: RESPECT FOR AUTHORITY – MANAGERIAL PREROGATIVE

In any human organization a person occupying a higher position and status needs to be respected, listened to and to have his or her communication and behaviour responded to favourably. Such respect for a higher-position holder is an integral part of a formal organization, since it is the authority of the superior to instruct and lead, and it is the responsibility of those who are subordinate to obey and to be led. The effectiveness of both the superior and the subordinate is to a large extent dependent upon the nature and extent of respect for authority adhered to in the given organization. As a corollary, the effectiveness of the organization as a whole is influenced accordingly.

An army is an institution from which many of the principles of management and organization originated, including the respect for authority. But such respect is to be seen and fostered as a consequence of the superior being accepted as both mentor and role model.

From the Spandan point of view, this value, as also the other values in the spectrum, has an umbilical relationship with the awareness and acceptance of and adherence to Transformational Human Values.

Discovery: Extent of Adherence

Tables 12.1 and 12.2 contain the relevant information.

Table 12.1 **Management and organizations: organizational human values: extent of adherence [research study, 2011 (N=58)]**

HV no.	Category	Human value	Extent of adherence (N=58)					
			Indian industry		One's own organization		One's own professional life	
			Mean	Rank	Mean	Rank	Mean	Rank
1.	Organizational	Accountability – Owning responsibility	5.1	XXIV	7.2	XVI	8.2	III
2.	Organizational	Autonomy in decision making – Flexible work culture – Accepting diversity and diversions	5.2	XXI	7.2	XVI	7.9	XIV
7.	Organizational	Commitment	5.5	XII	7.4	V	8.4	II
8.	Organizational	Community interest – Social good – Sustainable development	4.7	XXXII	7.1	XXI	7.5	XXIV
14.	Organizational	Customer satisfaction	5.8	VII	7.5	III	8.1	VII
17.	Organizational	Employee orientation	5.4	XV	7.0	XXII	7.8	XVIII
20.	Organizational	Fairness – Equity – Justice	5.2	XXI	7.4	V	8.1	VII
30.	Organizational	Respect for authority – Managerial prerogative	6.5	III	7.6	I	8.0	XI
Overall average			5.4		7.3		8.0	

Table 12.1 shows that respect for authority (30) has been rated as the top most value adhered to at the levels of Indian industry and one's own organization, with mean values of 6.5 and 7.6 respectively. At the level of one's own professional life, however, it is ranked lower, though with a mean average of 8.0. The second lowest value in this category, with an average of 7.8, is employee orientation (17), which was assessed the lowest (7.0) at the level of one's own organization. When we put these findings together, we have an image of industrial India with a higher respect for authority but a much lower adherence to the value of employee orientation. The image is not a commendable one. The image becomes more of a concern when we find that community interest (8) is the lowest (7.5) priority value in the category of one's own professional life, second lowest at the level of one's own organization (7.1) and lowest in Indian industry as a whole (4.7).

Table 12.2   Management and organizations: organizational human values: extent of adherence – perceptual gaps

Organizational human values	One's own professional life	One's own organization	Perceptual gap
1. Accountability	8.2	7.2	-1.0
2. Autonomy in decision making	7.9	7.2	-0.7
7. Commitment	8.4	7.4	-1.0
8. Community interest	7.5	7.1	-0.4
14. Customer satisfaction	8.1	7.5	-0.6
17. Employee orientation	7.8	7.0	-0.8
20. Fairness – Equity – Justice	8.1	7.4	-0.7
30. Respect for authority	8.0	7.6	-0.4
Overall average:	8.0	7.3	-0.7

Table 12.2 reveals the perceptual gaps between adherence to values in one's own professional life and at the level of one's own organization. Adherence in one's own professional life is considered higher than in one's own organization with reference to all eight organizational human values.

Development: The Spandan Approach: Functionally Humane Organization (FHO)

The four chapters of Part III thus far (Chapters 9–12) have discussed four groups of Transactional Human Values – personal, professional, group-oriented and organizational human values. At this point, given the values discussed are primarily intra-organizational, it will be useful to pause and have a look at the concept of the Functionally Humane Organization (FHO) – the intended output of the inculcation of the Spandan Spectrum of Human Values. Consequently the following chapter (Chapter 13) will deal with the Functionally Humane Organization (FHO), before continuing with the fifth group of Transactional Human Values – globalization-induced human values – in Chapter 14. The subject of the Functionally Humane Organization will then be returned to in detail in Part IV.

References

Ahmed, Abad. 1999. Management by Human Values: An Over View. *Journal of Human Values*, 5(1) (April): 15–23.

Bhattacharya, Abhijit. 2011. How Can Organizations Innovate? *Trinidad and Tobago Guardian*, 10 June. [Online]. Available at: http://www.guardian.co.tt/business-guardian/2011/06/09/how-can-organisations-innovate [accessed: 6 August 2013].

Bhaya, Hiten. 2000. Managing Self: The Indian Ethos of Management. *Journal of Human Values*, 6: 29.

Blanding, Michael. 2011a. Getting to Eureka: How Companies Can Promote Creativity. *HBS Working Knowledge*, 22 August.

——2011b. The Great Wall of Trust. *HBS Working Knowledge*, 19 December.

Bookchin, Murray. 1982. *The Ecology of Freedom: The Emergence and Dissolution of Hierarchy*. Palo Alto, CA: Cheshire Books.

Dyer, Jeff, et al. 2011. Five Discovery Skills that Distinguish Great Innovators, *HBS Working Knowledge*, 20 February.

Gellerman, William, et al. 1990. *Values and Ethics in Organization and System Development*. San Francisco, CA: Jossey-Bass.

Gibbons, R. and R. Henderson. 2012. Relational Contracts and Organizational Capabilities. *Harvard Business School (Working Paper)*, 18 January.

Heskett, Jim, et al. 2008. Ten Reasons to Design a Better Corporate Culture. *HBS Working Knowledge*, 22 December.

Kast, Fremont E. and James Irwin Rosenzwig. 1985. *Organization and Management: A Systems and Contingency Approach*, 4th edition. New York: McGraw-Hill.

Maira, Arun and Peter Scot. 1997. *The Accelerating Organization: Embracing the Human Face of Change*. New York: McGraw-Hill.

Narayana Murthy, N.R. 2009. *A Better India: A Better World*. New Delhi: Penguin.

Nobel, Carmen. 2011. The Most Powerful Work Place Motivator. *HBS Working Knowledge*, 31 October.

Price Waterhouse. 1998. *Straight from the CEO*. New York: Simon & Schuster.

Rao, G.P. 2002. *Self Control as a Managerial Value: An Odyssey in Diagnosis, Discovery and Development*. AICTE Emeritus Fellowship Study.

Schoemaker, Michiel et al. 2006. Human Value Management: The Influence of the Contemporary Developments of Corporate Social Responsibility and Social Capital on HRM. *Management Revue – The International Review of Management Studies*, 17(4): 448–65.

Senge, Peter M. 1990. *The Fifth Discipline: The Art and Practice of the Learning Organization*. New York: Doubleday.

Sharma, Subhash. 2007. *New Mantras in Corporate Corridors: From Ancient Roots to Global Routes*. New Delhi: New Age International

Thomas, Shalom Mary. 2009. Humanizing Management. *Business Line*, 9 December.

Van den Steen, Eric J. 2009. Authority versus Persuasion. *HBS Working Knowledge*, 5 August.

Watson, George W, et al. 2004. Understanding Values in an Organization: A Value Dynamics. *Journal of Human Values*, 10 (April): 23–39.

13

The Management of Organizations: The Functionally Humane Organization: The Inculcation of Human Values through the Spandan 3D Process

The Context and the Issue

Earlier in the book the overall perspective of the Spandan Approach, the Spandan 3D Process and Spandan Spectrum of Human Values was presented (Chapter 3). Furthermore, the Spandan 3D Process of Diagnosis, Discovery and Development was explained as a means of inculcating human values in an organization, with the sequential salient features of the process being:

a)   Develop, or revisit, the mission statement as an anchor of the organization and …

b)   weave the values into the work fabric …

c)   through experiential learning and …

d)   by integrating the values with HRD and strategic management …

e)   to achieve an optimal balance between results and relations as a means …

f)   to evolve a Functionally Humane Organization with …

g)   top management support and an effective core group as its executive arm.

It was also explained how adherence to Transformational Human Values would enable a person to develop a proper mind-set towards self and others. Consequently the first four chapters of Part III discussed the personal, professional, group-oriented and organizational human values required for a manager in his or her roles as a human being, a professional, a member of a group and a member of an organization respectively.

The current chapter looks at the management *of* organizations – as against the preceding chapter's subject matter of management *and* organizations. Thus after coming to know the suitable Transactional Human Values with which to interact with others in the said roles, the manager should now start to think about transforming the enterprise into a Functionally Humane Organization, characterized by a sustained optimal balance between results and relations. The aim, in other words, is to achieve results through relations. The Spandan Approach, its 3D Process and the Spectrum of Human Values are systematically to be made integral to the enterprise's mission statement, work ethic, HRD, strategic management and its interface with the environment.

The process of transformation towards a Functionally Humane Organization as visualized is presented in Figure 13.1.

The inputs are the Transformational Human Values and the four professional values symbolizing the concept of *karma yoga*. The transformation consists of select results-oriented and relations-oriented human values considered more closely associated with the intended Terminal Values of material comforts and happiness respectively.

The output expected is threefold:

1.   through Transformational Human Values – I, Terminal Values (Chapters 18 and 21)

2.   through professional values, the Spandan 51:49 leadership philosophy (Chapter 20)

3.   through Transformational Human Values – II, spirituality in management and spiritual democracy (Chapters 19 and 14)

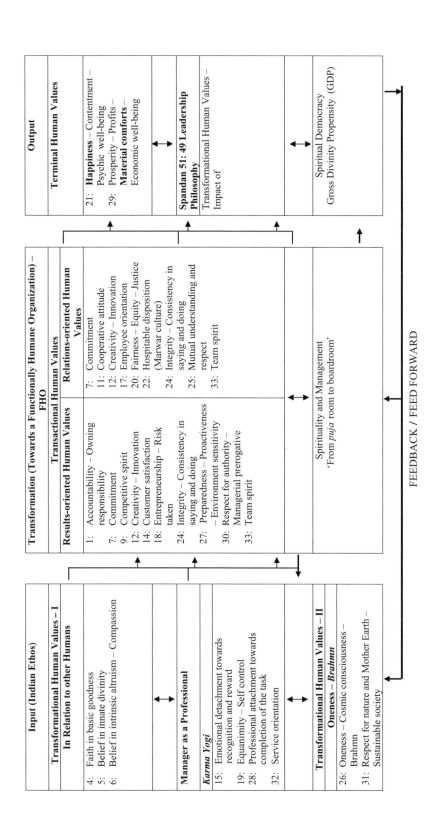

Figure 13.1 Remaking ourselves, enterprise and society: the Spandan Spectrum of Human Values and the Spandan 3D Process: human values – results and relations

The present chapter offers first-hand experience in conducting experiential learning as a means to sensitize one's self, group and organization. This is followed by a case study on the conduct of a typical *Spandan* workshop, including Focal Person–Resource Persons Interactive Sessions (FP–RP IS).

Experiential Learning: Insights of Mohan Bangaruswamy (Shangrila Management Consulting, Bangalore)

This section, by a member of *Spandan*, and one of my former students, delineates various aspects that are important in ensuring that experiential learning adds value to participants. It articulates the importance of facilitators inculcating some of the values espoused by the *Spandan* way. Many of the human values covered in the Spandan Spectrum of Human Values 2011 play a key role in ensuring the 'experiential learning' approach values both the uniqueness of the individual and the connectedness of the collective.

Experiential learning can be explained by viewing it through the lens of Kolb's learning cycle. Every event for an individual or a group of individuals is a learning experience. Experiential learning in the context of a 'learning intervention' is a semi-structured activity that enables individual(s) to engage with the activity and with each other. The description 'semi-structured' is the focal point as the facilitator can define the starting context and a few ground rules. What happens during the course of the activity is totally dependent on the participants' choices. These choices are affected values, beliefs, past experiences, meaning-making based on what others have said, and so on.

The processes that follow the activity enable learning to happen and to be integrated with the individual's life space. These processes pertain to aspects such as:

- 'reflecting on the experiences during the activity', 'looking at the meaning-making and the factors that impacted choice-making', 'the dynamics within the group', etc.;

- extracting themes, recurring patterns, functional and dysfunctional behaviour. Connecting these to conceptual frameworks, if required;

- deriving insights from the analysis in the previous steps for deploying in one's personal growth;

- setting the context for implementation in the 'back home' context. Concepts (themes/generalizations) that have been learnt during the programme will have to be deployed in different contexts. A context can be defined as a function of 'time, space, interaction with another person'. A change in any variable changes the context. The facilitator should enable this linkage to happen.

Experiential learning offers a way to bring congruence of thought, feeling and action. Feeling is one of the neglected aspects in day-to-day life. The logical, rational way reigns and people sometimes tend to bury feelings. This could result in a lack of nourishment in the growth process. Experiential learning activities enable participants to deal with the feeling side more effectively.

PRACTISING THE VALUES

Various values espoused by *Spandan* play a key role in enabling experiential learning to be an enriching experience. The role of a few of these values in various phases is stated below:

Value	Phase
Empathy (16)	Conducting activity and debriefing
Compassion (6)	Conducting activity and debriefing
Commitment (7)	Through all the phases
Trust (4)	Through all the phases
Self-control (19)	Through all the phases
Creativity and innovation (12)	Design and conducting the activity

EMPATHY (16) AND COMPASSION (6)

Empathy and compassion are discussed here under the same heading as they tend to have a similar impact on the interface with participants.

It was stated earlier that it is important for the facilitator to give space to participants during the activity. There are times when the facilitator may need to intervene and provide assistance. The author has encountered numerous situations where participants are stuck in an activity and do not seek help. Sometimes, joining in and triggering thoughts help them to move on. On other occasions, it could be related to providing them additional resources.

The author believes in the philosophy that as human beings 'we need help from time to time'. It is perfectly fine to offer to help the group if they need it. The choice is still left to the group to accept it.

Practising empathy and compassion allows the facilitator to connect with the universe of the participants and to make a choice which is wholesome for the process of learning. There are occasions when participants believe that a little bit of extra time will allow them to reach the goal. The facilitator may choose to go with their request. All of these are incidents that can be utilized during debriefing and while offering perspectives to participants.

These values play a key role in debriefing as this enables the participants to experience the humanness of the facilitator and their own humanness. It is accepted that the various meanings are the 'reality' of that individual's universe. All this adds to the richness of the learning. It also adds to the facilitator's meaning-making process as each group of participants is very different from the other.

COMMITMENT (7)

This value enables the facilitator to focus on delivering the results to the sponsor of the programme and the participants. It enables working towards customer satisfaction, which is the outcome of expectations being surpassed.

TRUST (4)

Trust is a two-way process in experiential learning. The facilitator needs authentic information from the organization to design the overall intervention and the experiential learning activities. The facilitator needs to establish trust to obtain the detailed information.

Trust as a factor helps the facilitator to bond with the participants during the activity and the debriefing. It enables the participants to seek the help they require, to ask questions without worrying, and so on.

During debriefing, the facilitator may choose to share personal experiences to help the participants gain different viewpoints. These may be stories of success and/or failure. Such sharing and making one's self vulnerable increases the trust factor. The participants also begin to share in a more authentic manner. This enriches learning for the collectivity.

In a way, trust in one's self (self-belief, trusting one's sensing of the situation) helps to enable learning. Self-trust combined with the philosophy of 'provisionalism instead of certainty' enables the facilitator to make hypotheses and offer perspectives during debriefing.

SELF-CONTROL (19)

The facilitator is as human as the next person and each facilitator can be quirky in their way. It is important for facilitators to be in touch with themselves, their meaning-making process and the significant themes in their lives at that point in time. Each of these will impact the process of facilitation. There can be times when the facilitator may be triggered by some of the goings-on in the group. While this is real and live, the facilitator needs to connect with the emotions within self and exercise self-control. At the moment, it is more important to be in touch with what is happening in the group and the participants' universe.

In this regard, experiential learning is very different from other forms of human process work such as encounter groups or 'labs'. In those situations, the facilitator joins in and expresses emotions that have been triggered in him or her. In typical experiential learning, which falls outside 'encounter groups', the facilitator needs to respect the role that he or she holds and stay with the dynamics of the participants. The facilitator can use 'clinic-ing' to work with his or her emotions at the end of the session or end of the day.

CREATIVITY AND INNOVATION (12)

This helps the facilitators to:

- design activities that would be relevant and meaningful for the participants

- make changes in the design during the course of the activity, if required.

TO SUM UP

Experiential learning offers an enriching mechanism to enable learning. It provides the means to work with participants with differing perspectives, beliefs and values. It helps in the process of building wholesomeness and integrating 'thought, feeling and action'.

Weaving experiential learning with the philosophy espoused by *Spandan* enhances the richness of the learning and contributes towards the replenishment of one's being.

Focal Person–Resource Persons Interactive Sessions (FP–RP IS): An Illustration

Figure 3.1, outlining the model of the Spandan 3D Process, contains two concurrent streams of sub-processes: institutional and individual. The institutional level activities, comprising Mission Statement, Diagnosis, Discovery and Development (of the 3D Process), and the Outcome (optimizing results and relations) are shown as the upper level stream of activities. The purpose in this stream is to bring in transformation at the institutional, systemic level. Experiential learning based upon Focal Person–Resource Persons Interactive Sessions (FP–RP IS) are shown in the lower stream. These interactive sessions aim at improving self-awareness, interpersonal skills and social sensitivity. The assumption is that a system is as good as its members.

The following illustrates the conduct of a typical *Spandan* workshop along with FP-RP IS and is taken from a document prepared by a participant in the workshop.

REMAKING AT ORGANIZATION LEVEL: AN ILLUSTRATION OF THE APPLICATION OF THE SPANDAN 3D PROCESS: SPANDAN MART INTERACTIVE SESSION, 10 APRIL 2012

Round 1: Diagnosis

MART's vision:

> *To become the most respected, employee-owned consultancy firm in the emerging markets, creating innovative and effective solutions in the sectors of our focus.*

At present, most businesses are made up of 'swollen heads and shallow hearts', but MART's philosophy is 'Business Mind – Social Heart', and this is the desired situation.

Round 2: Discovery

Round 2.1   MART vision: extent of achievement

Mean (on a ten-point scale)	Range	
	Minimum (n)	Maximum (n)
7.2	6.0 (2)	10.0 (4)

Round 2.2   **MART organizational values: the extent of their contribution to the achievement of the vision of the company**

MART Organizational values	Extent of adherence on a ten-point scale				CEO
	Partners/heads of the department (N=6)				
	Mean	Range			
		Minimum (n)	Maximum (n)		
1	2	3	4		5
1. Belongingness	8.0	6.5 (1)	10.0 (1)		6
2. Caring	8.2	6.5 (1)	9.3 (1)		7
3. Inter-dependence	8.1	6.5 (1)	10.0 (1)		6
4. Trust	8.9	7.4 (1)	10.0 (1)		8
5. Transparency	8.0	7.0 (2)	8.5 (4)		8
6. Team work	8.6	6.6 (1)	10.0 (1)		8
7. Shared leadership	7.9	6.0 (2)	9.8 (1)		8

Round 3: Development

How to strengthen shared leadership in MART?

	Solution offered by Team 1	Solution offered by Team 2
1	Build on other strengths to encourage leadership	Shared leadership is strengthened by demonstrating it
2	Identify and improve the individual leadership	Accountability and appraisal should be linked to improve shared leadership
3	Increase accountability and responsibility	Interdependency and trust are two values linked to shared leadership
4	Belongingness, team work, trust are three critical values to improve shared leadership	

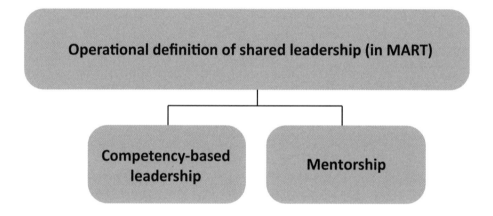

Round 4

Individual changes are required to change the organization:

- *Focal person*: top management, i.e. departmental head

- *Resource persons*: team members of department

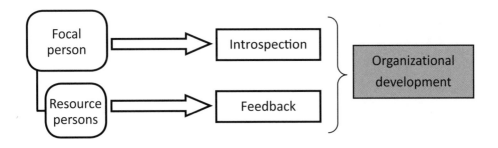

Round 5: Focal Person–Resources Persons Interactive Session (FP-RP IS)

Focal person: Pradeep Kashyap, CEO

Description	Resources persons: partners/ heads of departments (N=6)	CEO (self-assessment)
1	2	3
5.1: CEO leadership overall – on ten-point scale	9.5	9.0
5.2: CEO shared leadership – on a ten-point scale	9.2	9.0

5.3: As a founder, what are the strengths of Mr Kashyap?

Strength	Frequency of response	Rank
Logical	1	
Communication	1	
Family man	3	
Spiritual leadership	1	
Transparency	4	*1*
Passion for knowledge	1	
Team person	1	
Servant leadership	2	
Visionary	1	
Simplicity	1	
Clarity of thoughts	1	
Desire to improve	1	

5.4: As a founder, what are the areas of improvement for Mr Kashyap?

Strength	Frequency of response
Articulate more as a spiritual leadership	1
Articulate the vision to a larger level	1
Need to be more practical	1
Need to be more flexible	1

Areas of improvement articulated by Mr Kashyap (*introspection*):

- Need to setup formal process and rules (institutionalization)

- Need to be extrovert.

14

Management and Globalization: Globalization-induced Human Values

The Context and the Issue

On 30 January 2006 Pascal Lamy, Director General of the World Trade Organization (WTO), addressed a seminar on 'Humanizing Globalization' in Santiago de Chile, Chile. The seminar was also attended by Ricardo Lagos, President of Chile. His address is an important document on the subject relevant to this chapter.

Lamy (2006) defined globalization as

> a historical stage of accelerated expansion of market capitalism, like the one experienced in the 19th century with the industrial revolution. It is a fundamental transformation in societies because of the recent technological revolution which has led to a recombining of the economic and social forces on a new territorial dimension.

> We can today say that globalization and increased market opening has had very positive effects and some negative consequences.

> Globalization has enabled individuals, corporations and nation-states to influence actions an events around the world – faster, deeper and cheaper than ever before – and equally to derive benefits for them. Globalization has led to the opening of markets, the vanishing of many barriers and walls, and has the potential for expanding freedom, democracy, innovation, social and cultural exchanges while offering outstanding opportunities for dialogue and understanding.

> But the global nature of an increasing number of some worrisome phenomena – the scarcity of energy resources, the deterioration of the environment and natural disasters (including recently hurricane Katrina and the Asian tsunami), the spread of pandemics (AIDS, bird flu), the growing interdependence of economies and financial markets and the ensuing complexity of analysis, forecasts and predictability (financial crisis), and the migratory movements provoked by insecurity, poverty or political instability are also a product of globalization. ...

> It is this double face of globalization that we must seek ways of addressing if we want to 'humanize globalization'.

Diagnosis: Globalization-induced Human Values

As discussed in Chapter 7, a study was conducted in 2011 inviting select eminent persons from different walks of life to assess the extent of adherence to human values at the levels of one's own professional life, one's own organization and Indian industry as a whole. The Spandan Spectrum of Human Values 2011 (Chapter 7 Appendix) was forwarded to the approximately 200 invitees with a request to assess adherence to the 33 human values at the three levels cited. Fifty-eight invitees responded. Their average age was 50 years and average work experience 24 years.

Based on the responses received, an effort was made to identify what could be referred to as globalization-induced human values (diagnosis) and their adherence at the three levels mentioned. Adherence to these was compared with adherence to other Transactional Human Values, Fundamental and Terminal Human Values (discovery). Finally, policy implications were focused upon (development) for strengthening and balancing globalization-induced human values *vis-à-vis* other Transactional Human Values, in particular. The assumption and experience is that such a balance in human values would enable an organization to achieve an optimal balance between the two end state Terminal Human Values, viz. material comforts and happiness, i.e. prosperity and tranquillity

As also noted earlier, in Chapter 2, the advent and advance of globalization, during the last half century in particular, has brought a paradigm shift in human progress and development. The three cornerstones on which globalization has grown are global technology, global markets and global attitudes. These three critical components accordingly beckon corresponding cataclysmic changes in human thinking and mind-sets, as a prelude to carrying forward and coping with globalization effectively. Effective coping, to remind ourselves, is how best to achieve and maintain an optimal balance in human living and life. Also known as the work–life balance, the issue is striking and maintaining a balance between material comforts and happiness – that is to say, between head and heart at the individual level, between results and relations at the organizational level, and between technology and environment at the global level.

The Spandan Spectrum of Human Values 2011 has identified six human values as having been induced by globalization:

- 9: Competitive spirit

- 12: Creativity – Innovation

- 13: Cultural adaptiveness – Cross-cultural management

- 18: Entrepreneurship – Risk taking

- 22: Hospitable disposition (Marwar culture)

- 27: Preparedness – Proactiveness – Environmental sensitivity

That globalization has had a significant impact on management attitudes towards self and others has emerged in two ways. First, the Spandan Spectrum of 2011 consists of six globalization-induced human values as against three in the 2010 version. Second, these human values are qualitatively new and different. For instance, preparedness as a cluster comprising pro-activeness and environmental sensitivity finds a place in the spectrum. This is in addition to entrepreneurship, which continues to be in the spectrum as a separate human value.

Figure 14.1 presents globalization-induced human values within the conceptual framework of the book.

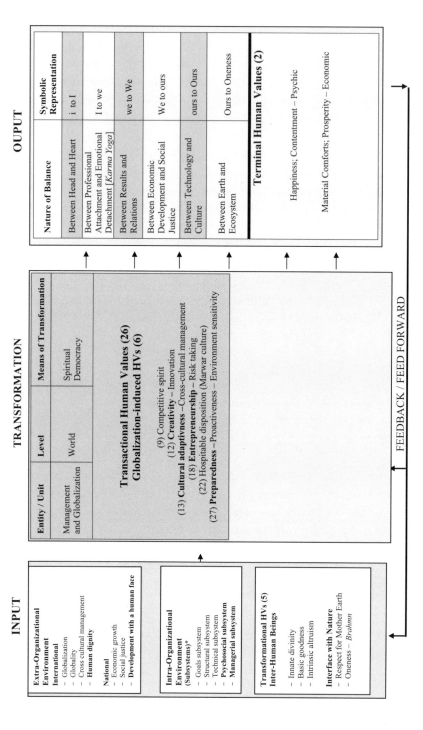

INPUT

Extra-Organizational Environment
International
– Globalization
  – Globality
  – Cross cultural management
  – **Human dignity**
National
– Economic growth
  – Social justice
  – **Development with a human face**

Intra-Organizational Environment
(Subsystems)*
  – Goals subsystem
  – Structural subsystem
  – Technical subsystem
  – **Psychosocial subsystem**
  – **Managerial subsystem**

Transformational HVs (5)
Inter-Human Beings
  – Innate divinity
  – Basic goodness
  – Intrinsic altruism

Interface with Nature
  – Respect for Mother Earth
  – Oneness – *Brahmn*

TRANSFORMATION

Entity / Unit	Level	Means of Transformation
Management and Globalization	World	Spiritual Democracy

Transactional Human Values (26)
Globalization-induced HVs (6)

(9) Competitive spirit
(12) Creativity – Innovation
(13) Cultural adaptivness –Cross-cultural management
(18) **Entrepreneurship** – Risk taking
(22) Hospitable disposition (Marwar culture)
(27) **Preparedness** –Proactiveness – Environment sensitivity

OUPUT

Nature of Balance	Symbolic Representation
Between Head and Heart	i to I
Between Professional Attachment and Emotional Detachment [*Karma Yoga*]	I to we
Between Results and Relations	we to We
Between Economic Development and Social Justice	We to ours
Between Technology and Culture	ours to Ours
Between Earth and Ecosystem	Ours to Oneness
Terminal Human Values (2)	
Happiness; Contentment – Psychic	
Material Comforts; Prosperity – Economic	

FEEDBACK / FEED FORWARD

Figure 14.1   Remaking ourselves as human beings, enterprise and society: Transactional Human Values: globalization-induced human values

Discovery: Extent of Adherence

Table 14.1 contains the relevant particulars on the extent of adherence to globalization-induced human values.

Cultural adaptiveness (13) has been considered the strongest of the globalization-induced human values at the personal and organizational levels with 7.7 and 7.5 mean values (on a ten-point scale) respectively. Competitive spirit (9) has been perceived as the weakest at the personal level with 7.1, and one of the weakest (6.9) at the organizational level. The need for strengthening competitive spirit at the personal and organizational levels is thus made clear. Such need becomes all the more relevant and possible since competitive spirit has been perceived as the strongest value at the level of Indian industry as a whole (7.1).

Table 14.1   **Management and globalization: globalization-induced human values: extent of adherence [research study, 2011 (N=58)]**

HV no.	Category	Human value	Extent of adherence (N=58)					
			Indian industry		One's own organization		One's own professional life	
			Mean	Rank	Mean	Rank	Mean	Rank
9.	Glob.-induced	Competitive spirit	7.1	II	6.9	XXIII	7.1	XXXII
12.	Glob.-induced	Creativity – Innovation	5.8	VII	7.2	XVI	7.5	XXVI
13.	Glob.-induced	Cultural adaptiveness – Cross-cultural management	5.8	VII	7.5	III	7.7	XXII
18.	Glob.-induced	Entrepreneurship – Risk taking	6.1	IV	6.9	XXIII	7.4	XXX
22.	Glob.-induced	Hospitable disposition (Marwar culture)	5.5	XII	6.9	XXIII	7.4	XXX
27.	Glob.-induced	Preparedness – Proactiveness – Environmental sensitivity	4.8	XXIX	6.9	XXIII	7.5	XXVI
Overall average			5.9		7.1		7.4	

An observation needs to be made regarding the assessments of adherence to competitive spirit, which is rated as the value most adhered to at the level of Indian industry as a whole, with a mean value of 7.1, yet the value least adhered to at the personal and organizational levels with values of 7.1 and 6.9 respectively. How can a value of 7.1 be the highest for competitive spirit at the level of Indian industry as a whole yet the lowest for the same human value at the level of one's own professional life? Further, the overall average at the personal level (7.4) is higher than that at the organizational level (7.1), which in turn is higher than that at the level of Indian industry as a whole (5.9). The same difference is discernible in other analyses, where adherence at the personal level is assessed to be higher than at the organizational and industry levels. This indicates the human tendency of assessing self higher compared to other entities like the organization and industry. Assessment at the level of one's own organization, although lower than at the level of self, is, however, always rated higher that at the level of industry as a whole!

Table 14.2   Management and globalization: globalization-induced human values: extent of adherence – perceptual gaps

Globalization-induced human values	One's own professional life	One's own organization	Perceptual gap
9. Competitive spirit	7.1	6.9	-0.2
12. Creativity – Innovation	7.5	7.2	-0.3
13. Cultural adaptiveness	7.7	7.5	-0.2
18. Entrepreneurship	7.4	6.9	-0.5
22. Hospitable disposition	7.4	6.9	-0.5
27. Preparedness	7.5	6.9	-0.6
Overall average	7.4	7.1	-0.3

Changes at the organizational level, as compared at the level of industry as a whole, are much more possible. Accordingly, Table 14.2 looks at the perceptual gap between the personal and organizational levels. The perceptual gap, defined as the difference between assessments at the levels of self and organization, is greatest with regards to preparedness, proactiveness and environmental sensitivity (-0.6). It is also significant to note that preparedness is perceived the weakest adhered to value at the level of Indian industry as a whole (4.8) (Table 14.1).

Turning to Table 7.5, the extent of adherence to other human values may now be compared to that of globalization-induced human values, so that areas for improvement can be identified.

The overall average for adherence to globalization-induced human values at the level of one's professional life is 7.4, which is lower than for all other Transactional Human Values groups: personal (7.9), professional (7.7), group-oriented (8.0) and organizational (8.0) human values. As noted earlier, competitive spirit – which was rated lowest at 7.1 – needs to be adhered to more. With stronger adherence to the Fundamental Human Values (8.0), it should not be a difficult task.

With regards adherence at the organizational level, the situation is not too discouraging, since the overall mean value of 7.1 for globalization-induced values is exactly in the middle of the average for other Transactional Human Values. The average for adherence to Fundamental Human Values is the same, at 7.1.

The picture at the level of Indian industry, however, changes dramatically. The respondents perceive that Indian industry is strongest in terms of globalization-induced human values at 5.9, as compared to its adherence to Transactional Human Values, all of which are bracketed at 5.4. Adherence to Fundamental Human Values is also lower at 5.0. The overall average for Terminal Human Values – material comforts and happiness – is also higher in this case (6.3) than for globalization-induced human values (5.9). This implies that the hard-earned benefits of globalization are perceived to be associated with higher material comforts and happiness. The same trend can perhaps be achieved with higher adherence to globalization-induced human values like, in particular, competitive spirit.

Development: Emeritus Fellowship Study Insights

Strengthening globalization-induced human values like competitive spirit at the professional and organizational levels is necessary for a country to gain an edge over other competing countries like China in the world globalization race. As noted at the beginning of this chapter, human values in an organization are to be anchored to its mission statement and integrated with its work ethic, organizational culture, human resources development and strategic management. An earlier study (Rao, 2001), found the following steps worthy of implementation for the purpose:

- leading by example

- selection, training and development, and performance appraisal to be dovetailed with the inculcation of human values as a means for higher employee empowerment, performance and identification with the organization

- an open, informal and relaxed organizational culture

- social and environmental responsiveness and responsibility.

The Spandan Perspective: Humanizing Globalization through Spiritual Democracy

I recently received an invitation from a management institution to participate in a seminar on 'Globalization – Unleashing India's Potential'. The theme overview of the seminar stated, 'India has to unleash its immense potential in the form of competition to face the onslaught of Chinese and other nations in international markets.' True, India like any other country, must strengthen its competitive edge – an important hallmark of globalization, no doubt – at the international level to reach and remain in the big league. Being effective in competition is necessary, however, but not sufficient when one is considering an appropriate role for a country like India – its leadership in the sphere of spiritualism being acknowledged the world over. India is perhaps more at home in the mode of cooperation and contribution rather than that of competition and a zero-sum game. In other words, the country should take up the responsibility to contribute to enabling other countries to achieve globalization without tears, such that humanity as a whole can enjoy equitably the fruits of economic growth and social justice.

Based on Vedantic philosophy, spiritual democracy entails 'the recognition of divinity in every man and woman' as well as 'everybody's inherent right to liberation or *moksha*'. Such spiritual democracy, howsoever laudable it might be, must subject itself to the overriding credo of *Vasudhaika Kutumbakam*, the concept of One World. When applied to globalization, the component of 'the recognition of divinity in every man and woman' would mean that all human beings, irrespective of their caste, creed, race and nationality, deserve to be and become rightful claimants to the benefits of globalization. The second component – 'everybody's inherent right to liberation or *moksha*' – indicates that all countries have a right to work out their own ways and means of participating in the globalization process. The overriding factor of *Vasudhaika Kutumbakam*, however, underscores the supremacy of the cosmos and enjoins that globalization, as well as the sharing of its gains, should not take place at the cost of the interests of others, but should also be such that the economic growth and social welfare of humankind as a whole are as great as possible.

Unleashing India's potential in the context of examining India's role in the globalization process should be aimed at humanizing globalization through value-based spiritual democracy, so that the process is humanistic and the sharing of its gains is just and equitable. Is it not significant that the concept of spiritual democracy was introduced by an Indian, Swami Vivekananda at the equally significant First World Parliament of Religions held in Chicago in September 1893? Is it not equally significant that a celebrated historian like Arnold Toynbee (1960) stated, 'It is already becoming clearer that a chapter which has a western beginning will have to have an Indian ending if it is not to end in the self destruction of the human race' (p. 54)? Finally, it may not be out of place to note that A.L. Basham, after an in-depth study of Indian civilization, came to the conclusion that 'the most striking feature of ancient Indian civilization is its humanity' (1954, p. 9). Not surprisingly his most famous study bears the title *The Wonder that was India*.

INDIAN INSIGHTS, EXPERIENCES AND PRACTICES

J.N. Tata, pioneer of the iron and steel industry in India, wrote a letter to Swami Vivekananda in 1898 in which he stated:

> *I very much recall at this moment your views on the growth of the ascetic spirit in India, and the duty, not of destroying, but of diverting it into useful channels. It seems to me that no better use can be made of the ascetic spirit than establishment of monasteries or residential halls for men dominated by this spirit where they should live with ordinary decency and devote their lives to the cultivation of sciences natural and humanistic ...*

> *If such a crusade were undertaken by a competent leader, ... it would greatly help asceticism, science and the good name of our country. (Ranganathan 2008)*

The Mother's Ministry of Management at the Sri Aurobindo Ashram at Auroville, Pondicherry comes perhaps nearest to implementing spiritual democracy at an institutional level:

> *Management is harmonizing men, material and methods towards the fulfillment of goals leading to human development social benefit and*

global welfare. However, MAN remains the basic factor in any field of human endeavour – it may be home, hospital, business, industry or any other profit/ non-profit socio-economic organization. By MAN we do not mean here only a lump of bones and flesh, nor an 'amalgam' of hands, feet and physical frame, but a 'conscious creature' designed by a Divine Craftsman. He has a spirit and a soul. Management of man, therefore, should not aim at mere regulation and control of his outer appearance but it should be developing his inner consciousness, his soul and his divinity. (Sri Aurobindo Society, 1990)

In recent times Indian industry has realized the role of values in an organization as a means of increasing employee commitment and productivity. Since the 1990s, when India joined the globalization process, such efforts at integrating values with organizational culture have been strengthened in order to enhance competitiveness at the international level. Infosys, for instance, claims to be 'Powered by Intellect, Driven by Values'. Narayana Murthy, as he stepped down as its chairman last year, stated that 'Infosys is not a company selling software, but a global corporation, with an enduring value system' (Srikanth 2006). Kumara Mangalam Birla [2005] feels the Birla group is facing five major challenges *vis-à-vis* its globalization process

> *[The] fifth set of these challenges ... involves making one's globalization character successful and sustainable. What bonds us are our values – integrity, speed, seamlessness, commitment and passion. We expect these values to define the character of our corporation.*

In the context of escalating competitive pressures, which is a hallmark of globalization, ITC Ltd.'s chairman, Y.C. Deveshwar, believes:

> *The enlargement of enterprise potential (therefore) requires Vision, Values and Vitality to be continuously recharged through practice and insight, revalidated for relevance and tested for appropriateness to the evolving competitive context. (Deveshwar 2006)*

In the milieu of mergers and acquisitions (M&A), which has become another important hallmark of globalization, human values as a means of creating the required equation in human interactions have become significant. Ratan Tata, for instance, recently stated (as reported in *The Times of India*) (*vis-à-vis* the Tata-Corus M&A) that Tata first evaluates a company's value system before acquiring or merging with it 'as values and human chemistry are very important to us'.

Quoting the Global Forum of Spiritual Leaders and Parliamentarians held in the Kremlin, in March 1990, will perhaps provide an appropriate conclusion to this discussion: 'A return to values is inescapable if we do not wish to hand over a dead stone to our children rather than a live planet.' The role of India in this process of a return to values can hardly be exaggerated.

References

Bartlett, Christopher A. and Paul W. Beamish. 2010. *Transnational Management: Text, Cases and Readings in Cross-Border Management*, 6th edition. New York: McGraw-Hill.

Basham, A.L. 1954. *The Wonder that was India*. London: Sidgwick and Jackson.

Benjamin, Michelle. 2011. Core Human Values for Ethical Entrepreneurship. [Online]. Available at: http://benjaminenterprises.com/2011/06/05/core-values-for-ethical-entrepreneurship/ [accessed: 6 August 2013].

Birla, Kumara Mangalam. 2005. Making of an Indian MNC. *The Times of India*, 8 October.

Bower, Joseph L. et al. 2012. Occupy Wall Street Protestors have a Point. *HBS Working Knowledge*, 15 February.

Chatterjee, Sameer R. 2005. Weaving the Threads of a Global Mindset in Work Organizations: Managerial Roles and Responsibilities. *Journal of Human Values*, 11 (April): 37–47.

Chumakov, Alexander. 1998. Human Values: The Key to Solving Global Problems. 20th World Congress of Philosophy, Boston, MA, November 1998.

Cohen, Ed. 2007. *Leadership without Borders: Successful Strategies from World Class Leaders*. New Delhi: Wiley India.

Deveshwar, Y.C. 2006. ITC Chairman's Speech. ITC 95th Annual General Meeting, 2006.

Genugten, Willem van et al. 2006. *The United Nations of the Future: Globalization with a Human Face*. Amsterdam: KIT Publishers.

George, Silby K. 2009. Hospitability as Openness to the Other: Levinas, Derrida and the Indian Hospitability Ethos. *Journal of Human Values*, 15(1) (January–June), 29–47.

Hanna, Julia. 2011. The Death of the Global Manager. *HBS Working Knowledge*, 8 August.

HBS Business Summit, Ethics in Globalization. *HBS Working Knowledge*, 13 October 2008.

HBS Cases, The Terror at Taj. *HBS Working Knowledge*, 24 January 2011.

Hettne, Bjorn (ed.). 2007. *Human Values and Global Governance*, vols 1 and 2. Basingstoke: Palgrave Macmillan.

Huntington, Samuel P. 1996. *The Clash of Civilizations and the Remaking of the World Order*. New York: Simon & Schuster.

Kumar, Nirmalya. 2009. *India's Global PowerHouses: How they are Taking On the World*. Boston, MA: Harvard Business Press.

Lamy, Pascal. 2006. *Humanizing Globalization*. Seminar held in Santiago de Chile, Chile, 30 January 2006.

McLuhan, Marshall and Bruce R. Powers. 1989. *The Global Village*. Oxford: Oxford University Press.

Nobel, Carmen. 2011. How Small Wins Unleash Creativity. *HBS Working Knowledge*, 6 September.

——2012a. Beyond Heroic Entrepreneur. *HBS Working Knowledge*, 18 January.

——2012b. Managing the Efficacy of the World's Manager. *HBS Working Knowledge*, 30 January.

Ranganathan, S. 2008. Many Ramayanas: In Pursuit of the History of the Foundation of IISc and NIAS. Paper prepared for the IISc and NIAS Wednesday Discussion Meeting, November 12, 2008. [Online]. Available at: http://alumni.iisc.ernet.in/ranganathan-foundation. pdf [accessed: 14 August 2013].

Salter, Malcolm S. 2004. Enron's Lessons for Managers. *HBS Working Knowledge*, 12 July.

Satish, D.P. 2008. Global Meltdown: America at Bay. *The Story Teller*, 27 October.

Sharma, Subhash. 2010. *Indian Management in the Era of Globalization: Towards New Mantras in Management and Leadership*. [Online]. Available at: http:// www.shunyacreations.com/Seven_Symbols_of_Indian_Management_ Philosophy.pdf [accessed: 21 July 2013].

Sirkin, Harold, et al. 2008. *Globality: Competing with Everyone from Everywhere for Everything*. New York: Business Plus, Hachette.

Smith, Joseph Wayne, et al. 1998. *Global Meltdown: Immigration, Multiculturalism and Nationalism in the New World Disorder*. Westport, CT: Preager.

Smith, Raymond D. 2010. The Role of Greed in the Ongoing Global Financial Crisis. *Journal of Human Values*, 16 (October): 187–94.

Sri Aurobindo Society, Auroville, Pondichery. 1990. *The Mother's Ministry of Management*. Pondicherry: Sri Aurobindo Society.

Srikanth, B.R. 2006. Murthy Logs Out of Infosys. *Hindustan Times*, 21 August. [Online]. Available at: http://www.hindustantimes.com/News-Feed/NM15/ Murthy-logs-out-of-Infosys/Article1-139667.aspx [accessed: 6 August 2013].

Toynbee, Arnold. 1960. *One World and India*. Calcutta: Orient Longmans.

UNESCO. 1999. *21st Century Talks: Humanize Globalization.* Paris: UNESCO Press, 15 September (No. 99-192).

Yunker, James A. 2005. *Rethinking World Government: A New Approach.* Lanham, MD: University Press of America.

PART IV

Towards a Functionally Humane Organization: Spandan Perspectives and Initiatives

15

The Management of Organizations: Towards a Functionally Humane Organization I: The Synergy of Human Values in Management between India and the West

The Context and the Issue

Human values, by their very nature, are situational and culture specific. It would therefore be unrealistic to think of 'transplanting' or 'transporting' values from one country or culture to another easily. One has to keep in mind the extent to which a particular human value which has been found to be effective in one context could be equally effective in the other. This could perhaps be done through cross-cultural studies. Today the world has become a global village with a remarkable and ever-increasing interface and interdependence between and among different nations. While India is one of the world's most populous countries and is developing as an economic and political power, the US today remains the most powerful and developed nation in the world. Since 1991, India has given special impetus to interfacing and interaction at the global level. Moreover, expatriate employment of Indians at the highest levels, in management and entrepreneurship, has further augmented a certain degree of synthesis and synergy in professional management at a cross-cultural level.

The following are considered key features of the wisdom of the East:

- selflessness and non-attachment

- servant leadership

- duty or right education (*dharma* in Sanskrit)

- *shanthi* (peace, harmony)

- self-realization

- unity

- nonviolence or *ahimsa*

As regards the West it is argued that a mutual learning and contribution with the East can be achieved by supplementing the current emphasis on leadership methods and processes with an Eastern approach to the leader and leadership virtues. This Eastern focus on the leader and his or her character derives nourishment from India's age-old spiritual traditions and beliefs This approach also provides an opportunity to the 'East' to do more than simply supplement the teaching of traditional management subjects, by building on its own rich heritage and ethos with its focus on the character of the individual leader.

It is in this context that the pioneering role played by Professor S.K. Chakraborty in developing a vast and deep corpus of knowledge applicable to management theory and practice emanating from Indian ethos, culture, traditions, philosophy, literature and arts and offering the same to academia and professionals alike in India and abroad becomes significant. A finance expert, S.K. Chakraborty started his career at the Indian Institute of Management, Calcutta (IIMC) in the early 1970s. Taking an interest in Indian philosophy and writings, he painstakingly collected material, organized it and during 1980s and 1990s started offering valuable literature, models and suitable management development programmes (MDPs). During this period Chakraborty convinced the management of the Institute to create a Centre for Human Values for the dissemination of knowledge, skills, attitudes and values to strengthen ethical behaviour in managers and management. The centre, called the Management Centre for Human Values (MCHV), stands as a tribute to an individual's dedication and determination resulting in, among others, a meaningful interface between management theory and practice emanating from Indian ethos.

The contribution of Professor Chakraborty in terms of his writings is, as mentioned, equally voluminous and significant. One such important contribution is his identification of 13 values emanating from the studies of Buddhism, Vedanta and yogic psychology as well as derivative epics and Puranic literature. Rooted in the deep structure of Indian culture and society, these 13 values are (Chakraborty 1990):

1.   the individual must be respected

2.   cooperation and trust

3.   jealousy is harmful to mental health

4.   *chitta-shuddhi* or purification of the mind

5.   top quality product/service

6.   work in worship

7.   containment of greed

8.   ethico-moral soundness

9.   self-discipline and self-restraint

10. customer satisfaction

11. creativity

12. the inspiration to give

13. renunciation and detachment

The Study

Keeping this in view, a simple research study was designed as a sequel to the study *Rekindling Innate Divinity in Human Beings* (2010) through the application of the Spandan Spectrum of Human Values 2011. Of the 58 respondents who had participated in the study, around 25 who had professional experience in India and the US were requested to answer two questions, as follows:

Q1: Of the 33 human values – or clusters thereof – included in the Spandan Spectrum of Human Values 2011, please identify those three human values which you think have been effective in India and could be recommended for inculcation in the West?

Q2: Of the 33 human values – or clusters thereof – included in the Spandan Spectrum of Human Values 2011, please identify those three human values which you think have been effective in the West and could be recommended for inculcation in India

Similarly, ten others with vast experience in both the Indian and the American working systems were invited to participate.

Ten respondents from the 58 who participated in the study of 2011, and five from the ten select invitees participated in this study.

Tables 15.1 and 15.2 present the values recommended for transfer from India to the West, and from the West to India respectively.

Columns 4 and 5 of Table 15.1 show the ranking of the ten human values recommended for inculcation in the West. Four of the 15 respondents recommended hospitable disposition (Marwar culture) (22), thereby placing the value in first position. Six values are bracketed in equal second position with three responses each: faith in the basic goodness of others – trust (4); belief in the intrinsic altruism in others – caring – sharing – compassion (6); cultural adaptiveness – cross-cultural management (13); empathy – transformative listening – social sensitivity (16); happiness – contentment – psychic well-being (21); humility – self-awareness (23).

The following values were ranked eighth with two respondents each: belief in the innate divinity in human beings – respect for others – self-respect (5); emotional detachment towards recognition and reward (15); employee orientation (17).

Table 15.1 Human values in an organization recommended for transfer from India to the West [research studies, February 2012 (N=15) and April 2011 (N=58)]

S. no.	Value no.	Human value	Human values recommended from India to West (N=15) Rank	No of respondents	Extent of adherence (2011 study, N=58) Indian industry Mean	Rank	One's own organization Mean	Rank	One's own professional life Mean	Rank	Extent of adherence in the US (N=2) Mean	Rank	Whether included in ICRC-HVs Yes/No	Rank	No. of groups
(1)	(2)	(3)	(4)	(5)	(6)	(7)	(8)	(9)	(10)	(11)	(12)	(13)	(14)	(15)	(16)
1	22	Hospitable disposition (Marwar culture)	I	4	5.5	XII	6.9	XXIII	7.4	XXX	4.0	XXXIII	No	-	-
2	4	Faith in the basic goodness of others – Trust	II	3	5.0	XXVI	7.3	IX	8.2	III	5.3	XXV	No	-	-
3	6	Belief in the intrinsic altruism in others – Caring – Sharing – Compassion	II	3	4.9	XXVII	7.3	IX	8.0	XI	4.5	XXVI	No	-	-
4	13	Cultural adaptiveness – Cross-cultural management	II	3	5.8	VII	7.5	III	7.7	XXII	6.3	XXI	No	-	-
5	16	Empathy – Transformative listening – Social sensitivity	II	3	4.9	XXVII	6.9	XXIII	7.8	XVIII	4.5	XXVI	No	-	-
6	21	Happiness – Contentment – Psychic well being	II	3	5.4	XV	6.9	XXIII	7.7	XX	4.5	XXVI	No	-	-
7	23	Humility – Self awareness	II	3	5.3	XVIII	6.7	XXXI	7.6	XXIII	4.5	XXVI	No	-	-
8	5	Belief in the innate divinity in human beings – Respect for others – Self-respect	VIII	2	5.3	XVIII	7.4	V	8.5	I	8.3	III	No	-	-
9	15	Emotional detachment towards recognition and reward	VIII	2	4.6	XXXIII	6.1	XXXIII	6.9	XXXIII	7.5	XIV	No	-	-
10	17	Employee orientation	VIII	2	5.4	XV	7.0	XXII	7.8	XVIII	6.0	XXII	No	-	-

A perusal of the aforementioned human values offers certain interesting insights:

a)   Inculcation of all three Transformational Human Values in relation to other human beings – namely faith in the basic goodness of others (4), belief in the intrinsic altruism in others (6), and belief in the innate divinity in human beings (5) – have been perceived important enough to be strengthened in Western work ethics. Similarly, the personal value humility – self-awareness (23) and the relational-oriented value empathy (16), have also been warranted important enough. The aim, therefore, appears to be to make the Western work ethic more self-oriented.

b)   The above human values have been compared with perceptions regarding the extent to which these human values are adhered to in the West. Columns 12 and 13 show that the least adhered to human value in the West, with a value of 4.0 (on a ten-point scale), and therefore ranked 33rd, is hospitable disposition (Marwar culture) (22). The next least adhered to human values, ranked equal 26th, are: belief in the intrinsic altruism in others (6); empathy (16); happiness (21); and humility (23). Thus there appears to be a rationale in the selection of the ten human values for inculcation in Western culture. The only exception appears to be belief in the innate divinity in human beings (5), which is ranked third in the Western context. The endorsement that belief in the innate divinity of human beings is cross-cultural and cross-national thus offers a positive note in the human endeavour for self-transformation.

c)   The extent of adherence data from the study of 2011 are offered in columns 6 to 11, with a view to assessing the extent to which the human values recommended for Western culture are being adhered to in the country. Emotional detachment towards recognition and reward (15), as noted earlier, was perceived to be the least adhered to human value at all three levels of Indian industry, one's own organization, and one's own professional life. Belief in the innate divinity of human beings (5) is ranked first at the level of one's own professional life, and ranked fifth at the level of one's own organization – but eighteenth in Indian industry as a whole.

Table 15.2   Human values in an organization recommended for transfer from the West to India [research studies, February 2012 (N=15) and April 2011 (N=58)]

S. no.	Value no.	Human value	Human values recommended from West to India (N=15) Rank	No of respondents	Extent of adherence (2011 study, N=58) Indian industry Mean	Rank	One's own organization Mean	Rank	One's own professional life Mean	Rank	Extent of adherence in the US (N=2) Mean	Rank	Whether included in ICRC-HVs Yes/No	Rank	No. of groups
(1)	(2)	(3)	(4)	(5)	(6)	(7)	(8)	(9)	(10)	(11)	(12)	(13)	(14)	(15)	(16)
1.	1	Accountability	I	7	5.1	XXIV	7.2	XVI	8.2	III	8.5	II	Yes	I	7
2.	2	Autonomy in decision making – Flexible work culture – Accepting diversity and divergence	II	4	5.2	XXI	7.2	XVI	7.9	XIV	8.0	VI	No	-	-
3.	12	Creativity – Innovation	II	4	5.8	VII	7.2	XVI	7.5	XXIV	7.5	XIV	Yes	IV	2
4.	17	Employee orientation	II	4	5.4	XV	7.0	XXII	7.8	XVIII	6.0	XXII	No	-	-
5.	28	Professional attachment towards completion of the task	II	4	5.9	V	7.4	V	8.2	III	8.3	III	Yes	IV	2
6.	9	Competitive spirit	VI	3	7.1	II	6.9	XXIII	7.1	XXXII	8.3	III	No	-	-
7.	18	Entrepreneurship – Risk taking	VI	3	6.1	IV	6.9	XXIII	7.4	XXX	7.5	XIV	No	-	-
8.	27	Preparedness – Proactiveness – Environmental sensitivity	VI	3	4.8	XXIX	6.9	XXIII	7.5	XXVI	8.0	VI	Yes	IV	2

Table 15.2 looks at human values in an organization drawn from Western culture and recommended for inculcation in India:

a)   Accountability (1) ranked first with seven out of 15 respondents recommending its inculcation in India. The four values ranked second, with four respondents each, are: autonomy in decision making (2); creativity – innovation (12); employee orientation (17); professional attachment towards completion of the task (28). Autonomy in decision making (2) and professional attachment (28), like accountability (1), aim at improving upon managerial performance at the professional level. It may be recollected that Table 15.1 indicated the need for managers in the West to strengthen themselves at the individual level.

b)   The three values ranked 6th, with three respondents each, are: competitive spirit (9); entrepreneurship – risk taking (18); preparedness – proactiveness – environmental sensitivity (27). These three values, along with creativity – innovation (12), are globalization-induced human values. The message here is therefore to strengthen management in India with stronger adherence to and practice of globalization-oriented human values.

c)   Extent of adherence in the West (columns 12 and 13): accountability (1) is ranked 2nd; professional attachment towards the completion of the task (28) and competitive spirit (9) are bracketed together in 3rd; and autonomy in decision making (2) and preparedness (27) are bracketed in equal 6th position. Five of the eight human values identified for transfer from the West for inculcation in India are strongly adhered to in the West. This perception thus lends credibility to the selection of the said human values.

d)   Extent of adherence, 2011 study [N=58]: professional attachment towards completion of the task (28) stands strongest in 3rd place at the level of one's own professional life and 5th at the levels of Indian industry and one's own organization. The plausible rationale is that although India is strong in its professional orientation, it is not strong enough for the global arena.

Table 15.3   Human values recommended for transfer from India to the West: their rankings compared to those for: (a) perceived adherence at the levels of industry, one's own organization and one's own professional life [research study, 2011 (N=58)]; (b) Institutional Civic Responsibility to Community through Human Values (ICRC-HVs) [research study, 2011 (N=25)]; (c) infusion of family values [research study, 2011 (N=25)]

S. no.	Value no.	Human value	Human values recommended from India to West	Extent of adherence (2011 study, N=58)			Extent of adherence in the USA/West (N=2)		Institutional Civic Responsibility to Community through Human Values (ICRC-HVs)	Infusion of family values in management
			Rank	Indian industry Rank	One's own organization Rank	One's own prof. life Rank	Mean	Rank	Rank	Rank
(1)	(2)	(3)	(4)	(5)	(6)	(7)	(8)	(9)	(10)	(11)
1	22	Hospitable disposition (Marwar culture)	I	XII	XXIII	XXX	4.0	XXXIII	-	I
2	4	Faith in the basic goodness of others – Trust	II	XXVI	IX	III	5.3	XXV	-	-
3	6	Belief in the intrinsic altruism in others – Caring – Sharing – Compassion	II	XXVII	IX	XI	4.5	XXVI	-	-
4	13	Cultural adaptiveness – Cross-cultural management	II	VII	III	XXII	6.3	XXI	-	-
5	16	Empathy – Transformative listening – Social sensitivity	II	XXVII	XXIII	XVIII	4.5	XXVI	-	-
6	21	Happiness – Contentment – Psychic well being	II	XV	XXIII	XX	4.5	XXVI	-	-
7	23	Humility – Self-awareness	II	XVIII	XXXI	XXIII	4.5	XXVI	-	-
8	5	Belief in the innate divinity in human beings – Respect for others – Self-respect	VIII	XVIII	V	I	8.3	III	-	VIII
9	15	Emotional detachment towards recognition and reward	VIII	XXXIII	XXXIII	XXXIII	7.5	XIV	-	-
10	17	Employee orientation	VIII	XV	XXII	XVIII	6.0	XXII	-	-

Table 15.3 compares the rankings for perceived adherence to human values recommended for transfer from India to the West to (a) Institutional Civic Responsibility to Community Through Human Vales (ICRC-HVs) (N=25) and (b) infusion of family values (N=25).

Table 15.3 (Column 10) reveals that none of the seven values considered important values for ICRC-HVs is among the ten values recommended for adherence in the West. However, four values perceived important for transfer from the West to India (Table 15.4, Column 10) are among the seven under ICRC-HVs. These are accountability (1); creativity innovation (12); professional attachment towards completion of the task (28); and preparedness (27). These values are similar to those found in Table 15.3 with reference to their adherence in the West. The message which thus keeps on repeating itself is three-fold:

a)   Indian managers need to strengthen themselves professionally;

b)   they need to gear up in terms of their knowledge, skills, attitudes and values to be successful in the process of globalization world over; and

c)   they need to strengthen themselves professionally with a global orientation so as to contribute the might of their organizations for the welfare of the community and society.

THE INFUSION OF FAMILY VALUES IN MANAGEMENT

Table 15.3 shows that two of the ten human values identified as suitable for transference from India to the West emanate from family values. These are:

●   22: Hospitable disposition (Marwar culture): emanating from the family value of 'being hospitable to everyone who comes to your home, irrespective of cast, creed, financial position or status' (family value no. 5, see Chapter 17).

●   5: Belief in the innate divinity in human beings – Respect for others – Self-respect: emanating from the family value of maintaining 'respect, obedience, courtesy, decorum and discipline towards, and in the presence of, elders' (family value no. 1, see Chapter 17).

None of the eight human values recommended for transfer from the West to India emanates from Indian family values (Table 15.4, column 11).

Table 15.4 Human values recommended for transfer from the West to India: their rankings compared to those for: (a) perceived adherence at the levels of industry, one's own organization and one's own professional life [research study, 2011 (N=58)]; (b) Institutional Civic Responsibility to Community through Human Values (ICRC-HVs) [research study, 2011 (N=25)]; (c) infusion of family values [research study, 2011 (N=25)]

S. no.	Value no.	Human value	Human values recommended from the West to India Rank	Extent of adherence (2011 study, N=58)			Extent of adherence in the USA/West (N=2)		Institutional Civic Responsibility to Community through Human Values (ICRC-HVs) Rank	Infusion of family values in management Rank
				Indian industry Rank	One's own organization Rank	One's own prof. life Rank	Mean	Rank		
(1)	(2)	(3)	(4)	(5)	(6)	(7)	(8)	(9)	(10)	(11)
1	1	Accountability	I	XXIV	XVI	III	8.5	II	I	-
2	2	Autonomy in decision making – Flexible work culture – Accepting diversity and divergence	II	XXI	XVI	XIV	8.0	VI	-	-
3	12	Creativity – Innovation	II	VII	XVI	XXIV	7.5	XIV	IV	-
4	17	Employee orientation	II	XV	XXII	XVIII	6.0	XXII	-	-
5	28	Professional attachment towards completion of the task	II	V	V	III	8.3	III	IV	-
6	9	Competitive spirit	VI	II	XXIII	XXXII	8.3	III	-	-
7	18	Entrepreneurship – Risk taking	VI	IV	XXIII	XXX	7.5	XIV	-	-
8	27	Preparedness –Proactiveness – Environmental sensitivity	VI	XXIX	XXIII	XXVI	8.0	VI	IV	-

References

Aleve, Ergenc Kathril et al. 2006. Congruence of Family and Organizational Values in Relation to Organizational Citizenship Behavior. *Journal of Human Values*, 12 (April): 81–9.

Arunachalam, K. 1985. *Gandhian Way of Management*. Madurai: Tamilnad Gandhi Smarak Nidhi.

Baha'i International Community. 2011. National Spiritual Assembly: Trusteeship is the Answer. *Times of India*, 21 April.

Chakraborty, S.K. 1990. *Human Response Development: Exploring Transformational Values*. New Delhi: Wiley Eastern.

Eccles, Robert G. and George Serafeim et al. 2011. Leading and Lagging Countries in Contributing to a Sustainable Society. *HBS Working Knowledge*, 23 May.

GCEG (Global Community Earth Government) Community. 2007. *Earth Governance and Management*, 10 June 2007, Editorial Page. [Online]. Available at: www.globalcommunitywebnet.com/GPA/globalgovernance.html [accessed: 9 August 2013].

Global Community U.S. 2010. *Societal Sustainability*. [Online]. Available at: www.goodweave.org/index.php?cid=148gold=Cmis3f717rgCFYRV4godbo AUA [accessed: 9 August 2013].

Hall, Jeremy and Harrie Vredenburg. 2003. The Challenges of Innovating for Sustainable Development. *MIT Sloan Management Review*, 15 October.

Independent India at 60. 2007. *The Hindu*, special supplement, 15 August.

Institute for Communitarian Policy Studies. 2000. *Communitarianism Explained (Four Basic Tenets of Communitarianism: Human Dignity, Liberty, Responsibility and Open Discussions*. [Online]. Available at: www.debate.uvm.edu/handbookfile/pubpriv/046.html [accessed: 15 August 2013].

Kalam, Abdul. 2007. *Vision 2020 Mission: PURA Mission and Model*, 14 November 2007. [Online.] Available at: www.apjabdulkalam.com [accessed: 26 July 2013].

Kleinman, Arthur. 1998. *Experience and its Moral Modes: Culture, Human Conditions and Disorder*, The Tanner Lectures on Human Values, Stanford University, 13–16 April 1998.

Maira, Arun M. 2004. *Remaking India: One Country, One Destiny*. New Delhi: Sage.

Nilekani, Nandan 2009, *Imagining India: Ideas for the New Century*, revised and updated. London: Penguin.

Prahalad, C.K. 2004. *Fortune at the Bottom of the Pyramid*. Upper Saddle River, NJ: Pearson Education / Prentice Hall.

Prasad, M.G. 2011. *Some Basic Features of Indian Heritage*. [Online]. Available at: http://www.docstoc.com/docs/129875237/SOME-BASIC-FEATURES-OF-INDIAN-HERITAGE-M [accessed: 15 August 2013].

Pruzan, Peter. 2004. Blending the Best of East and West in Management Education; A View from Northern Europe. In Ananda Das Gupta (ed.), *Human Values in Management*. Aldershot: Ashgate, pp. 3–18.

Stone, Lawrence. 1994. *Family Values in a Historical Prospective, and Family Values in 1993*, The Tanner Lectures on Human Values, Harvard University, 16 November 1994.

World Commission on Environment and Development. 1987. *Our Common Future*. Oxford: Oxford University Press.

16

Management and Society: Towards a Functionally Humane Organization II: Institutional Civic Responsibility to the Community through Human Values (ICRC-HVs): A Case Study of Jaipur Rugs Co., Jaipur

The Context and the Issue

The concept of Institutional Civic Responsibility (ICR) arose from the felt need that contributions made by management and organizations to the community and society could, and should, be wider and deeper than they currently are – although initiatives such as Corporate Social Responsibility (CSR) are laudable and doing their best. In terms of widening the scope, it is considered that organizations other than large, profitable organizations as well as institutions involved in other economic, social and educational spheres of activity have an equally important role to play. Deepening of the scope, on the other hand, requires management initiatives meeting needs other than simply the 'social' needs of society. 'Civic' responsibility is considered more basic and generic – enabling the development of proper 'citizens' would then be the objective of the initiative. Hence, the focus here is Institutional Civic Responsibility (ICR). The Western concept of communitarianism, in particular, which sees values as being the instruments of institutional contribution,[1] added strength to this line of thinking. The activities of smaller and not widely-known organizations, such as Jaipur Rugs Company, Jaipur, India, clinched the issue. Application of the Spandan 3D Process and the use of the Spandan Spectrum of Human Values has lead us to create the initiative we here refer to as Institutional Civic Responsibility to Community through Human Values (ICRC-HVs).

This chapter recounts the efforts of the Jaipur Rugs Company, Jaipur, India, as a case study.

Jaipur Rugs

THE COMPANY

Jaipur Rugs is an India-based organization engaged in the manufacturing and exporting of hand knotted products since 1999. It manufactures elegantly designed and exquisitely finished, customized, handmade rugs, woven with wool and silk threads. The company is directly associated with around 40,000 weavers working 3,400 looms in ten states of India, providing employment to rural artisans at their doorstep. The extended family concept, technology sharing, quality control and customer satisfaction are a few of its strengths, helping it to sustain itself as a 100 per cent export unit with potential annual growth of 35 per cent.

In 2004 the company launched the Jaipur Rugs Foundation (JRF) as a social initiative with the prime objective of promoting sustainable livelihood opportunities as a means to uplift deprived communities of rural artisans and weavers. These artisans and weavers are the real champions of the carpet industry's success story. Thus the foundation's aim is to empower rural artisans to become entrepreneurs by availing them of opportunities to earn a regular income and to be motivated to make savings. JRF is also the apparatus through which the company takes action to look into and improve other areas of the weavers' lives through welfare activities related to health and sanitation, education, livelihood, the empowerment of women and so on. The foundation is also helping the weavers to connect with other government and agency schemes such as helping in the making of Artisan Credit Cards

---

1   Robert N. Bellah (1995–1996), for instance, gives the following as four central values of 'Democratic Communitarianism': 1) sacredness of the individual, 2) solidarity, 3) 'complementary association' and 4) participation as both a right and a duty.

or obtaining insurance under the Rajiv Gandhi Bima Yojna programme and so on.

VISION

The company's vision can be summed up as 'Sustainable livelihoods for people engaged in the carpet value chain, empowering them to become entrepreneurs.'

MISSION

The Jaipur Rugs Foundation is a non-profit organization that promotes sustainable livelihoods for the rural poor to become artisans engaged in the rug value chain in India by empowering them to establish community-level enterprises through enhancing their artisanal and business skills.

OBJECTIVES

The company's strategic plan is to build on the experiences of JRF since 2004 and to propel the foundation along a high-growth trajectory during the next three years by:

- expanding operations across ten states and issuing new artisan cards for 20,000 artisans;

- providing education and health services to 30,000 artisans;

- identifying, developing and training 15,000 new artisans to make international quality carpets;

- upgrading the skills of 25,000 existing artisans;

- setting up 200 village factories, 500 Community Entrepreneurship Groups (CEGs) and two Common Facility Centres (CFCs);

- achieving an annual turnover of Rs 20 crores (200 million) by the end of the financial year 2014.

JRF also aims to provide artisans with a voice and a platform for improving the quality of their lives and most importantly giving them the collective strength to combat the exploitative practices of middle men, including eliminating child labour. Further, JRF has been working at remote locations, where livelihood options are limited, and has engaged people from the most disadvantaged segments of the society including Scheduled Castes (SC), Scheduled Tribes (ST), minorities and women. Indeed 70 per cent of those employed by JRF are women, who also constitute one of the most vulnerable groups in rural India and make up part of the BPL (Below the Poverty Line) category.

The Role of HR in Uplifting the Weaving Community

TRAINING

Training covers the basic skills of weaving, making people artisans, and also the skill upgrades required to help weavers learn the finer aspects of the weaving process. Training also helps improve time efficiency.

INCENTIVES

Bonuses are provided to weavers who complete rugs in a shorter time span. In other words, if a carpet is manufactured in a shorter period of time than expected, the artisan receives higher compensation from the company.

EXPOSURE VISITS

Such visits have been arranged by the Human Resources department to help weavers gain wider experience and to familiarize them with the working environment.

RECRUITMENT

From the pool of artisans, the organization identifies those with the potential to be deployed effectively in office posts such as master trainer, branch manager, quality supervisor etc., thus providing opportunities for promotion from field jobs to office work.

POLICY ON CHILD LABOUR

As the art of weaving is transferred from one generation to another, in such livelihoods where art and craft is involved children often become part of the household's labour force. The practice of employing child labour, however, is strictly condemned by the organization. Consequently the organization is RugMark certified for its prevention of child labour policy.

STATEMENT FROM JAIPUR RUGS CMD

> *I believe in nurturing rural artisans to make them self employed and self sufficient with control over their lives. I believe in carrying forward traditional values and I also believe that as each day passes we approach each step in our system to enhance productivity at the initial level, and then each day one enjoys a different level of prosperity. I want to transfer more and more ownership to those who work at grassroots. The business is scaling up each year. We want to develop more natural leaders who can take care of profits and society as well. Proficiency means more efficiency and better systems.*

Uplifting the Weaving Community

SEVEN INITIATIVES

To achieve the objective of uplifting the weaving families who make rugs in Jaipur and elsewhere in India, a foundation was created within the company. Furthermore, a qualified and experienced functionary was appointed at senior management level and a team was created with a young and committed professional from Romania inducted as its secretary in direct liaison with the company's CMD, Nand Kishore Chaudhury.

Seven initiatives have been identified as follows:

1. communicate the vision, mission and culture of the Jaipur Rugs Company;

2. ensure: efficiency of supply chain; use of technology; planning-processes; ownership-delegation;

3. uphold and spread dignity of artisans;

4. create a strategy to allows two ways of communication (bottom-up and top-down);

5.   do social research to get to know the artisans, their potential and
      needs (database assessment);

6.   employ training and development (internal);

7.   aim for a target of assimilating / preparing 60,000 new artisans
      (planning and training methods).

Diagnosis: Human Values Considered Important for the Initiative

A day-long *Spandan* work shop on human values was conducted at the Jaipur
Rugs Centre on 29 February 2012 to crystallize thoughts with reference to the
seven initiatives stated above.

The 25 participants were divided into five groups. Four of these groups
were assigned initiatives one, two, six and seven respectively. These
groups were assigned the task of identifying five human values considered
important for translating the concerned initiative into action. Of these five
values, the groups were to identify three from the Spandan Spectrum of
Human Values 2011; the remaining two could, if desired by the group,
be from outside the spectrum. The fifth group was assigned the task of
identifying the five human values considered important for translating all
four initiatives selected for discussion into reality. The results of the group
exercise are shown in Table 16.1.

Table 16.1 contains both group-wise and initiative-wise responses:

Group initiatives

Group A: 1. Culture of Jaipur Rugs (morals + values)

Group B: 2. Efficiency of supply chain

Group C: 6. Training and development

Group D: 7. More artisans (60,000)

Group E: Overall – all seven initiatives

Table 16.1 Institutional Civic Responsibility to Community through Human Values (ICRC-HVs): Jaipur Rugs Foundation (JRF) for uplifting the weaving community – seven initiatives, human values perceived as important and assessment of the extent of their adherence [Spandan Workshop at Jaipur Rugs Co., Jaipur]

| | | | Overall ranking | | Human values perceived as relevant – group and initiative wise | | | | | |
S. no.	Value no.	ICRC-HVs	Rank	No. of groups with 5 members each (N=5)	Group A — 1. Culture of JR (M+V)*	Group B — 2. Efficiency of supply chain	Group C — 6. Training and development	Group D — 7. More artisans (60,000)	Group E — Overall – all seven initiatives	Total (cols. 5–10)
(1)	(2)	(3)	(4)	(5)	(6)	(7)	(8)	(9)	(10)	(11)
1	1	Accountability	I	5	Yes	Yes	Yes	Yes	Yes	5
2	2	Autonomy in decision making	VIII	1	-	-	Yes	-	-	1
3	3	Behavioural flexibility	VIII	1	-	-	-	Yes	-	1
4	7	Commitment	VIII	1	-	Yes	-	-	-	1
5	8	Community interest	II	2	Yes	-	-	Yes	-	2
6	9	Competitive spirit	VIII	1	-	Yes	-	-	-	1
7	12	Creativity – Innovation	II	2	-	Yes	-	-	Yes	2
8	13	Cultural adaptiveness	VIII	1	-	-	Yes	-	-	1
9	16	Empathy	VIII	1	-	-	Yes	-	-	1
10	18	Entrepreneurship	VIII	1	-	-	-	Yes	-	1
11	24	Integrity	II	2	Yes	-	-	-	Yes	2
12	27	Preparedness	II	2	-	-	-	Yes	Yes	2
13	28	Professional attachment towards work	II	2	Yes	Yes	-	-	-	2
14	33	Team spirit	II	2	-	-	Yes	-	Yes	2
		Other than spectrum values			– Sharing ideas – Sense of belonging	-	-	Ethical leadership	-	3

* M + V = morals and values

In brain-storming sessions the five groups identified 14 of the 33 human values in the Spandan Spectrum of Human Values 2011.

Columns 4 and 5 reveal that accountability (1) was identified by all five groups as relevant in the successful execution of the JRF initiative of uplifting the weaving community, thereby placing the value in first position. The remaining six values – each picked by two groups – bracketed at equal second position are preparedness – proactiveness – environmental sensitivity (27); team spirit (33); professional attachment towards completion of the task (28); community interest – social good – sustainable development (8); creativity – innovation (12); and integrity – consistency in saying and doing (24).

The remaining seven values – each picked by one group – are bracketed together in eighth position.

Discovery: Extent of Adherence

An attempt was made to assess the extent of adherence to the top seven human values selected by the workshop groups as perceived by the 58 select invitee respondents at the levels of Indian industry, one's own organization and one's own professional life (Table 16.2, columns 6–11). Professional attachment towards the completion of the task (28) was perceived as the most adhered to value, ranked 5th at the levels Indian industry and one's own organization, and 3rd in one's own professional life. Integrity – consistency in saying and doing (24) stands second, ranked 14th at the level of Indian industry, 9th at the level of one's own organization and 3rd in one's own professional life. The implication therefore is that Indian industry and its management has a long way to go to make social initiatives like ICRC-HVs effective.

Table 16.2 Institutional Civic Responsibility to Community through Human Values (ICRC-HVs): human values perceived as important and assessment of the extent of their adherence [Spandan Workshop at Jaipur Rugs Co., Jaipur]

S. no.	Value no.	ICRC-HVs	Human values perceived as important		Extent of adherence (2011 study, N=58)								Whether figuring in human values from India to the West and the West to India		
			Rank	No. of groups with 5 members each	Indian industry		One's own organization		One's own professional life				Yes/No	Rank	No.
					Mean	Rank	Mean	Rank	Mean	Rank					
(1)	(2)	(3)	(4)	(5)	(6)	(7)	(8)	(9)	(10)	(11)			(12)	(13)	(14)
1	1	Accountability	I	5	5.1	XXIV	7.2	XVI	8.2	III			Yes	I	4
2	27	Preparedness – Proactiveness – Environmental sensitivity	II	2	4.8	XXIX	6.9	XXIII	7.5	XXVI			Yes	II	3
3	33	Team spirit	II	2	5.7	X	7.1	XX	7.9	XIV			No	-	-
4	28	Professional attachment towards completion of the task	II	2	5.9	V	7.4	V	8.2	III			Yes	IV	2
5	8	Community interest – Social good – Sustainable development	II	2	4.7	XXXII	7.1	XX	7.5	XXIV			No	-	-
6	12	Creativity – Innovation	II	2	5.8	VII	7.2	XVI	7.5	XXIV			Yes	IV	2
7	24	Integrity – Consistency in saying and doing	II	2	5.1	XXIV	7.3	IX	8.2	III			No	-	-

Table 16.3 Institutional Civic Responsibility to Community through Human Values (ICRC-HVs): rankings compared to those of (a) industry, one's own organization and one's own professional life [research study, 2011 (N=58)]; (b) synergy study on human values to be recommended for transfer from India to the West and vice versa (N=15); and (c) infusion of family values (N=25)

S. no.	Value no	Human value	Human values perceived as important	Extent of adherence by CMD Jaipur Rugs Company, Jaipur, India			Extent of adherence (2011 study, N=58)			Human values recommended from- (N=15)		Infusion of family values in management
				Indian industry	One's own orgn.	One's own prof. life	Indian industry	One's own orgn.	One's own prof. life	India to the West	West to India	
			Rank	Rank	Rank	Rank	Rank	Rank	Rank	Rank	Rank	Rank
(1)	(2)	(3)	(4)	(5)	(6)	(7)	(8)	(9)	(10)	(11)	(12)	(13)
1.	1	Accountability	I	II	III	II	XXIV	XVI	III	-	I	-
2.	27	Preparedness-Proactiveness-Environment Sensitivity	II	III	II	II	XXIX	XXIII	XXV	-	II	-
3.	33	Team Spirit	II	II	III	III	X	XX	XIV	-	-	II
4.	28	Professional Attachment towards Completion of the task	II	II	IV	III	V	V	III	-	IV	-
5.	8	Community Interest – Social Good-sustainable development	II	III	II	II	XXXII	XX	XXIV	-	-	-
	12	Creativity – Innovation	II	II	II	III	VII	XVI	XXIV	-	IV	-
	24	Integrity – Consistency in saying and doing	II	II	III	III	XXIV	IX	III	-	-	IV

STUDY OF SYNERGY BETWEEN INDIAN AND WESTERN HUMAN VALUES (TABLE 16.3, COLUMNS 11 AND 12)

None of the ten values recommended for transfer from India to the West is included in the top seven human values comprising ICRC-HVs (Table 16.3, column 11). Four human values, however, out of the eight identified for inculcation in India from the West are included in the seven values of the ICRC-HVs. These are accountability (1); preparedness – proactiveness – environmental sensitivity (27); professional attachment towards completion of the task (28); and creativity – innovation (12). These four values are related to professional advancement (accountability and professional attachment) and preparedness for coping with globalization processes (preparedness and creativity).

INFUSION OF FAMILY VALUES IN MANAGEMENT (TABLE 16.3, COLUMN 13)

Two human values from the ICRC-HVs emanate from Indian family values:

Human Values	Family Values[2]
33: Team spirit	4: Maintaining strong bonds with family members as well as relatives
24: Integrity	3: Never compromising on integrity for the purpose of prosperity

References

Bellah, Robert N. 1995–1996. Community Properly Understood: A Defense of 'Democratic Communitarianism'. *The Responsive Community*, 6(1) (Winter): 49–54.

---

2   See Chapter 17, in which nine Indian family values are identified: 1. maintaining respect, obedience, courtesy, decorum and discipline towards, and in the presence of, elders; 2. living peacefully and respecting each other's rights; 3. never compromising on integrity for the purpose of prosperity; 4. maintaining strong bonds with family members as well as relatives; 5. being hospitable to everyone who comes to your home, irrespective of caste, creed, financial position or status; 6. treating guests as God (*atithi devo bhava*); 7. remembering and bowing to God first thing in the morning; 8. practising yoga and meditation; 9. always taking the advice of elders on important decisions.

17

Towards a Functionally Humane Organization III: The Infusion of Family Values in Management

The Context and the Issue

A human being plays different roles concurrently, interacting with different persons in different places and situations. At home a human being is a member of her family; at work she is a member of an organization. She has her own set of personal values; her family has its own values – influenced and evolved by the society of which both the family and the human being are members. An organization or institution has its own values – again as a part of society, but equally as part of the country or economy. The organization and its values are thus impacted by the society and the country and their values. Thanks to globalization, no country or industry is immune from the effects of – good or otherwise – events at the global level. One can thus see the 'flow' of interactions, emotions and activities of different entities (sub-systems) – from individual to family to organization to society to country and to the world – both within, between and among such entities. Equally important is how a human being, family, organization and society (as part of a country and the world) weave relationships and evolve values to achieve their goals as well as the common goals of the entities interacting together. It is in this context that values play an important role. Knitting together the values of human beings, families, organizations and society is an opportunity as much as a challenge. It is an opportunity to work together effectively (results) and harmoniously (relations) towards commonly set objectives. When accomplished successfully, values become a glue, a binding force, a bond between and among cooperating entities. If, on the other hand, values are inculcated too strongly, the system and its members develop rigidity, lack flexibility and will not be able to respond effectively to the changes in other systems and the environment. Values then become deterrents to 'remaking' ourselves, enterprise and society. The key challenge and the opportunity, therefore, is how to infuse, synthesize, synergize and synchronize values at the various levels such that an optimal balance between results and relations is obtained and maintained throughout.

Lawrence Stone (1994), in his Tanner Lectures on Human Values delivered at Harvard University in 1994, offered certain observations relevant to this context. He delivered two lectures under the overarching title of *Family Values in a Historical Perspective*: 'Family Values in the Past' and 'Family Values in 1993'.

In the first lecture Stone stated that family values can be seen as 'the values needed for members of the lower middle class to obtain self respect and to get on in the world: namely, hard work, self discipline, [etc.]' (1994, p. 70). He felt that in the past obedience had been the most important family value.

In the second lecture, on family values in 1993, Stone expressed that there had been a remarkable change in family values in Western society over a period of time. As a result of the emergence of the nuclear family, the disruption of the joint family system, industrialization and the need for family members to be scattered to different places for employment and careers, and the consequent social and health problems, Western society as a whole had to pay rather a heavy price in terms of several far-reaching social, economic and psychological consequences.

> *What is needed to turn our society around is a politics based on hope not fear, a moral code based on the acceptance of personal responsibility for one's actions, and greater family and community cooperation rather than the selfish pursuit of the marriage of individual happiness, regardless of its effect on others. (1994, p. 110)*

This chapter addresses the idea of infusing family values in business and management, taking India as its frame of reference.

Family Businesses

When the Industrial Revolution got underway in the mid-eighteenth century, its initiation, functioning, consolidation and expansion was undertaken by the communities and segments of society which were engaged in trade and commerce, which was family-owned and managed. The concept of the joint stock company came into being later with the growth of manufacturing industries, plantations, mines and other large-scale economic activities that required pooling resources from society at large.

Indian society is classified into castes based upon the principle of the division of labour, known as *varnashrama dharma*. The activities of society were divided between large groups: (i) scholastic, preaching, teaching and priestly work; (ii) law and order, protection of the kingdom and people; (iii) trade, commerce and business; and (iv) menial work such as cleaning, sweeping, sanitation. These four broad groups of activities were applied to four groups of castes, *Brahmin, Kshatriya, Vysya* and *Shudra* respectively. These castes and their functioning were defined by birth, thus someone born into a Brahmin family was ordained to undertake the activities and responsibilities of a Brahmin.

When the process of industrialization began in India in the mid-nineteenth century, its leadership was assumed by essentially the *Vysyas*. The managing agency system came into being with three major functions: ownership, finance and management. The family values of the business communities along with the values of Indian society shaped the business principles and practices in India. Their effect is still strong, although the managing agency system was abolished in 1956.

Certain valuable insights have been offered by Gopal Srinivasan, Founder, Chairman and Managing Director of TVS Capital Funds – part of the highly respected TVS group of Companies – on the role and relevance of the values of family businesses in the Indian context. Srinivasan (see Bagchi 2011) sums up his insights on managing a family-owned business as follows:

- The best multi-generational family businesses strive for very meritocratic management because it is in their best interest to sustain their wealth.

- You want to leave your legacy a little bit better than when you got it.

- All family businesses that have been hugely successful were built on very strong links to society.

The best way to think about a multi-generational family business is a flow across time ... from the past, the present and inheritance of the legacy your passing to the future! So, in many ways, good families have this strong sense of what I call institutional loyalty versus individual loyalty. It is loyalty to what TVS stands for: the reputation we have; the way it opens doors; you want to leave it a little bit better than where you got it. (Bagchi 2011)

Indian Family Values System: The Study

Values can be defined as certain attitudes and beliefs that a person follows in his conduct.

In the Indian culture, there are certain rules and regulations that each and every child is taught right from his childhood. (iloveindia.com)

Some such important family values in India are:

- maintaining respect, obedience, courtesy, decorum and discipline towards, and in the presence of, elders

- living peacefully and respecting each other's rights

- never compromising on integrity for the purpose of prosperity

- maintaining strong bonds with family members as well as relatives

- being hospitable to everyone who comes to your home, irrespective of caste, creed, financial position or status

- treating guests as God (*atithi devo bhava*)

- remembering and bowing to God first thing in the morning

- practising yoga and meditation

- always taking the advice of elders on important decisions (adapted from: iloveindia.com)

An attempt has been made to understand the relevance of the above Indian family values to work situations in India, and the extent to which these values are adhered to in Indian industry as a whole, in one's own organization and in one's own professional life. For this purpose, a response sheet was developed and administered personally and online to select respondents, individuals and institutions known for being successful family-managed businesses in India.

This study on the relevance of and adherence to family values in management was conducted in two organizations: the Jaipur Rugs Company in Jaipur and MART in Noida. Both are entrepreneur-driven organizations with a strong ethical orientation and an adherence to family culture and values in their working systems. Both are small in terms of employees – around 200 and 60 respectively. Jaipur Rugs is involved in the manufacture and sale of rugs. MART is a non-governmental organization (NGO) that offers expertise in rendering services in rural marketing and development.

The response sheet (see Appendix) was administered to the two institutional heads and their immediate work groups consisting of 14 heads of departments (HODs) (Jaipur Rugs) and nine partners / HODs (MART). The responses sought and analysed relate to:

a)   extent of relevance of family values in business and management

b)   extent of adherence to family values at the level of Indian industry as a whole

c)   extent of adherence to family values in one's own organization

d)   extent of adherence to family values in one's own professional life

Table 17.1 contains the relevant data on the extent of relevance of family values in business with reference to the nine family values stated as perceived by the CMD of Jaipur Rugs and his 14 heads of departments, and the CEO of MART and his nine partners / heads of departments. The table reveals that 'Being hospitable to everyone who comes to your home, irrespective of caste, creed, financial position or status' (family value no. 5) is ranked as the most relevant family value with a mean average of 8.5. The table also shows the relevant value from the Spandan Spectrum of Human Values 2011, wherever applicable, that is most similar to the given family value. Being hospitable, for instance, is considered similar to the human value hospitable disposition (Marwar culture) (22).

Table 17.1   Infusion of family values in management: extent of relevance of family values in business – perception of: CMD and HODs (N=14), Jaipur Rugs Co., Jaipur; and CEO and HODs/partners (N=9), MART, Noida

S. no.	Family value	Human value most similar to the family value	Extent of relevance to the work situation (extent of desirability on ten-point scale)									
			Jaipur Rugs Company, Jaipur				MART, Noida (N=10)				Overall (N=25)	
			CMD (N=15)		HODs (N=14)		CEO		Partners – HODs (N=9)			
			Mean	Rank	Mean	Rank	Mean	Rank	Mean	Rank	Mean	Rank
1.	Respect, obedience, courtesy, decorum and discipline towards, and in the presence of, elders	5: Belief in innate divinity – Human dignity – Self-respect	7.5	VII	8.4	III	6.0	V	8.7	I	8.4	II
2.	Living peacefully and respecting each other's rights	25: Mutual understanding and respect – Psychological contract	8.0	III	7.6	VI	8.0	II	7.6	VII	7.6	VI
3.	Never compromising on integrity for the purpose of prosperity	24: Integrity – Consistency in saying and doing	8.5	II	7.5	VIII	10.0	I	7.7	VI	7.7	IV
4.	Maintaining strong bonds with family members as well as relatives	33: Team spirit	8.0	III	7.6	VI	7.0	III	8.6	III	8.0	III
5.	Being hospitable to everyone who comes to your home, irrespective of caste, creed, financial position or status	22: Hospitable disposition (Marwar culture)	8.0	III	8.7	I	7.0	III	8.4	IV	8.5	I
6.	Treating guests as God (*atithi devo bhava*)	-	7.0	VIII	7.8	V	6.0	V	7.8	V	7.7	IV
7.	Remembering and bowing to God first thing in the morning	-	8.0	III	8.5	II	4.0	VII	6.1	IX	7.4	VIII
8.	Practising yoga and meditation	-	9.0	I	7.9	IV	4.0	VII	6.3	VIII	7.5	VII
9.	Always taking the advice of elders on important decisions	-	7	VIII	6.9	IX	4.0	VII	8.7	I	7.4	VIII

The family values ranked second and third are 'Respect, obedience …' (family value no. 1) and 'Maintaining strong bonds with family members …' (family value no. 4) respectively.

Tables 17.2, 17.3 and 17.4 refer to the extent of adherence to family values at the levels of Indian industry and one's own organization, and in one's own professional life. At all three levels the family value of being hospitable to everyone is ranked as the most important family value – sharing, however, this first rank position with family value no. 1, that is 'Respect, obedience …', at the level of one's own professional life. This family value turns out to be the second most relevant family value for management (see Table 17.5). This finding is significant in two more respects. One, it indicates that obedience, which Lawrence Stone has stated was the most important family value in the past in the Western context, appears still to be functional in the Indian situation. Two, as shown in the tables, this human value equates to 'Belief in the innate divinity of human beings – Human dignity – Self-respect' (5) in the Spandan Spectrum of Human Values 2011.

Table 17.5 presents a summary of the data of the preceding four tables – that is, data on the extent of relevance of and the extent of adherence to family values at the three levels of Indian industry, one's own organization and one's own professional life. The picture that emerges is that family values no. 1 and no. 5 – corresponding to human values 'Belief in the innate divinity of human beings' (5) and 'Hospitable disposition (Marwar culture)' – are perceived the two most relevant and adhered to values at the level of one own professional life today. The two values bracketed together in third position are family value no. 3 – corresponding to 'Integrity' (24) – and family value no. 4 – corresponding to 'Team spirit' (33). The human value 'Mutual understanding and respect' (25), regarded as emanating from family value no. 2 'Living peacefully and respecting each other rights', stands as the fifth most relevant and adhered to value. It is, therefore, rather significant that all five family values (out of a total of nine) with corresponding human values in the Spandan Spectrum of Human Values 2011 are perceived to be the five most relevant and adhered to family-cum-human values in the present-day Indian context. This is, one should think, an indication of the liveliness and relevance of family values in Indian society, and equally a mark of the ability of Indian industry to try to infuse these value in its functioning.

Table 17.2   Infusion of family values in management: extent of adherence to family values in work situations in Indian industry – perception of: CMD and HODs (N=14), Jaipur Rugs Co., Jaipur; and CEO and HODs/partners (N=9), MART, Noida

S. no.	Family value	Human value most similar to the family value	Extent of adherence in work situations – on a ten-point scale									
			Jaipur Rugs Company, Jaipur (N=15)				MART, Noida (N=10)				Overall (N=25)	
			CMD		HODs (N=14)		CEO		Partners – HODs (N=9)			
			Mean	Rank	Mean	Rank	Mean	Rank	Mean	Rank	Mean	Rank
1.	Respect, obedience, courtesy, decorum and discipline towards, and in the presence of, elders	5: Belief in innate divinity – Human dignity – Self-respect	8.0	II	7.9	VI	7.0	I	6.7	II	7.4	III
2.	Living peacefully and respecting each other's rights	25: Mutual understanding and respect – Psychological contract	7.0	VII	7.9	VI	7.0	I	6.0	IV	7.1	VI
3.	Never compromising on integrity for the purpose of prosperity	24: Integrity – Consistency in saying and doing	8.0	II	8.1	V	5.0	VI	5.1	VIII	6.9	VIII
4.	Maintaining strong bonds with family members as well as relatives	33: Team spirit	5.0	IX	8.2	III	6.0	III	5.9	V	7.2	IV
5.	Being hospitable to everyone who comes to your home, irrespective of caste, creed, financial position or status	22: Hospitable disposition (Marwar culture)	8.0	II	8.8	I	6.0	III	6.7	II	8.3	I
6.	Treating guests as God (atithi devo bhava)	-	9.0	I	7.9	I	6.0	III	5.9	V	7.1	VI
7.	Remembering and bowing to God first thing in the morning	-	8.0	II	8.2	III	4.0	VIII	5.8	VII	7.2	IV
8.	Practising yoga and meditation	-	8.0	II	8.4	II	4.0	VIII	4.0	IX	6.6	IX
9.	Always taking the advice of elders on important decisions	-	7.0	VII	7.9	VI	5.0	VI	7.2	I	7.5	II

Table 17.3   Infusion of family values in management: extent of adherence to family values in work situations in one's own organization – perception of: CMD and HODs (N=14), Jaipur Rugs Co., Jaipur; and CEO and HODs/partners (N=9), MART, Noida

S. no.	Family value	Human value most similar to the family value	Extent of adherence in work situations – on a ten-point scale									
			Jaipur Rugs Company, Jaipur				MART, Noida (N=10)				Overall (N=25)	
			CMD (N=15)		HODs (N=14)		CEO		Partners – HODs (N=9)			
			Mean	Rank	Mean	Rank	Mean	Rank	Mean	Rank	Mean	Rank
1.	Respect, obedience, courtesy, decorum and discipline towards, and in the presence of, elders	5: Belief in innate divinity – Human dignity – Self-respect	8.0	IV	8.4	V	9.0	II	8.2	VI	8.3	VI
2.	Living peacefully and respecting each other's rights	25: Mutual understanding and respect – Psychological contract	8.0	IV	8.7	III	8.0	IV	8.8	IV	8.7	III
3.	Never compromising on integrity for the purpose of prosperity	24: Integrity – Consistency in saying and doing	8.0	IV	8.9	II	10.0	I	9.4	I	9.1	II
4.	Maintaining strong bonds with family members as well as relatives	33: Team spirit	7.0	IX	8.6	IV	8.0	IV	7.7	VII	8.2	VII
5.	Being hospitable to everyone who comes to your home, irrespective of caste, creed, financial position or status	22: Hospitable disposition (Marwar culture)	10.0	I	9.3	I	9.0	II	9.4	I	9.4	I
6.	Treating guests as God (*atithi devo bhava*)	-	9.0	II	8.3	VI	8.0	IV	8.8	IV	8.5	IV
7.	Remembering and bowing to God first thing in the morning	-	9.0	II	8.0	IX	7.0	VIII	6.2	IX	8.0	VIII
8.	Practising yoga and meditation	-	8.0	IV	8.2	VIII	5.0	IX	6.4	VIII	7.4	IX
9.	Always taking the advice of elders on important decisions	-	8.0	IV	8.3	VI	8.0	IV	9.0	III	8.5	IV

Table 17.4   Infusion of family values in management: extent of adherence to family values in work situations in my own professional life – perception of: CMD and HODs (N=14), Jaipur Rugs Co., Jaipur; and CEO and HODs/partners (N=9), MART, Noida

S. no.	Family value	Human value most similar to the family value	Extent of adherence in work situations – on a ten-point scale								
			Jaipur Rugs Company, Jaipur				MART, Noida				Overall (N=25)	
			CMD (N=15)		HODs (N=14)		CEO		Partners – HODs (N=9)			
			Mean	Rank	Mean	Rank	Mean	Rank	Mean	Rank	Mean	Rank
1.	Respect, obedience, courtesy, decorum and discipline towards, and in the presence of, elders	5: Belief in innate divinity – Human dignity – Self-respect	9.0	I	9.0	II	9.0	II	9.0	I	9.0	I
2.	Living peacefully and respecting each other's rights	25: Mutual understanding and respect – Psychological contract	9.0	I	8.1	VII	9.0	II	8.4	VI	8.3	V
3.	Never compromising on integrity for the purpose of prosperity	24: Integrity – Consistency in saying and doing	7.0	VIII	8.5	V	10.0	I	9.0	I	8.7	III
4.	Maintaining strong bonds with family members as well as relatives	33: Team spirit	7.0	VIII	8.7	III	9.0	II	8.9	III	8.7	III
5.	Being hospitable to everyone who comes to your home, irrespective of caste, creed, financial position or status	22: Hospitable disposition (Marwar culture)	9.0	I	9.2	I	9.0	II	8.8	V	9.0	I
6.	Treating guests as God (atithi devo bhava)	-	9.0	I	8.2	VI	8.0	VII	8.0	VII	8.2	VI
7.	Remembering and bowing to God first thing in the morning	-	9.0	I	8.6	IV	9.0	II	5.8	IX	7.6	IX
8.	Practising yoga and meditation	-	8.0	VII	7.6	VIII	7.0	VIII	5.9	VIII	7.9	VIII
9.	Always taking the advice of elders on important decisions	-	9.0	I	7.5	IX	6.0	IX	8.9	III	8.0	VII

Table 17.5 Infusion of family values in management: extent of relevance of and adherence to family values in business: perception of: CMD and HODs (N=14), Jaipur Rugs Co., Jaipur; and CEO and HODs/partners (N=9), MART, Noida

S. no.	Family value	Human value most similar to the family value	Extent of relevance (N=25)		Extent of adherence (N=25)					
					Indian industry		One's own organization		One's own professional life	
			Mean	Rank	Mean	Rank	Mean	Rank	Mean	Rank
1.	Respect, obedience, courtesy, decorum and discipline towards, and in the presence of, elders	5: Belief in innate divinity – Human dignity – Self-respect – Respecting others	8.4	II	7.4	III	8.3	VI	9.0	I
2.	Living peacefully and respecting each other's rights	25: Mutual understanding and respect – Psychological contract	7.6	VI	7.1	VI	8.7	III	8.3	V
3.	Never compromising on integrity for the purpose of prosperity	24: Integrity – Consistency in saying and doing	7.7	IV	6.9	VIII	9.1	II	8.7	III
4.	Maintaining strong bonds with family members as well as relatives	33: Team spirit	8.0	III	7.2	IV	8.2	VII	8.7	III
5.	Being hospitable to everyone who comes to your home, irrespective of caste, creed, financial position or status	22: Hospitable disposition (Marwar culture)	8.5	I	8.3	I	9.4	I	9.0	I
6.	Treating guests as God (*atithi devo bhava*)	-	7.7	IV	7.1	VI	8.5	IV	8.2	VI
7.	Remembering and bowing to God first thing in the morning	-	7.4	VIII	7.2	IV	8.0	VIII	7.6	IX
8.	Practising yoga and meditation	-	7.5	VII	6.6	IX	7.4	IX	7.9	VIII
9.	Always taking the advice of elders on important decisions	-	7.4	VIII	7.5	II	8.5	IV	8.0	VII

Table 17.6 Infusion of family values in management: rankings compared to those of: (a) industry, one's own organization and one's own professional life [research study, 2011 (N=58)]; (b) synergy study on human values to be recommended for transfer from India to the West and vice versa (N=15); and (c) Institutional Civic Responsibility to Community through Human Values (ICRC-HVs) (N=25)

S. no.	Family value	Human value most similar to the family value	Extent of relevance (N=25) Rank	Extent of adherence (N=25)			Extent of adherence (2011 study, N=58)			Human values recommended from- (N=15)		Institutional Civic Responsibility to Community through HVs (ICRC-HVs) Rank
				Indian industry Rank	One's own orgn. Rank	One's own prof. life Rank	Indian industry Rank	One's own orgn. Rank	One's own prof. life Rank	India to the West Rank	The West to India Rank	
(1)	(2)	(3)	(4)	(5)	(6)	(7)	(8)	(9)	(10)	(11)	(12)	(13)
1.	Respect, obedience, courtesy, decorum and discipline towards, and in the presence of, elders	5: Belief in innate divinity – Human dignity – Self-respect – Respecting others	II	III	VI	I	XVIII	V	I	VIII	-	-
2.	Living peacefully and respecting each other's rights	25: Mutual understanding and respect – Psychological contract	VI	VI	III	V	XXIX	XXXII	XXVII	-	-	-
3.	Never compromising on integrity for the purpose of prosperity	24: Integrity – Consistency in saying and doing	IV	VIII	II	III	XXIV	IX	III	-	-	IV
4.	Maintaining strong bonds with family members as well as relatives	33: Team spirit	III	IV	VII	III	X	XX	XIV	-	-	-
5.	Being hospitable to everyone who comes to your home, irrespective of caste, creed, financial position or status	22: Hospitable disposition (Marwar culture)	I	I	I	I	XII	XXIII	XXX	I	-	II

Table 17.6 contains the data from three related phenomena. The first is the extent of adherence at the levels of Indian industry, one's own organization and one's own professional life, as perceived by the 58 select invitee-respondents in the study of 2011. The second is the study of human values recommended for transfer from India to the West, and vice versa, for the strengthening of work ethics. The third is the Institutional Civic Responsibility to Community through Human Values ICRC-HVs, being the *Spandan* initiative on an organization's contribution to society.

A) EXTENT OF ADHERENCE (N=58) (SEE CHAPTER 7) – TABLE 17.6, COLUMNS 8 TO 10

'Respect, obedience ...' (family value no. 1), corresponding to the human value 'Belief in the innate divinity in human beings' (5) is rated as the most adhered to value in one's own professional life. Family value no. 2 (Living peacefully and respecting each other's rights) – corresponding to human value 'Mutual understanding and respect' (25) – has been ranked rather low at all three levels. Out of the total of 33 human values in the Spandan Spectrum, this value is placed 29th (Indian industry), 32nd (one's own organization) and 27th (one's own professional life).

B) SYNERGY STUDY ON RECOMMENDING HUMAN VALUES BETWEEN INDIA AND THE WEST (SEE CHAPTER 15) – TABLE 17.6, COLUMNS 11 AND 12

Of the ten human values recommended for transfer from India to the West (Table 15.1), two are from the nine family values covered in this study. Of these, family value no. 5 ('Being hospitable to everyone ...') – corresponding to the human value 'Hospitable disposition (Marwar culture)' (22) – is ranked the most important. The perception that the value 'Hospitable disposition (Marwar culture)' (22) is the least adhered to human value in the West (Table 15.1, column 13) lends support to the recommendation. The next most recommended family value for transfer from India to the West is 'Respect, obedience ...' (family value no. 1) – corresponding to the human value 'Belief in the innate divinity of human beings' (5).

C) INSTITUTIONAL CIVIC RESPONSIBILITY TO COMMUNITY THROUGH HUMAN VALUES (ICRC-HVS) (SEE CHAPTER 16) – TABLE 17.6, COLUMN 13

Of the human values considered important for effectively carrying out ICRC-HVs, two are family values. These are: no. 3: 'Never compromising on integrity ...' – corresponding to the human value 'Integrity' (24); and no. 5: 'Being hospitable to everyone' – corresponding to the human value 'Hospitable disposition (Marwar culture)' (22). However, as 'Being hospitable ...' is primarily an individual characteristic, the fact that this ranks 30th at the level of one's own professional life while being ranked second in the ICRC-HV column suggests this matter needs some attention.

Finally, Table 17.7 offers a bird's-eye view of the top five human values in terms of their relevance and adherence as perceived by all 25 respondents representing both the Jaipur Rugs Company, Jaipur and MART, Noida.

It is significant that family value no. 3 ('Never compromising on integrity for the purpose of prosperity') is considered the most important desirable family value to be infused in management. Meanwhile family value no. 5 ('Being hospitable to everyone who comes to your home, irrespective of caste, creed, financial position or status') is perceived to be the most adhered to family value in management. These two family values correspond to 'Integrity' (24) and 'Hospitable disposition (Marwar culture)' (22) respectively in the Spandan Spectrum of Human Values 2011.

Table 17.7   Infusion of family values in management: extent of relevance and adherence – a bird's-eye view: perception of: CMD and HODs (N=14), Jaipur Rugs Co., Jaipur; and CEO and HODs/Partners (N=9), MART, Noida

Description/values	Extent of relevance		Extent of adherence (on a ten-point scale)		Whether common in both
	Overall		Overall		
	n: weighted value	Rank	n: weighted value	Rank	
1. Respect, obedience, courtesy, decorum and discipline towards, and in the presence of, elders	3:7	V	8:36	II	
2. Living peacefully and respecting each other's rights	2:7	I	5:21		
3. Never compromising on integrity for the purpose of prosperity	3:13	I	8:31	III	
4. Maintaining strong bonds with family members as well as relatives	3:11	II	7:19		
5. Being hospitable to everyone who comes to your home, irrespective of caste, creed, financial position or status	3:11	II	12:50	I	
6. Treating guests as God (*atithi devo bhava*)	2:2		6:20		
7. Remembering and bowing to God first thing in the morning	2:7		8:22	IV	
8. Practising yoga and meditation	3:8	IV	2:08	II	
9. Always taking the advice of elders on important decisions	1:3		4:16		

Note: family or home can be read as company or organization

TO SUM UP

Despite paradigm changes taking place throughout the world, consequent upon globalization in particular, the family as a social institution continues to play a crucial role in economic development across the globe. Around 95 per cent of businesses in Asia, the Middle East, Italy and Spain are family controlled. In other European countries it varies between 75 and 85 per cent. Even in the United States, still the most advanced country in the world, the corresponding figure is estimated at between 60 and 70 per cent.

Like other sectors of the economy and segments of society the world over, family-owned industries were also hit in the recent economic downturn. They could, however, cope better because of their

> *inherent competitive advantage to ensure they survive and prosper despite the poor business and financial climate. According to Randel Carlock [an authority on family business and entrepreneurial leadership], this advantage encompasses committed owners, long term strategies, industry knowledge accumulated over generations, and values such as trust, stewardship, and longevity. ...*

> *'Family businesses are unique in two main ways', Carlock says. 'First, they hold a long term perspective: and, second, they are driven by values ... It is all about "professional-emotional" families – combining family passion with professional management.'* (Karabell 2009)

MART: Business Mind, Social Heart: A Case Study

In Chapter 13, on the application of the Spandan 3D Process as integral to evolving a Functionally Humane Organization (FHO), the organization MART was used to illustrate the role of experiential learning in self-awareness and development.

MART, a consultancy firm, had won the Spandan IBA Annual Award in Human Values for Professionals for the year 2011. Excerpts from MART CEO Pradeep Kashyap's acceptance speech are presented below as additional comments on the subject of family values.

MART CEO PRADEEP KASHYAP'S ACCEPTANCE SPEECH: CREATING AN ENDEARING ORGANIZATION

For the first 20 years of my professional life I worked with 3 multinational companies in India. During this period I acquired a fair amount of material wealth and creature comforts. But the inner richness was missing from my life and a hollow feeling kept bothering me. It was around the same time that I had met my spiritual guru. He encouraged me to inquire into the purpose of life. The year I turned 40, I decided with the guidance of my guru that I should change the course of my life. I voluntarily opted out of the corporate sector to serve the poor. In the initial years as a consultant to some NGOs and the government I got the opportunity to travel through the length and breadth of the country and experienced rural poverty first hand. I realized I had to do something to improve the condition of the poor

I decided to start a professional organization to help create large-scale livelihoods for the poor. But having experienced the impersonal and 'what's in it for me' selfish culture of multinationals, I was determined that my organization would offer a strong sense of belonging and self-giving among its employees. I studied the different types of institutions in society – government organization, private company, not-for-profit NGO, and even the institution of marriage. I realized that 'Family' is the only institution to which we continue to belong throughout our lives. So MART was established in 1993 on 'Family values'.

1. In a family we do not have one fixed designation. I am husband, father, son, brother and more. So in MART too no one has a designation and therefore there is no hierarchy. We are a flat organization.

2. 'No one leaves his family' is our shared belief and we put this to practice. On completing ten years' service in MART every employee becomes a partner with 2.5 per cent shareholding gifted by the company. We have already inducted nine partners this way and in the next few years my hope is that MART would become a fully employee-owned organization.

    We are a team of 75 professionals. In the last five years only five people have left us, of which three have rejoined. The remaining two have also expressed a keenness to return. Against an average attrition of 10 per cent in industry, not even 1 per cent of employees have left MART.

3.   Transparency: A close knit family shares problems, joys and information with each other. At MART we have taken transparency to an extreme. Every employee knows every other employee's salary. We celebrate all the happy occasions of the family members and reach out whenever any member has a problem.

Rajiv joined us two years ago as a management trainee. Last month his father, who was visiting Rajiv in Delhi from Patna, suddenly complained of chest pain. Rajiv rushed him to hospital where he was diagnosed with two blocked arteries which needed immediate stenting. The hospital admitted his father and advised Rajiv to deposit two and half lakh rupees by the evening. A distraught Rajiv rushed to the office and broke down in front of his senior expressing his helplessness in arranging such a large sum of money at such short notice. By the evening the required amount was collected through personal contributions by the staff and deposited with the hospital. The stenting was carried out successfully the next day. Rajiv's father returned to Patna, sending the money which was returned immediately to the contributors. I was away in Bangladesh when this happened. On my return an emotional Rajiv met me and said 'How can I ever leave my MART Family?'

4.   As Head of the MART Family my role extends much beyond that of a CEO of a company. For example, most professionals have joined MART straight out of college and several of them have got married while working with us. Many a times, the father-in-law-to-be wanted to see me before meeting the boy's father, to check out the career prospects of the 'groom in consideration'.

Pankaj an MBA who had worked with MART for five years was unsuccessful in finding himself a bride, despite persistent efforts by his parents. Reasons for rejection – the boy is neither in government service nor does he work for a bank or a known private company. He works for some small, unknown consulting firm. What is this consultancy business anyway? So Pankaj decided to leave us. He joined a well-known American organization and within a year found himself a lovely bride. Mission accomplished, he rejoined MART. Four years into MART in his second innings he is the proud head of a happy family.

5.   At home no work is considered menial. The same is true at MART. We even scrub toilets and wash utensils when the cleaning person

doesn't show up. In keeping with this philosophy we do not have any written job descriptions at MART because we are ready to do any work that needs to be done.

I am sure by now many of you must be thinking that whilst this family approach may work for a small set up like MART, surely large organizations cannot follow a family culture? There will be chaos. Well Toyota and many other Japanese companies follow the life-time employment philosophy and host employees' wedding receptions because the company considers itself head of a large family.

References

Alev, Ergenic Kathril et al. 2006. Congruence of Family and Organizational Values in Relation to Organizational Citizenship Behavior. *Journal of Human Values*, 12 (April): 81–9.

Bagchi, Subroto. 2011. Gopal Srinivasan: Values of Family Businesses. *India Forbes*, 21 October.

Beresford, Philip. 1997. Report on Asian Millionaires in Britain. *Sunday Times* (London), 17 February.

Carlock, Randel and John L. Ward. 2010. *When Family Businesses are Best: The Parallel Planning Processes for Family Harmony as Business Success.* Houndmills: Palgrave Macmillan.

iloveindia.com. no date. *Indian Family Value System.* [Online.] Available at: http://www.iloveindia.com/indian-traditions/family-value-system.html [accessed: 27 July 2013].

Karabell, Shellie. 2009. Family Values: Leading the Way Out of the Downturn. *INSEAD Knowledge*, 22 September 2009. [Online]. Available at: http://knowledge.insead.edu/business-finance/family-business/family-values-leading-the-way-out-of-the-downturn-1431 [accessed: 15 August 2013].

Kashyap, Pradeep. 2012. Acceptance Speech at Spandan IBA Fifth Annual Award in Human Values for Professionals, IBA, Greater Noida, India, March 2012.

Shah, Grishma. 2008. *The Impact of Economic Globalization on Work and Family Values in India.* Newark, NJ: Rutgers University.

Stone, Lawrence. 1994. *Family Values in a Historical Perspective*, The Tanner Lectures on Human Values at Harvard University, 16–17 November 1994.

Appendix: Infusion of Family Values in Management – Response Sheet

Description/value*	Extent of relevance in business (on 10-point scale)**	Extent of adherence in (on 10- point scale)*		
		In my own professional life	In my own organization	Indian industry
1 Respect, obedience, courtesy, decorum and discipline towards, and in the presence of, elders				
2 Living peacefully and respecting each other's rights				
3 Never compromising on integrity for the purpose of prosperity				
4 Maintaining strong bonds with family members as well as relatives				
5 Being hospitable to everyone who comes to your home, irrespective of cast, creed, financial position or status				
6 Treating guests as God (*atithi devo bhava*)				
7 Remembering and bowing to God first thing in the morning				
8 Practising yoga and Meditation				
9 Always taking the advice of elders in any important decisions				

Note: family, home can be read as company or organization

*   Base: www.iloveindia.com, Indian family value system

**   10-point scale:

```
 1      2      3      4      5      6      7      8      9      10
 |      |      |      |      |      |      |      |      |      |
Very Low      Low           Medium            High          Very High
```

RESPONDENT PROFILE

1.   Name:

2.   Designation/status:

3.   Name of the organization:

4.   Educational and professional background:

5.   Work experience (years):

   a.   In the present organization:

   b.   Total:

6.   Date of Birth:

COMMENTS AND OBSERVATIONS, IF ANY

18

Towards a Functionally Humane Organization IV: Human Values: Material Comforts and Happiness

The Context and the Issue

Harry Frankfurt (2004), in his Tanner Lectures on Human Values, entitled 'Taking Ourselves Seriously', states that humans seem to be the only things around that are even *capable* of taking themselves seriously, adding:

> *Two features of our nature are centrally implicated in this: our rationality and our ability to love. Reason and love play critical roles in determining what we think and how we are moved to conduct ourselves .... It is reason and love – the directives of our heads and of our hearts – that we expect to equip us most effectively to accomplish this. (pp. 169–70)*

> *We care about things only for their instrumental value. They are intermediate goals for us. we need final ends ... I believe our final ends are provided and legitimized by love. (p. 185)*

In his second lecture, 'Getting it Right', Frankfurt zeroes in on the matter further, stating 'it is *whole-hearted love* which is our final end' (p. 201).

There is much thinking along these lines (see Lear 1999, Wolf 2007), thinking that advocates introducing love and affection to our work lives in order to balance it with the goals of material comfort and economic wellbeing.

The 'diminishing effectiveness' of economic growth on human happiness, meanwhile, is the subject of concepts such as Richard A. Easterlin's 'Easterlin

Paradox' (1974 and 2010), Barry Schwartz's 'Paradox of Choice' (2004) and Felix Fitzroy's 'Happiness Paradox' (2011). These concepts reveal that the average happiness of developed nations has not generally increased with growth of the Gross Domestic Product (GDP) per capita over the past few decades, and in China has even declined despite its spectacular economic growth.

It is against this backdrop that the efforts of Bhutan in developing a Gross National Happiness (GNH) Index is to be understood and assessed (Tashi, Prakke and Chettri 1999, Tideman 2008). Rooted in the Buddhist philosophy of the eightfold path, GNH presents a paradigm shift in development economic and social theory. As observed by Tideman (2008, p. 242), the GNH represents an amalgam of Richard Barrett's model of seven levels of consciousness, Maslow and Vedic principles, and Bhutan's Four Pillar definition of GNH.

Diagnosis: Terminal Human Values

The first part of this book presented, among others, the essence of the Spandan (Heartbeat) Approach based upon faith in the basic goodness of others and belief in the innate divinity and intrinsic altruism of human beings, all three values together postulated as the bedrock of human existence and growth. Transactional Human Values are related to the translation of these Transformational Human Values into appropriate actionable behaviour in the context of a human being's interactions with others in his or her personal, professional, group, organizational and societal roles.

The Transformational and Transactional Human Values thus developed are grouped as:

Transformational Human Values (5 values)

I – In relation to other humans (3)

II – In relation to Mother Earth and the universe (2)

Transactional Human Values (26 values)

Personal human values (4)

Professional human values (4)

Group-oriented human values (4)

Organizational human values (8)

Globalization-induced human values (6)

The question that now arises is: what is the ultimate objective of adherence to the Transformational and Transactional Human Values? There are two answers. One is that adherence to transformational values results in the remaking of ourselves as human beings, while adherence to transactional values enables human beings to remake the organization, enterprises or institutions and the society of which they are members.

The other answer relates to the expected outcome(s) of these transactions. Each entity with which human beings interact and upon which they mutually depend has its own set of objectives, of which survival and growth can be taken as the generic twin objectives of any living organism or collectivity. This growth can be viewed in terms of physical, material and economic dimensions as reflected in higher standards of living, material comforts and economic well-being. It can also be understood in terms of psychic, emotional and social aspects as reflected in happiness, contentment and psychic well-being. This brings us to the Terminal Values identified in the Spandan Spectrum of Human Values:

- 29: Material comforts – prosperity – profits – higher standards of living – economic well-being

- 21: Happiness – contentment – satisfaction – psychic well-being.

Discovery: Extent of Adherence

Table 18.1 shows that adherence to happiness is perceived as lower at the levels of Indian industry and one's own organization, as compared to adherence to material comforts. This indicates that the degree of happiness being enjoyed at these levels is perhaps lower compared to that of material comfort. At the level of one's own professional life, however, the reverse is to be found. Happiness is measured at 7.7 as against 7.1 for material comforts. If an individual is happy in her professional life, compared to the level of her economic status, it is perhaps necessary, especially at the level of higher management, for that individual to spread her happiness and joy throughout the team and organization.

Table 18.1   Material comforts and happiness: extent of adherence

HHV no.	Category	Human value	Extent of adherence (N=58)					
			Indian industry		One's own organization		One's own professional life	
			Mean	Rank	Mean	Rank	Mean	Rank
21.	Terminal	Happiness – Contentment – Psychic well-being	5.4	XV	6.9	XXIII	7.7	XX
29.	Terminal	Prosperity – Profits – Material comforts – Economic well-being	7.2	I	7.3	XI	7.1	XXXII
Overall average			6.3		7.1		7.4	

Table 18.2 confirms the phenomenon of a discrepancy between the figures for adherence at the levels of one's own organization and one's own professional life. The perceptual gap is negative to the tune of -0.8 in the case of happiness between these two levels.

Table 18.2   Material comforts and happiness: extent of adherence – perceptual gaps

Terminal Human Values	One's own professional life	One's own organization	Perceptual gap
21. Happiness – Contentment – Psychic well-being	7.7	6.9	-0.8
29. Material comforts – Prosperity – Economic well-being	7.1	7.3	+0.2
Overall average	7.4	7.1	-0.3

Table 18.2 compares the various groups of human values and reveals certain interesting insights. The overall average for Terminal Human Values – material comforts (29) and happiness (21) – at the level of one's own professional life is 7.4, which is equal to the lowest of the various Transactional Human Values at the same level (globalization-induced human values, 7.4). However, the overall average for Terminal Human Values at the level of one's own organization is 7.1, which is very close or equal to all groups of Transactional Human Values at the same level. This indicates that there is a greater synchronization between Terminal Human Values and Transactional Human Values at the level of one's own organization than in one's own professional life.

Development: The Spandan Initiative: Identifying Human Values Related to Efficiency and Happiness

Chapter 13, Figure 13.1 outlined the specific Transactional Human Values oriented towards results and relations respectively. These human values are:

Results-oriented human values

HV no.	Category	Human value
1	Organizational	Accountability – Owning responsibility
7	Organizational	Commitment
9	Globalization-induced	Competitive spirit
12	Globalization-induced	Creativity – Innovation
14	Organizational	Customer satisfaction
18	Globalization-induced	Entrepreneurship – Risk taking
24	Personal	Integrity – Consistency in saying and doing
27	Globalization-induced	Preparedness – Proactiveness – Environmental sensitivity
30	Organizational	Respect for authority – Managerial prerogative
33	Group-oriented	Team spirit

Relations-oriented human values

HV no.	Category	Human value
7	Organizational	Commitment
11	Group-oriented	Cooperative attitude
12	Globalization-induced	Creativity – Innovation
17	Organizational	Employee orientation
20	Organizational	Fairness – Equity – Justice
22	Globalization-induced	Hospitable disposition (Marwar culture)
24	Personal	Integrity – Consistency in saying and doing
25	Group-oriented	Mutual understanding and respect
33	Group-oriented	Team spirit

As discussed in subsequent chapters (Chapters 15, 16 and 17) *Spandan* has introduced three initiatives to improve the balance of transactional values: the synergy of human values between India and the West (Chapter 15); Institutional Civic Responsibility to Community through Human Values (ICRC-HVs) (Chapter 16); and the infusion of family values in management (Chapter 17). These are referred to as Spandan Initiatives I, II and III respectively.

Concurrently, *Spandan* has been working, through workshops and interactive sessions, to identify human values specific to efficiency – as indicative of results and material comforts – and employee satisfaction – as indicative of relations and happiness. Table 18.3 shows the efficiency-related and happiness-related human values as the composite outcomes of three different workshops in which participants were drawn from upper and middle management.

It is significant that autonomy in decision making (2) is considered important both as an efficiency-oriented human value and as a happiness-oriented one.

An Indian Approach: The Indian Conception of Well-being

S.K. Kiran Kumar, in his scholarly work on the above theme (2003), offers two observations worthy of consideration:

1. EXPANSION OF CONSCIOUSNESS AND REALIZATION OF A TRANSCENDENT SELF

> *Statistically speaking, a vast majority share a collective perspective occupying the area comprising the second and third quartile of a normal probability curve, with those sharing hedonistic and the transcendental perspectives occupying first and fourth quartiles respectively. The three perspectives can be placed on a continuum of human evolution, from animal, to human, and to divine as understood by Indian sages and seers. Thus in Indian thought the ideal well-being is understood as a resultant of the expansion of consciousness and realization of a transcendent Self whose very nature is bliss.*

2. CONCEPT OF DHARMA AND ITS ROLE IN ENSURING THE WELLBEING OF ALL

> *The term* dharma *is derived from the Sanskrit root dhr, which means to uphold, to sustain, and to hold together.* Dharma *is a most complex concept to define and it has different connotations. Ancient thinkers tried to use this umbrella concept to cover all values related to all the aspects of life. Broadly speaking, the concept stands for the fundamental order in social affairs and in moral life and is a principle which maintains the stability of society.* Dharma *connotes precepts that aim at securing the material and spiritual sustenance and growth of the individual and society .*

Table 18.3   Terminal Human Values: efficiency-oriented human values and happiness-oriented human values: extent of adherence

HV no.	Category	Human value	Rank	Extent of adherence (N=58)					
				Indian industry		One's own organization		One's own professional life	
				Mean	Rank	Mean	Rank	Mean	Rank
		Efficiency-oriented Human Values							
2	Organizational	Autonomy in decision making – Flexible work culture – Accepting diversity and divergence	I	5.2	XXI	7.2	XVI	7.9	XIV
7	Organizational	Commitment	II	5.5	XII	7.4	V	8.4	II
19	Professional	Equanimity – Self-control	II	5.5	XII	6.8	XXX	7.4	XXVII
18	Globalization-induced	Entrepreneurship – Risk taking	II	6.1	IV	6.9	XXIII	7.4	XXX
		Efficiency: Employee performance		*5.6*		*7.1*		*7.8*	
		Happiness-oriented Human Values							
2	Organizational	Autonomy in decision making – Flexible work culture – Accepting diversity and divergence	I	5.2	XXI	7.2	XVI	7.9	XIV
23	Personal	Humility – Self-awareness	II	5.3	XVIII	7.4	XXXI	6.7	XXIII
22	Globalization-induced	Hospitable disposition (Marwar culture)	II	5.5	XII	6.9	XXIII	7.4	XXX
6	Transformational Human Values	Belief in the intrinsic altruism in human beings – Caring – Sharing – Compassion	II	4.9	XXVII	7.3	IX	8.0	XI
8	Organizational	Community interest – Social good – Community service	II	4.7	XXXII	7.1	XX	7.5	XXIV
		Happiness		*5.4*	*XV*	*6.9*	*XXIII*	*7.7*	*XX*

Light grey shaded boxes indicate the highest ranked human values.
Dark grey shaded boxes indicate the lowest ranked human values.

Table 18.4 Terminal Values: efficiency-oriented human values and happiness-oriented human values: diagnosis and discovery

HV no.	Category	Human value	Extent of adherence (N=58)					
			Indian industry		One's own organization		One's own professional life	
			Mean	Rank	Mean	Rank	Mean	Rank
		Results-oriented						
1	Organizational	Accountability – Owning responsibility	5.1	XIV	7.2	XVI	8.2	III
7	Organizational	Commitment	5.5	XII	7.4	V	8.4	II
9	Organizational	Competitive spirit	7.1	II	6.9	XXIII	7.1	XXXII
12	Globalization-induced	Creativity – Innovation	5.8	VII	7.2	XVI	7.5	XXVI
14	Organizational	Customer satisfaction	5.8	VII	7.5	III	8.1	VII
18	Globalization-induced	Entrepreneurship – Risk taking	6.1	IV	6.9	XXIII	7.4	XXX
24	Personal	Integrity – Consistency in saying and doing	5.1	XXIV	7.1	IX	8.2	III
27	Globalization-induced	Preparedness – Proactiveness – Environmental sensitivity	4.8	XXIX	6.9	XXIII	7.5	XXVI
30	Organizational	Respect for authority – Managerial prerogative	6.5	III	7.6	I	8.0	XI
33	Group-oriented	Team spirit	5.7	X	7.1	XX	7.9	XIV
		Overall average	5.8	-	7.2	-	7.8	-
		Terminal Value – 29: Material comforts	7.2	I	7.3	IX	7.1	XXXII
		Relations-oriented						
7	Organizational	Commitment	5.5	XII	7.4	V	8.4	II
11	Group-oriented	Cooperative attitude	5.6	XI	7.3	IX	8.1	VII
12	Globalization-induced	Creativity – Innovation	5.8	VII	7.2	XVI	7.5	XXVI
17	Organizational	Employee orientation	5.4	XV	7.0	XXII	7.8	XVIII
20	Organizational	Fairness – Equity – Justice	5.2	XXI	7.4	V	8.1	VII
22	Globalization-induced	Hospitable disposition (Marwar culture)	5.5	XII	6.9	XXIII	7.4	XXX
24	Personal	Integrity – Consistency in saying and doing	5.1	XXIV	7.1	IX	8.2	III
25	Group-oriented	Mutual understanding and respect	5.2	XXI	7.3	IX	8.0	XI
33	Group-oriented	Team spirit	5.7	X	7.1	XX	7.9	XIV
		Overall average	5.4	-	6.5	-	7.1	-
		Terminal Value – 21: Happiness	5.4	XV	6.9	XXIII	7.7	XX

Light grey shaded boxes indicate the highest ranked human values.
Dark grey shaded boxes indicate the lowest ranked human values.

References

Achor, Shawn. 2012. Positive Intelligence. *Harvard Business Review*, January–February.

Barrett, Richard. n.d. Seven Levels of Consciousness Model. [Online]. Available at: http://www.valuescentre.com/culture/?sec=barrett_model [accessed: 16 August 2013].

Bhattacharya, Sonali. 2010. Relationship between Three Indices of Happiness: Material, Mental and Spiritual. *Journal of Human Values*, 16 (April): 87–125.

Bhaumik, Mani. 2011. Science of Happiness. *The Speaking Tree (Times of India)*, 23 January.

Diwakar, R.R. 1986. The Science of Human Values, *The Hindu*, 17 June.

Easterlin, Richard A. 1974. Does Economic Growth Improve the Human Lot? Some Empirical Evidence. In Paul A. David and Melvin W. Reder (eds), *Nations and Households in Economic Growth: Essays in Honor of Moses Abramovitz*. New York: Academic Press, pp. 89–125.

Easterlin, Richard A. et al. 2010. The Happiness Income Paradox Revisited. *PNAS*, 13 December.

Fitzroy, Felix. 2011. Happiness Paradox, *The New Scientist*, 4 May.

Fox, Justin. 2012. The Economics of Well Being. *Harvard Business Review*, January–February.

Gilbert, Daniel. 2006. *Stumbling on Happiness*. New York: Alfred A. Knopf.

Frankfurt, Harry. 2004. *Taking Ourselves Seriously*, The Tanner Lectures on Human Values, Stanford University, 14–16 April, 2004.

Herr, Harveen. 1997. Corporate Management: The New Corporate Mantra. *LifePossible*, April. [Online.] Available at: http://www.lifepositive.com/mind/work/corporate-management/corporate-mantra.asp [accessed: 28 July 2013].

Hosie, Peter et al. 2007. The 'Happy Productive Worker Thesis' and Australian Managers, *Journal of Human Values*, 13(2): 151–76.

Kant, Immanuel. 1998. *Ground Work of the Metaphysics of Morality*, ed. Mary Gregor and Jens Timmermann. Cambridge: Cambridge University Press.

Kiran Kumar, S.K. 2003. An Indian Conception of Wellbeing. In J. Henry (ed.), *European Positive Psychology Proceedings 2002*. Leicester: British Psychological Society. [Online]. Available at: http://www.ipi.org.in/texts/kirankumar/kk-indian-conception-ofwellbeing.php [accessed: 28 July 2013].

Layard, Richard. 2005. *Happiness: Lessons from a New Science*. London: Penguin.

Loy, David R. 2003. *The Great Awakening: A Buddhist Social Theory*. Boston, MA: Wisdom Publications.

Morse, Gardiner. 2012. The Science Behind the Smile: An Interview with Daniel Gilbert. *Harvard Business Review*, January–February.

Schwartz, Barry. 2004. *The Paradox of Choice: Why More is Less*. New York: HarperCollins.

Seligman, Martin. 2002. *Authentic Happiness: Using the New Positive Psychology to Realize Your Potential for Lasting Fulfillment*. New York: Simon & Schuster.

Sharma, Subhash. 2011. *Karma Capital: Towards New Age ADAM Model for Prosperity, Justice and Peace (PJP)*. Paper Presented at the symposium on Human Development in Indian Tradition, Department of Psychology, University of Allahabad, 18–20 December 2011.

Spotlight: The Happiness Factor. 2012. *Harvard Business Review*, January–February.

Spreitzer, Gretchen and Christine Porath. 2012. Creating Sustainable Performance. *Harvard Business Review*, January–February.

Strearns, Peter N. 2012. The History of Happiness. *Harvard Business Review*, January–February.

Swami Jnaneshvara Bharathi. no date. Maslow's Needs Hierarchy and Advanced Yoga Psychology. [Online.] Available at: http://www.swamij.com/maslow-yoga.htm [accessed: 28 July 2013].

Tashi, Khenpo Phuntsho, Diederik Prakke and Saamdu Chettri. 1999. Gross National Happiness: Concepts for the Debate. In *Gross National Happiness: Discussion Papers*. Thimpu: The Centre for Bhutan Studies, pp. 104–15.

Tideman, Sander G. 2008. Gross National Happiness: Towards a New Paradigm in Economics. In *Proceedings of the First International Conference on Operationalization of Gross National Happiness*. Thimpu: Centre for Bhutan Studies, pp. 222–47.

19

Spirituality and Management: Changing Perspectives

The Context and the Issue

Subhash Sharma (2010) broadly categorized the evolution of management thought over the last hundred years in terms of three distinct eras: the Scientific Management era (beginning around 1900); the Human era (beginning around the 1960s); and the New Mantras era (beginning around 2000) wherein human and spiritual values are echoed in management thought. During the Scientific Management era, management thought was deeply influenced by the disciplines of engineering and economics and during the Human era, by psychology and related disciplines. With the acceptance of yoga and meditation as stress management tools for corporate managers, the disciplines of spirituality and the inner sciences started influencing management thought leading to many new mantras in management and leadership.

The evolution of management thought has also been influenced by ideas contributed by different nations. Initially management thought was dominated by American management concepts. This continued until the 1970s. Then emerged the idea of Japanese management, wherein technology and culture were integrated and many new ideas such as team building, quality circles and so on emerged. Taking inspiration from this thought revolution, many scholars in India, such as Profs. J.B.P. Sinha, Rajen Gupta, B.R. Virmani, S.K. Chakraborty and others, worked on the cultural dimension of management to suggest some new ideas.

In 1997–98 I conducted a research study on Spirituality and Management in India. This was a period when Indian industry was 'discovering' itself in the wake of the 1991 paradigm shift in government thinking and policy that had resulted in the Indian economy and industry opening its doors to privatization, liberalization and globalization. Until then the Indian market had remained closed, despite the fact that the processes of globalization were already underway elsewhere across the globe. The decision to keep Indian markets closed had been made mainly because the Government of India had hoped in this way to be able to strike a balance between economic development and social justice. The government's epoch-making policy shift caught industry and its leaders off guard, and for a few years they were a little dazed by the situation. It was in this context that my research on Spirituality and Management in India took place. Until then – and even now, to a considerable extent – spirituality and business were considered two separate disciplines. Spiritual pursuits were considered the domain of one's personal beliefs and acts. Consequently, spirituality in business or industry was generally confined to philanthropic activities like the construction of temples and providing amenities to the public.

The following sections offer, first, an abridged version of the study conducted in 1997–98 with the involvement of a dozen select academics and management professionals known for their interest and involvement in the field, and second, details of a short update of the study undertaken in 2012 with the involvement of three eminent persons as respondents to certain questions. A summary and conclusions are offered with special reference to the Spandan Approach.

Spirituality and Management in India[1]

THE GLOBAL SCENARIO

> *Never before was man so educated yet so ignorant; so profusely equipped yet so insecure; so much in plenty, yet in such penury; so highly civilized yet morally so low.*
>
> – *Swami Tathagatananda, Ramakrishna Mission, Calcutta, India, 1996*

The world at large is at a crossroads. The ingenuity and intellectual abilities of human beings can achieve remarkable heights in science and technology, resulting in incredible developments in those aspects of human living related to materialism. Tragically, however, the spiritual and humane abilities of humankind are not utilized to a corresponding degree. Consequently, we are

---

1   This section is comprised of an edited and abridged version of G.P. Rao, Spirituality and Management in India (unpublished research study, 1998).

unable to understand, much less take control of, ourselves and the others with whom we live and work. As the celebrated behavioural scientist Elton Mayo stated, we can achieve high technical skills but have very low social skills. The wide and deep chasm between the maximum utilization of human intellect resulting in materialism and the almost dismal utilization of our spiritual and humane abilities resulting in insecure human beings is the real tragedy of today. We are now therefore at the crossroads, not knowing what to do next: How do we ensure that the undesirable consequences of industrialization, urbanization, technological development etc. are in future arrested? What can we do to help human beings understand themselves and others better, such that the insecurity that haunts them is in future minimized? How, in brief, do we bridge the gap between the disproportional utilization of the human intellect and the human spirit such that human endeavour achieves not only prosperity but also peace for ourselves as well as others.

The Club of Rome provides an example of human endeavour attempting to achieve such a balance between materialism and spiritualism. Formed by a small group of individuals from ten countries at Rome in 1968, the Club has become an important institution dedicated to an understanding of the global system. According to the Club, a human is considered not only a biological organism, or an economic unit, but all its manifestations: 'Man is a spiritual and rational creature, a playful one, an artistic and dreaming one: we consider him in the work span of his personality and not just as a body and a customer' (Meadows 1974).

Understandably, management as a profession and the manager as a professional are at a point of dilemma. Management as a profession is age-old, yet management as a discipline, as an area of study and as an educational process, is only a century old. During this hundred or so years academicians, thinkers and researchers have occasionally collaborated with practitioners in management to try to develop theories, techniques, models in the different spheres of organization and management in order that organizations can become effective in contributing towards the well-being of society while also meeting the needs of their employees. This odyssey started with scientific management and moved on to human relations theory, socio-technical systems and systems approach, contingency theory and so on. Some of the major related aspects of management on which such theorizing has focused are motivation, leadership and managerial effectiveness. However, we are still not in a position to offer any theory of organization, leadership and motivation that can stand the tests of time and place. The primary reason for this, I believe, lies in the fact that we have been laying greater and greater emphasis on the utilization of intellect:

Science and Technology → Materialism → Higher Standard of Living
(society being the beneficiary)

and failed to attain corresponding, concurrent progress in the utilization of human spiritual abilities:

Self Understanding and Empathy → Spiritualism → Higher Standard of Life
(humans being the beneficiaries)

In other words, the head won, over the heart.

The enormity of the problem can be better gauged by taking cognizance of the far-reaching consequence of industrialization that is the division of society into managers and the managed. As Alexander Lindsay, the British philosopher put it,

> *Industrialism has introduced a new division into society. It is the division between those who manage and take responsibility and those who are managed and have responsibility taken from them. This is a division more important than the division between the rich and the poor. (Quoted in Andrews 1989, p. 60)*

In this context, achieving a balance between organizational goals and the individual's needs becomes much more formidable.

THE INDIAN CONTEXT

Such a dilemma – the dichotomy between the head and heart of management, and between theories and practices – is much more acute in India primarily because of the historical necessity – in the absence of models of management developed in the country – of having to teach and use models developed abroad – in the West and then Japan. Since, however, management by definition is situational, attempts at the transplantation of theories of leadership and motivation from one culture to another are bound to fail – as happened in India.

It must, however, be noted that academicians and practitioners in management in India – as elsewhere – have of late realized the need to find a better balance between the head and the heart in management theories and practices. Looking back at the growth of management and management education in India, particularly following the establishment of the first two Indian Institutes of Management (at Ahmedabad and Calcutta) in the early 1960s, which signalled the commencement of professionalism in management education in the country, it is clear that such efforts have accelerated. The early 1970s, for example, saw the publication of a doctoral thesis on consciousness management based on the fundamental spiritualism of oneness, by academician Gary Jacobs. Academicians started looking into the Indian ethos to develop models of management and leadership suitable for the country with a special emphasis on value systems. Indian concepts emanating from Indian scriptures and other ancient writings came to the fore – for example, *karma yoga* (doing one's best without hankering for recognition and reward), *guru shisya parampara* (the mentor–disciple tradition), yoga, transcendental meditation, and an emphasis on one's duty (*dharma*) rather than rights. Finally, attempts were initiated, that have been gaining ground over a period of time, to develop course structures and content, with instruments of learning including cases, problems, theories and techniques based on Indian situations, as the basis for and elements of a typical MBA programme.

BRIDGING THE GAP BETWEEN DESIRABILITY AND PRACTICABILITY

The first part of this section described in brief the increasingly felt need at the global level for the societies and organizations to become more altruistic and spiritual in their approaches such that a proper balance between heart and head can be restored and maintained. The second part offered an outline of the role and relevance of spiritualism in management and management education in India. This part deals with two specific issues emanating from the preceding discussion. The first is to understand the extent to which management professionals desire and practise a spiritual approach in their personal lives and in their careers. The second relates to how the gap between the desirability and practicability of adhering to spirituality, if any, can be minimized through suitable steps in the work situation and through the instruments of management education, that is teaching, research, training and consultancy.

The gap between desirability and practicability

In 1995–6, as Sir Ratan Tata Visiting Fellow at the Indian Institute of Management, Calcutta, I conducted a research study on 'Human Values in Industrial Organizations' (Rao 1996), with the aim of addressing this issue.

The study involved 396 respondents – including 37 non-Indians – comprising managers, supervisors, faculty, students and administrators, all of whom answered a questionnaire which was supplemented with interviews. Of the 396 respondents 349 were male, 47 female. The objective of the study, among others, was to examine the desirability and practicability of applying human values accorded by respondents in their personal lives and their work situations. Material Comforts–Spiritual Pursuits was one of the 21 value dyads covered in the study.

The study's findings can be summarized as:

1.   Spiritual Pursuits was perceived as a more desirable human value than Material Comforts in personal value systems, particularly by non-Indian respondents.

2.   Material Comforts was perceived as one of the top three human values practised in industrial organizations, while Spiritual Pursuits was perceived as one of the bottom three.

3.   Certain subtle significant differences were discernible nationality-wise and gender-wise.

4.   The lack of ability to translate into action what is perceived as desirable appears to be quite substantial.

Bridging the gap

The issue of bridging the gap between the desirability and practicability of spirituality in management was addressed in a brief study I conducted which aimed at:

a)   understanding the meaning given by select experienced practitioners and academicians on spirituality as a value in the work situation and as a managerial value,

b)   knowing the extent to which they are able to practise spirituality in their personal lives and their work situation,

c)   seeking their suggestions for making a spiritual approach in management more practicable based on their experiences,

d)   understanding the nature and extent of coverage of spirituality in management teaching, research, training and consultancy in the educational institute in which the respondents are working,

e)   seeking their suggestions for inculcating human values including spirituality in the different components of management education as above, and

f)   examining whether the human values in spirituality could be inculcated elsewhere.

The study involved 12 respondents comprising six academics-cum-academic administrators and six practitioners. Their mean age was 55 years with a range of 39 to 74 years; and their mean work experience was 32 years with a range of 13 to 50 years. The following offers an overview and samples of the responses in each of the areas covered.

a)   Meaning of spirituality

Item (b) 1 in the questionnaire was:

A dictionary defines spirituality as 'the state or quality of being concerned with spiritual matters'.

According to me, spirituality

(i) in work situations means: _____
_____

(ii) as a managerial value means: _____
_____

The perceptions of the respondents, understandably, had a wide range, on both spirituality in work situations and spirituality as a managerial value. Some of the responses suggested: spirituality in work situations is in essence 'focusing on work' with sincerity, dedication and concentration; relating one's own work to the supreme/divinity is a complementary dimension to this; the concept of *karma yoga* as enunciated in the *Bhagavad Gita* can be seen as the essence of spirituality as a managerial value – the concept denotes that one should do one's best in achieving the given task without craving any fruits from the completion of the task; 'Compelling Humanism' is another insightful meaning given to spirituality as a managerial value.

b)   Desirability and practicability

Table 19.1   Spirituality: its desirability and practicability in one's personal life and work situations (N=12)

Desirability/Practicability	One's Personal Life		One's Work Situations	
	Range	Mean (N=12)	Range	Mean (N=12)
Desirability	8–10	9.5	4–10	9.2
Practicability	6–10	8.4	2–10	7.2

Table 19.1 reveals that, in one's personal life, the desirability of spiritual pursuits is 9.5 (out of a possible maximum of 10), but the extent to which they are practicable is 8.4. In the case of one's work situations, the corresponding figures are 9.2 and 7.2 respectively. One can thus discern that:

1.   the ability of respondents to practice spiritual pursuits is lower than what they consider desirable with reference to their personal and work lives; and,

2.   both the desirability and practicability of engaging in spiritual pursuits are lower in work situations than in one's personal lives.

c)   Suggestions for making spirituality more practicable in management

•   Cognitive level:

   –   'Regular reading of a page or two of the writings of a great soul keeps inner motivation alive.'

•   Conation – Individual level:

   –   Meditation and yoga (n=3)

   –   Practising humanism (n=2)

- Conation – Institutional level:

    – Systematic encouragement of the practice of a spiritual approach to management (n=2).

    – 'Some fear (legal or otherwise) is necessary for people to realize that ethical values are important for the overall wellbeing of society.'

d)   Role of spirituality in management education

The coverage of spirituality in human values in management teaching, research, training, consultancy and others as undertaken in the educational institutions where the academicians cum academic administrators are working. Propagation of human values and spirituality is undertaken through offering foundational courses, complemented by advanced studies to those interested. Similarly, seminars, conferences and interactive sessions are organized. Training is offered to professionals working in profit and non-profit organizations.

e)   Suggestions for inculcating human values including spirituality in management education

Respondents offered suggestions with reference to teaching, research, training and consultancy in management education. Meditation and yoga again came up as frequent and important suggestions in terms of teaching, research and training. Another important suggestion is that persons involved in all four aspects of management – teaching, research, training and consultancy – should be clear about the concerned aspects.

f)   Inculcation of human values including spirituality elsewhere

It was suggested that spirituality and other human values could be inculcated at the levels of family, school and college as well as work situations. In this regard, the family was considered the most potent force for inculcating the appropriate human values in a human being (N=8). According to one respondent, spirituality can be inculcated 'by practising morally coded affection, love and respect within the limited means of the family members.' School was also seen as an important factor in moulding the character of an individual (N=8). School teachers and parents are expected to be role models for their students and children respectively. The judgment of Justice M. Karoagavinayagam of the Madras

High Court in a case of ragging by a college student is relevant in this context: 'Teachers and parents should take a pivotal role in cultivation of human values in the minds of the younger generation. If education does not teach students to love all and serve all, education will become meaningless' (*The Hindu*, 9 November 1997). In work situations, it was suggested that institutionalizing spirituality and other human values in an organization must be supported by the unstinting commitment of the management. Neighbourhood and social and cultural organizations were perceived as other contributory factors in inculcating human values, including spirituality, in managers.

POLICY IMPLICATIONS

Spirituality in management – implying, as one respondent in the study said, 'Compelling Humanism' – is not only desirable but also necessary if managers the world over are to realize their felt need to translate their desirability and willingness into practicability and action. The task needs to be addressed and undertaken jointly by both management and management education. Policy implications include:

- Management profession: commitment and support from top management in making the inculcation of spirituality and other human values an on-going institutionalized activity.

- Management education: 'These issues tend to be absorbed if participants experience the values in the social organization of the institution.' Experiential learning is to be the pivot; yoga/meditation/mind-stilling exercises are to be the instruments at the cognitive and conative levels.

- Education at school and college levels: the school level needs to be more effective in view of the age and the stage of growth of the students. Teachers are to be role models; yoga, meditation, ethics and moral science are to be incorporated in the curricula.

- Family: family is perhaps the most effective and enduring force. Value orientation and implementation is to be a way of life. The neighbourhood is also important.

India could perhaps play a subtle but decisive role in the process because of its rich spiritual past and the continuity of spiritualism into the modern age via seers such as Swami Vivekananda, Ramakrishna Paramahansa and Mahatma Gandhi. This discussion on spiritualism and management could perhaps best be summed up and concluded by quoting Mother Teresa. Addressing a National Convention organized by the Calcutta Management Association in 1979, Mother Teresa stated:

> It is you who hold the responsibility of the vocations in your organizations, hold the lives of many people. But how much do you know your people. It is something that you owe to god for these people have been entrusted to your care. The reason for a manager knowing his people as a prelude to loving and serving them is that, maybe just right there in your office, in your home, there may be somebody who feels unwanted, unloved uncared.

She then added:

> Management is a great work because it involves dealing with people and people need love and compassion. It is not enough just to pay them a job. It is something more than you would need to have and respect for the person working with you and for you, for that person is your brother, and your sister. (Mother Teresa 1979)

The Present-day Scenario (2012)

AN UPDATED STUDY (N=3)

The following responses were given by three eminent persons to the same question on the meaning of spirituality as detailed above, that is:

> A dictionary defines spirituality as 'the state or quality of being concerned with spiritual matters'.
>
> According to me, spirituality
>
> (i) in work situations means: _____
> _____
>
> (ii) as a managerial value means: _____
> _____

Respondent 1

(i) In work situations means: Seeing unity in diversity, and accepting all people, situations, and circumstances, both good and bad, as a manifestation of God.

(ii) As a managerial value means: The ability to interact and make managerial decisions based on Truth, Righteousness, Peace, Nonviolence, and Love because the manager understands that everything is a manifestation of God. As a result, the manager will be compelled to 'Love All, Serve All', to 'Help Ever, Hurt Never', because he/she has the right vision, i.e. the manager prays with his/her eyes open, or essentially sees God in everything.

Respondent 2

(i) In work situations means: Complete commitment to one's work.

(ii) As a managerial value means: Creating confidence and making the work interesting.

Respondent 3

Dictionary defines spirituality as 'the state or quality of being concerned with spiritual matters'. This definition is sadly inadequate. According to me, spirituality

(i) In work situations means: Spirituality in all situations means the same. Humans cannot be someone or some state at work and in another state while not at work. Values reside in the depth of the iceberg of the subconscious brain. Ability to do something about housing such values by regulating responses, taking and acting upon decisions lies in the frontal brain. We take the same brain to work or play.

Spirituality: The ability to step away from the self and view situations in a detached way.

That is [the definition] according to me. This definition has its base in neuroscience.

(ii) As a managerial value, spirituality means: As a managerial value spirituality, as defined above, is a palpable asset. A spiritual person acts with fairness, transparency, empathy and balance. The ability to view oneself objectively motivates inner discipline. Discipline involves restraint, appropriate responsibility, adaptability and balance which are visible traits which quickly earn respect and compliance from others.

Spirituality helps people to live with mindfulness. Mindfulness results in Presence. Authentic Presence is essential to Leadership.

One could note a sea-change in the perception of what constitutes spirituality in work situations and as a managerial value.

Spirituality, Sustainable Development and Earth Governance

Traditionally, spirituality has been perceived as a matter of personal faith and religious outlook. Spiritual pursuits were accordingly confined to the room of worship, known in India as the *puja* room. With an increasing spiritual orientation, beginning from the West in particular, more managers are becoming spiritualistic. This is reflected in their growing realization that human effort, howsoever sincere and hardworking it might be, may not always yield the desired results. There is a supreme power – called Lady Luck, Destiny, Fate, Predetermination theory. The essence is a growing belief in divine power. This is in stark contrast to the concepts of scientific management, operations research, and management by results, which assume the supremacy and infallibility of the human intellect, logic and reasoning. Situational leadership theory, however, came very close to accepting that situations may at times overshadow human intelligence.

Furthering the implications of situational leadership on the limits of the leader and combining the concept of *karma yoga* as applicable to the manager as a professional (see Chapter 10), I wish to offer, in the following chapter, the Spandan 51:49 leadership philosophy, which aims at understanding further the boundaries and limits mutual to the leader and to those being led within the matrix of an enterprise, organization or institution.

Another area in which spirituality is leading the world is sustainable development, along with its sister concept of earth governance. Worshipping God, acts of charity, philanthropy and the recently initiated 'Giving Pledge' are current manifestations of spiritualism. The increasing degradation of the world's natural resources due to human greed has reached a stage where the virtual collapse of the earth and its inhabitants has become imminent. Worshipping the earth, the conservation of resources, restoration of the ecological balance and sustainable development are considered at least equally important tasks and priorities for humankind. The relevance and need for adherence to the Spandan Spectrum Transformational Human Value, 'Respect for nature and Mother Earth – Sustainable development' (no. 31) can hardly be exaggerated.

It may in this context be noted further that the importance of an ecological balance was very much in evidence in the past throughout the world – and to tribals the world over even today. The respect shown to all animate and inanimate beings, and the care taken to preserve them is amazing – and worthy of emulation by the so-called civilized world.

References

Andrews, Kenneth Richard (ed.). 1989. *Ethics in Practice: Managing the Moral Corporation*. Boston, MA: Harvard Business School Press.

Birla, Rajshree. 2011. Spirituality: A Way of Life. *Speaking Tree* (*Times of India*), 20 December.

Jue, Arthur L. 2007. The Demise and Reawakening of Spirituality in Western Entrepreneurship. *Journal of Human Values*, 13 (April): 1–11.

Learue, Gerald A. 1998. Human Values for the 21st Century. *Humanism Today*, 12: *Globalization and Humanism* (North American Committee for Humanism). [Online.] Available at: http://www.humanismtoday.org/vol12/larue.html [accessed: 29 July 2013].

Meadows, Donella H., Jorgen Randers, Dennis L. Meadows and William W. Behrens. 1974. *The Limits to Growth: A Report for the Club of Rome's Project on the Predicament of Mankind*, 2nd edition. New York: Universe Books.

Misra, Narayanji. 2008. *Better Management and Effective Leadership through the Indian Scriptures*. Delhi: Pustak Mahal.

Mother Teresa. 1979. Manager Must Remember (Address to Calcutta Management Association (CMA), Calcutta, India). *The CMA Newsletter*, October.

Pruzan, Peter et al. 2007. *Leading with Wisdom: Spiritual-based Leadership in Business*. Sheffield: Green Leaf Publishing.

Rao, G.P. 1996. *Human Values in Industrial Organizations: Feminine Perspective*. New Delhi: Sage.

—1998. Spirituality and Management in India. Unpublished research study.

Appendix: Spirituality as a Managerial Value

RESPONSE SHEET

1. Dictionary defines spirituality as 'the state or quality of being concerned with spiritual matters'.
    According to me, spirituality …

    a)   in work situations means: _____

    b)   as a managerial value means: _____

2. Spirituality, as understood above, I am able to adhere to …

    a)   in work situations: — (out of 10)

    b)   as a managerial value: — (out of 10)

    c)   in my personal life: — (out of 10)

3. The occasions or incidents wherein I had adopted a spiritual approach in dealing with others in my career, along with the results/consequences, are as follows:

4. The steps I suggest for making a spiritual approach more effective in the management of organizations are as follows:

5. Any other comments, suggestions and insights:

20

Spandan 51:49 Leadership Philosophy: The Spandan Perspective

The Context and the Issue

Forty-seven of us who constituted the first batch of management students at the Indian Institute of Management, Calcutta (IIMC) were waiting in the classroom for the arrival of the teacher. A highly-experienced professional with equally impressive academic credentials, the professor came to the class. After exchanging pleasantries, he made the following statement:

(1) $B = f(I, S)$, where

B = (Human) Behaviour

I = Individual

S = Situation

In simple terms, the equation means that what a person does, or does not, depends upon the individual (self) and the situation (consisting of people, 'others' and the inanimate environment).

Further discussion brought out the following insights:

- Whether one does, or does not, depends upon the willingness or otherwise, and ability or otherwise, of the self and of others.

(2) $B = f (I (W, A), S (W, A))$, where
W = Willingness
A = Ability

- Whether one is willing or not, and whether one is able or not, depends upon the Knowledge (K), Skills (S) and Attitudes (A) one possesses.
  Knowledge: Awareness, *what*; Skills: Doing, *How*; and Attitudes: Predisposition to persons and issues, *why*.
  (3) $B = f (I (W, KSA; A, KSA), S (W, KSA; A, KSA))$, where
  K = Knowledge
  S = Skills
  A = Attitudes

- Attitudes being perhaps most important and most difficult to acquire, it becomes necessary that positive and strong attitudes are to be inculcated and adhered to. Strongly held positive attitudes are defined as values. Since the individual and others are human beings, it is human values – i.e. strongly held positive attitudes – which are to be identified (diagnosis), assessed (discovery) and inculcated (development). The inculcation of suitable human values, complemented by the appropriate knowledge and skills, thus becomes the critical factor in the modification of human behaviour. Behaviour modification, or remaking ourselves, is thus a function of (i) diagnosis, discovery and development of human values in the work ethic, and (ii) the transmission of quality education and skills development.
  (4) $B = f (I (W, KSA; A, KSA); S (W, KSA; A, KSA) \times K (QE), S (SD), A (3D HVs))$, where
  QE = Quality Education
  SD = Skills Development
  3D HVs = Inculcation of Human Values through the 3D Process of Diagnosis, Discovery and Development
  or
  Behaviour modification or remaking ourselves is a function of quality education, skills development and the inculcation of human values.
  (5) $BM, RO = f (QE, SD, 3D HVs)$, where
  BM = Behaviour Modification
  RO = Remaking Ourselves

- Since the inculcation of human values (3D HVs) is relatively more important but more difficult, equation (5) can be restated as:
  (6) BM, RO = f (qe, sd, 3D HVs)
  Lower case initials indicate the relatively lesser challenges to be faced in quality education (qe) and skills development (sd).
  By retaining RO and 3D HVs, and stating
  (7) RO = f (3D HVs)
  we come to the conclusion that remaking ourselves as human beings is largely dependent upon the inculcation of human values in an institution.

The issue therefore is how to move from

(1) B = f (I, S)

to

(7) RO = f (3D HVs)

The Spandan Approach, with its 3D Process of inculcation and Spectrum of Human Values – consisting of Transformational, Transactional and Terminal Human Values – becomes the catalyst in the transformation of human beings through human values.

This chapter explains the Spandan 51:49 leadership philosophy and its role in the Spandan Approach and other initiatives discussed in the book.

Leadership Behaviour: The Leader, the Led, the Organization and the Environment

Applying leadership behaviour to equation (1), B = f (I, S), we can see that

(8) LB = f (L, S), where

LB = Leadership Behaviour

L = Leader

S = Situation

LEADERSHIP IS RELATIONAL, SITUATIONAL AND A PROCESS

Relational

Between the leader and the led, in particular, and other work group members comprising superior(s), colleague(s) and peer(s).

(9) LB = f (L, l, s, c, p), where

L = Leader

l = led

s = superior(s)

c = colleague(s)

p = peer(s)

Situational

The organization, enterprise or institution is the immediate frame of reference; the organization being in its turn, a subsystem of society, the economy and the country.

(10) LB = f (O, S, G), where

O = Organization

S = Society

G = Government

A process

Leadership is a process of influence, of trying to modify the thought processes and actions of others. Two aspects of this process need to be considered here. First, when the leader is the focal person, her attempts will be to influence her team members (the led), in particular, and her other work group members (superior(s), colleague(s), peer(s) and others – within and outside the organization). However, the process of influence is reciprocal: just as the leader will try to influence others, others will also try to influence her behaviour. In this case, the others assume the role of focal persons.

Secondly, the process of influence – whether instigated by the leader, or by the led or others as focal persons – is affected by the organization, its objectives, management philosophy and work ethic. The nature and extent of the willingness and ability to influence exerted by the leader on others – and by others on the leader – is determined by the organization, its policies and practices, and by society and the government of which the leader, led, others and the organization are a part.

Leadership effectiveness, as a process, is thus a function of the relational (equation 9) and situational (equation 10) dimensions of the environment within which the leader functions.

The Spandan Perspective on the Leadership Process and its Effectiveness

After stating in equation (1) B = f (I, S) that human behaviour is a function of the self (Individual) and the environment (Situation) within which the leader operates, and having incorporated Willingness and Ability (W, A), Knowledge, Skills and Attitudes (K,S,A), and Human Values as strongly-held positive attitudes (3D HVs), we arrived at equation (7) RO = f (3D HVs), which stated that in the ultimate analysis remaking ourselves (RO) is determined by the nature and extent of the inculcation of human values in a given organization complemented by quality education and skills development.

We may restate equation (7), with reference to leadership and its effectiveness, as:

Equation (11): LE = f (Relational (I), equation 9; and, Situational (O, S, G), equation 10), where

LE = Leadership Effectiveness

I = Individual

O = Organization

S = Society

G = Government

The attempt here is to understand further, along with the role of the Spandan 3D Process, the role of the Spandan Spectrum of Human Values in the Spandan Approach being the catalyst for a leader or manager to develop as a Spandan 51:49 leader.

The Spandan Spectrum of Human Values 2011 and Leadership

The Spandan Spectrum aims to identify an inventory of human values considered suitable for an organization to adhere to in order to maintain an optimal balance between results and relations as a means to evolve into a Functionally Humane Organization (FHO). As such, the Spandan Spectrum of Human Values 2011 has developed into an inventory of 33 human values, divided into three categories: Transformational, Transactional and Terminal.

Chapter 8 discussed Transformational Human Values. These are fundamental human values that deal with (a) human beings in relation to other human beings (Transformational HVs – I), and (b) human beings in relation to Mother Earth and the universe (Transformational HVs – II). The former group consists of three human values: faith in the basic goodness of others (no. 4), belief in the innate divinity in human beings (no. 5) and belief in the intrinsic altruism of human beings (no. 6). The inculcation of and adherence to these three values by human beings includes leaders, the led and others within and outside the given organization. Such inculcation by all concerned is expected to modify their perception, attitudes and motivation such that their mind-set accepts the idea that human dignity, divinity, self-respect and respecting others is normal in all of us. This results in mutual respect and trust, which is the pivot on which the very existence, not to speak of the growth and development, of an organization depends. The proposition here, therefore, is that adherence to these values provides an adequate relational basis (equation 9) for an effective leadership process.

Equation no. 9:

(9) LB = f (L, l, s, c, p), where

LB = Leadership Behaviour

L = Leader

l = led

s = superior(s)

c = colleague(s)

p = peer(s)

can therefore be restated as:

LB (Relational) = f (Transformational HVs – I)

Transactional Human Values are those human values which enable human beings, in their different roles, to evolve functional and humane transactions and interactions with others. Chapters 9–12 and 14 dealt with the Transactional Human Values with reference to the manager as a human being – personal values (Chapter 9) – the manager as a professional – professional values (Chapter 10) – management and groups – group-oriented values (Chapter 11) – management and organizations – organizational values (Chapter 12) – and management and globalization – globalization-induced values (Chapter 14).

Chapter 13 dealt with the process needed (Spandan 3D Process) and the type of leadership required (from the Spandan Approach) with special reference to the adherence to Transformational Human Values – I as the bedrock of a Functionally Humane Organization. Figure 13.1 incorporated the concept of *karma yoga* (doing one's best, but not craving for recognition and reward) as the most effective role for any manager or leader. Accordingly, adherence to the four professional values is recommended for a manager assuming the role of a *karma yogi*. These are: equanimity (19), professional attachment towards the completion of the task (28), emotional detachment towards recognition and reward (15) and service orientation (32). The proposition here, therefore, is that the suitable leadership style in an organization (equation 10) is that of *karma yogi*.

Equation no. 10:

(10) LB = f (O, S, G), where

LB = Leadership Behaviour

O = Organization

S = Society

G = Government

may therefore be restated as:

LB (Situational) = f (Professional Values (*karma yogi*))

Equation (11) combined equations (9) and (10) thus:

(11): LE = f (Relational (I), equation 9; and Situational (O, S, G), equation 10)

When restated with reference to leadership, equation 11 would be:

LB Relational = f (Transformational HVs – I)

LB Situational = f (Professional Values (*karma yogi*))

To sum up, Spandan 51:49 leadership consists of:

1.   the inculcation of and adherence to Transformational Human Values – faith in the basic goodness, belief in the innate divinity and belief in the intrinsic altruism of human beings; and

2.   *karma yoga* adopted as the management style, which means adherence to the professional Transactional Human Values – equanimity, professional attachment towards task completion, emotional detachment towards recognition and reward, and service orientation.

The Significance of 51:49

When Transformational Human Values – I and professional human values are adhered to by the leader, the led and the organization, the assumption is that this will result in the leader and the led doing their best voluntarily. The question, however, is what does 51:49 in the Spandan leadership philosophy mean and what is its significance. When, both the leader and the led are doing their best, their relative contributions to the completion of the task or achievement of the objective can be understood in terms of three possible ratios:

1. Leader contribution being higher than that of the led:
    >50 : <50

2. Leader contribution being the same as or similar to that of the led:
    50 : 50

3. Leader contribution being lower than that of the led:
    <50 : >50

Of the three possible relative contributions, the leader contribution being lower than that of the led (ratio no. 3) is certainly not desirable. The leader contribution being the same as or similar to that of the led (ratio no. 2) indicates that in terms of competence, knowledge, skills and attitudes, the leader is no different to the led, his subordinates and the work group. In that situation, the leader might have been designated as a superior, but is not perceived as such by others. Thus, the leader contribution under the Spandan Approach, based upon adherence to the transformational and professional human values, should be higher than that of the led (ratio no. 1). The gap should not, however, be too large and for long periods. This would mean that the leader needs to re-examine his or her mentoring role.

The Spandan 51:49 Leadership Philosophy: A Response

While working on the concept of the Spandan 51:49 leadership philosophy, I prepared a note, and asked my former students to consider its meaning and message. The note read:

> *Behaviour is a function of Individual and Situation.*
>
> *   *By vs. Through*
>
> *   *Every saint has a past; and every sinner a future*
>
> *   *Human beings as antennae*
>
> *   *Agricultural approach*

- *Lord Anjaneya, Hanuman, Bajrangbali (character in the* Ramayana)

- *You cannot motivate others*

IN SEARCH OF THE SPANDAN 51:49 LEADERSHIP PHILOSOPHY: A RESPONSE FROM G. REVATHI, PROFESSOR, CHENNAI, INDIA, 11 APRIL 2012

If leaders had sole responsibility for their subordinates' behaviour or performance, these latter would be machines, not humans. On the other hand, if every individual employee was solely responsible for his behaviour there would be no need for leaders. In reality, although every human being has immense potential, many often do not know how to unlock it. Hence a person's performance requires both his own individual effort as well as leadership that helps him tap his potential: leadership that lets him know that there is always hope even when one has failed, that success is often achieved after many failures. Leadership is thus the differentiating factor that changes sub-standard performance into mediocre, and mediocre into excellent performance.

Such changes can be brought about in the short-term through the use of traditional extrinsic motivators. Transactional leaders use a quid-pro-quo psychological contract. However for sustained or long-lasting change, there needs to be a shift in one's beliefs and value systems. Such intrinsic motivation can be achieved by transformational leaders who inspire people to change from within. Thus, with not just the right facilities and resources, but with the right guidance and inspiration, every person – even one who is currently under-performing – has the capability to excel.

Nurturing and inspiring leaders would not therefore look at a 50:50 leader–follower relationship, as that would be transactional. They would believe that it is the leader's responsibility to always give more than the follower: *to be always one step ahead, to anticipate needs and provide appropriate support, to be patient and forgiving when the follower makes mistakes, to inspire him when his confidence fails, and to help him discover his potential and channelize it in the right direction. Most importantly, the leader has to be the change that he desires to see in his subordinate. He has to become a role model for the follower to emulate. That would be the best way to influence others – to 'walk the talk'; to be seen as practising what one preaches.*

But first, leaders need to be their own role models. When they feel unsure of their ability to do something, they need to motivate themselves. They need to tell themselves that with a little more effort they can cross the winning line. They need to remind themselves of past successes however small, and set those successes as benchmarks for each new effort.

Second, they should always remember that it is a small step backward from success to failure. Hence they should be ever-watchful for signs of complacency, and keep raising the bar to do better each time, and not worse.

Third, if in spite of their best efforts they do fail, they should try and try again. This would not only lead to attainment of the objective, but would make them role models of perseverance for others to follow.

51:49 Leadership Philosophy

My understanding of '51:49' is that it is not an exact proportion, but an implication that there should be more of the leader's contribution *(symbolized by 51 per cent) as compared to the follower's contribution (symbolized by 49 per cent) in order to obtain optimum performance from the follower. This means that while the follower's performance depends both on himself as well as on his leader, the latter's role is more vital.*

Hence leaders should be willing to give more *(in terms of nurturance and influence) than they* receive *(in terms of their subordinates' self-motivation and effort). Thus the philosophy of leadership:* not '50:50' but '51:49'.

Similar Approaches

WHOLESOME LEADERSHIP

This concept comes from a deep connection to the heart, and also exhibits skill in action. This gives a leader the courage to follow a large and an ethical vision. It allows him/her to enable others to act, because they

see the latent power and beauty hidden in each person; it helps them be
appreciative and encourage the unfolding of spirit.

—*Arun Wakhlu, Founder and Chairman, Spiritually inspired*
Leadership Education and Consultancy Firm,
Pragati Leadership Institute, Pune, India

MINDFUL LEADERSHIP

Mindful leadership is another leadership style and philosophy similar to that of Spandan's 51:49 leadership philosophy. The Harvard Business School has taken a lead in this direction, with Professor William George talking of when East meets West. Sean Silverthorne, introducing his interviewee, George, writes: 'Asian beliefs, philosophies and practices are influencing everything from the way we treat the ill to how we make cars' (Silverthorne 2010). Similarly, both East and West can benefit mutually through the concept of mindfulness. George explains:

> *Mindfulness is a state of being fully present, aware of oneself and other people, and sensitive to one's reactions to stressful situations. Leaders who are mindful tend to be more effective in understanding and relating to others, and motivating them towards shared goals. (Silverthorne 2010)*

George, significantly, has associated with Tibetan philosopher Yongey Mingyur Rinpoche in his activities on mindful leadership.

TRANSCENDENTAL LEADERSHIP

Mitch Maidique, Visiting Professor at Harvard Business School, developed a six-level, purpose-driven model of leadership ranging from sociopath to transcendent. One of the key concepts in this model comes in the form of a question to be asked of a leader: Whom do you serve? Yourself? Your group? Your society? The answer to this question often reveals more about leaders than knowing their personality traits, level of achievement, or whether they are 'transformational' or 'transactional' leaders.

The six levels of leadership are: sociopath, opportunist, chameleon, achiever, builder, and transcended. The sixth level leader, 'transcended', is so called because she transcends her political party, her ethnic or racial group, and even her institution. She focuses on how to benefit all of society. She is a 'global citizen', in the words of Howard Gardner's recent book, *Truth, Beauty, and Goodness Reframed*, who watches out not only for 'number one' but for the wider public as well. Nelson Mandela, the first black president of South Africa provides an excellent living example of transcendental leadership.

DISPERSED LEADERSHIP

The University of Exeter, UK, conducted a review of leadership theory (Bolden et al. 2003), based upon a review of the major theories of leadership developed so far. The review concludes with an introduction to the notion of 'dispersed leadership', and a description of the distinction between the process of leadership and the socially constructed role of leader. Not necessarily confined to organizational hierarchy, it is argued that anyone, anywhere could influence and become a leader:

> *The changing nature of work and society, it is argued, may demand new approaches that encourage a more collective and emergent view of leadership and leadership development and of sharing the role of leaders more widely within the organisation. (Bolden et al. 2003, p. 2)*

CORPORATE SUFI

The term 'corporate Sufi' appears at face value to be an oxymoron, yet when fully understood it is a profound concept. A corporate Sufi is a person who is business-centric, driven and productive but also heart-centred, principle-based and balanced. A concept developed by Azim Jamal (2005), the corporate Sufi takes a holistic view of life's meaning, seeking both material and spiritual advancement to become truly rich.

References

Advantage Ascent 2011: A Milestone in Leadership. *Times of India*, 28 December 2011.

Bhargava, Shivganesh. 2004. *Transformational Leadership: Value-based Management for Indian Organizations*. New Delhi: Sage; Response Books.

Bolden, R. et al. 2003. *A Review of Leadership Theory and Competency Framework*. Exeter: University of Exeter, Centre for Leadership Studies.

Cotterell, Arthur et al. 2010. *Leadership Lessons from the Ancient World*. New Delhi: Wiley India.

Gardner, Howard. 2011. *Truth, Beauty, and Goodness Reframed: Educating for the Virtues in the 21st Century*. New York: Basic Books.

George, Bill. 2011. Why Leaders Lose Their Way? *HBS Working Knowledge*, 6 June.

Jamal, Azim. 2005. *The Corporate Sufi*. Mumbai: Jaico.

——2012. *Corporate Sufi: Business, Balance and Beyond*. Mumbai: Jaico.

JRD QV (Quality Value) Award of the TATA Group of Companies. *The Hindu*, 1 August 1999.

Maidique, Mitch. 2011. Are You a Level Six Leader? *HBS Working Knowledge*, 6 July.

Nadkarni, Anant G. 2011. Enlightened Business. *The Speaking Tree* (*Times of India*), 21 December.

Nobel, Carmen. 2011. Looking in the Mirror: Questions Every Leader Must Ask. *HBS Working Knowledge*, 18 July.

Porter, Michel E. and Mark R. Kramer. 2011. Creating Shared Value. *Harvard Business Review*, January–February.

Pratap, Ram. 2009. *Gandhi and Management: The Paragon of Higher Order Management*. Mumbai: Jaico.

Schoemaker, Michiel et al. 2006. Human Value Management: The Influence of the Contemporary Developments of Corporate Social Responsibility (CSR) and Social Capital (SC) on Human Recourses Management (HRM). Contribution to the Proceedings of the 10th Annual Conference by the Reputation Institute, May 2006, New York.

Sheldrake, Peter and James Hurtley. 2000. The Good Manager in a World of Change. *Journal of Human Values*, 6(2) (October): 131–4.

Silverthorne, Sean. 2007. Growing CEOs from the Inside. *HBS Working Knowledge*, 14 November.

——2010. Mindful Leadership: When East Meets West, an interview with William W. George. *HBS Working Knowledge*, 7 September.

Smith, Raymond D. 2002. A Case for the Centrality of Ethics in Organizational Transformation. *Journal of Human Values*, 8(1) (January): 3–16.

21

The Spandan Approach, Perspectives and Initiatives: In Retrospect and Prospect

The Context and the Issue

The first effort to communicate to the academic fraternity the launching of *Spandan* as a foundation for the propagation and inculcation of human values in management and management education took place in 2002 (Rao 2002). The ten or so years since then has been full of experiences and experiments between and among the small group determined to do whatever possible to achieve the foundation's objective. Whatever the results, the efforts have always been memorable and rewarding. Earlier chapters, Chapter 3 in particular, proved how essential the Spandan Approach, its 3D Process and Spectrum of Human Values can be. The current chapter takes a retrospective look at *Spandan* to see what lessons can be drawn for the future from its insights and experiences.

Since the inception of *Spandan*, a certain issue has repeatedly grabbed our attention: the distance, difference or discrepancy between the admiration for and implementation of human values in action. At different fora of academicians, practitioners, professionals, leaders and entrepreneurs, the importance of human values in life is invariably acknowledged; and eagerness and interest is shown by one and all to improve upon the situation such that humankind moves from a value-less – or at best value-free – to a value-oriented society. The rub, though, comes when one is asked to prepare for and to start the process: the issues involved, the difficulties, the limitations, apprehensions at individual and institutional levels all make the task at best formidable, and at worst abominable.[1] The major focus of this chapter, therefore, is to try to understand the issues involved as perceived and experienced by individuals and institutions, to examine what attempts have been made to tackle these issues, and to consider what can and needs to be done in future in the light of the experiences gained so far.

This chapter has two objectives. One, to take a retrospective look at *Spandan* as a movement for the propagation and inculcation of human values in management, and thus draw lessons for the future. Two, to take stock of the *Spandan* perspectives and initiatives discussed in the book as a means for moving ahead.

Translating Admiration into Action: A Decade in Retrospect

The role of an 'agent', 'a facilitator', such as *Spandan* is to kindle self-awareness by creating conditions conducive to the purpose. As Vipin Dewan, a founder member of *Spandan*, states,

> *Market driven economies are focused on individualism and materialism. The quest for higher standards of living in every part of the world has weakened the emotional and social fabric of both the individual and society. Reversal of this trend is impossible. It will move ahead with ever-increasing acceleration and is required too to eliminate poverty, disease and destitution from the earth.*

> *How do we ensure that our moral and social values not only remain intact but are gainfully employed to achieve the desired economic goals? Spandan may have an answer! You could join the odyssey of an uncharted territory within you and your organization and discover an invaluable treasure.[2]*

---

1   Remarkably similar findings emanated from the author's earlier work on *Human Values in Industrial Organisations: Feminine Perspective* (New Delhi: Sage, 1996), completed as the Sir Ratan Tata Visiting Fellow at MCHV, IIM Calcutta. The findings, characterized as 'awareness unaccompanied by action', referred to the inability of a person to translate what he or she believes as desirable into practice – and, more often than not, doing exactly the opposite to what should have been done. The group of 396 respondents participating in the study felt that self-control was not one of the top 10 values most desirable in a work situation, but were honest enough to place controlling others as the highest value practised in industry. In other words, while we know what is good for us, we may in practice still end up doing exactly the opposite!

2   Vipin Dwan, personal email communication.

PREPAREDNESS AND NECESSARY CONDITIONS

Based on the assumptions and beliefs stated above, a process of values orientation has been – and still is being – evolved – the bedrock of which is *self-awareness, awakening and action* – at individual and institutional levels. Other related conditions necessary for engaging in an effective process of values orientation are:

1. *Top management/support* – To be active and offer facilitative leadership through, essentially, the core group.

2. *Core group* – Members representing different functional streams, levels and stakeholders (around a dozen in each organization). The roles of the core group are:

   a) to be the executive arm of the value orientation process;

   b) conducting feedback and other in-house research work;

   c) monitoring, reviewing and recommending suitable modifications to the top management on an on-going basis;

   d) functioning with an external facilitator and eventually becoming facilitator(s) on their own.

3. *Facilitators* – (honorary, full time and core group) – to be catalysts in the inculcation of values.

4. *Leading by example* – The only means of transmitting, teaching, propagating and inculcating values – to become the substance of the style of leadership.

5. *Integration* – of selected values, or cluster of values, with the system of selection, appraisal, training and career development.

6. *Networking* – between and among those involved in teaching, research, training and facilitation, and institutions.

Four major instruments have been so far evolved; three for propagation and one for inculcation (the latter is comprised of three elements).

PROPAGATION

1.   interactive sessions

2.   workshops on select themes

3.   seminar courses

INCULCATION OF HUMAN VALUES

1.   *Objectives and duration* – Human values anchored to the mission statement of the given organization, enveloping in its ambit: selection, appraisal, training and development, and the organization's culture and commitment. Seven to nine weeks duration, involving 16 to 20 contact days with *Spandan* as the facilitator to complete one cycle of the inculcation of human values.

2.   *Process* – The process involves a 3D approach consisting of diagnosis, discovery and development and is based on experiential learning. The core group plays the roles of executive arm, organizer of research, advisor to top management and change agent subsequent to the completion of the tasks of *Spandan* as the facilitator of the given cycle of inculcation.

3.   *On-going activity* – The core group, with *Spandan* making periodic visits, continues the process, which is to be understood as an ever-continuing activity.

IN RETROSPECT

Propagation

During the ten or so years of its existence, *Spandan* has organized around 200 interactive sessions involving 6,000 participants in different parts of India. These interactive sessions were mainly held at management institutions, industrial organizations and professional bodies such as local chapters of the All India Management Association (AIMA). The participants were academicians, professionals, entrepreneurs, industrialists, management students, consultants and social workers. The purpose was to spread the message and mission of **Spandan**. While the purpose was propagation, the assumption was that it might lead some organizations to explore the idea of inculcating values as a means to develop their work ethic, culture and organization.

In addition, half-day or one-day workshops on themes relevant to the given industrial organizations and management institutions numbering around ten and 20 each were conducted.

Thirdly, a seminar course of 20 sessions was offered to two succeeding batches of management students at a management institution in New Delhi.

Inculcation

Three industrial organizations and one large government research institution in northern India have completed the process of one cycle of the inculcation of values lasting a year or so. An IT-related organization has completed one cycle, and is continuing the process as an on-going activity. At present an industrial organization in Mysore, one in Andhra Pradesh and two in the NCR (National Capital Region) are going through the process of inculcation. It is perhaps significant that the Andhra Pradesh Police Academy has initiated the process recently with the objective of involving police officials throughout the state.

An assessment

In the first three years of its existence, when we first took stock of its progress, it was difficult to decide the extent to which *Spandan* had fulfilled its mission of the propagation and inculcation of human values. As stated, 200 organizations and professional bodies have now been addressed at interactive sessions and 30 workshops held. At all of these events there was widespread appreciation of the concept and effort. Indeed on many occasions very senior functionaries became quite emotional over the failure of humankind to progress in terms of value orientation. The irony, however, is that out of 230 organizations, only four opted to undergo the process of inculcation. Considering the several limitations within which it has to function, *Spandan* could only do its best. Considering, however, the importance of the task it has undertaken, the professional potential it has within, and the endless need to propagate, inculcate, sustain and continue the odyssey of values orientation in society, *Spandan*'s contribution is only a drop in the ocean. The purpose of declaring this rather limited achievement is not to be defeatist, but to indicate the vastness of the opportunities beckoning us to carry on. The following part of this chapter, accordingly, addresses what can be considered the key issue in triggering the process of values orientation: translating admiration into action and inculcation.

THE TASK AHEAD: TRANSLATING ADMIRATION INTO ACTION AND INCULCATION

The requirement now is to examine what can be done to translate admiration for the concept of values orientation into sustained activity at individual and institutional levels – preceded, understandably, by a look at the possible deterrents to taking up the process. Based on the experience gained so far, such deterrents could broadly be viewed as:

- extra-organizational or environmental

- intra-organizational – related to systems and structures

- transformational or inherent in the process of the inculcation of human values, as woven into the fabric of the given organization with its mission as the anchor.

While all three are equally important, greater focus will be placed on the third – that is, the issues inherent in the very approach adopted as outlined under the necessary conditions.

Environmental factors

Globalization, for example, characterized by 'cutting edge' competition, in particular where the sole focus becomes output – that is, a tangible, measurable and saleable output in terms of goods and services – is one important environmental factor. Three entrepreneurs from the IT and related industries, although keen to experiment with the inculcation of values in their enterprises, could not initiate the process because of the extreme pressure and competition in India and from abroad under which they are functioning.

Organizational factors

1. indifference, apathy, suspicion and cynicism from top management and concerned coordinating departments – particularly when the process requires overhauling the total system in terms of attitudes and values;

2.   lack of required interest and motivation in training in general, at all levels in the given organization;

3.   the effectiveness of transformational change processes will only be perceived after a period of time, yet top management fails to be patient and perseverant enough to see the process through, and thus shuns the budgets required for such activities.

Transformational factors – specific to the Spandan Approach

A perusal of the conditions necessary for the effective inculcation of values indicates that three critical determinants are: (1) top management role and support, (2) the core group, and (3) the integration of values with the mission statement and organizational policies and practices.

1.   *Top management role and support*: Since the inculcation of values needs (i) to envelop all members of the given organization, (ii) to be a continuous process and (iii) to be anchored to the mission statement and integrated with HRD and other policies and practices, the role of the top management becomes highly critical. While the lack of top management support is a limitation, too much support is equally to be avoided. When, in other words, the rank and file feel that the process of the inculcation of values is the management's 'baby', the total commitment and involvement of one and all – which is essential for the process to be effective – may be eroded and become limited.

Our efforts, however, have revealed that eliciting the required commitment from top management for the value orientation process, which lasts several months, is not easy. While they are appreciative of the concept of values and aware of the need to enrich their organization with suitable values, they appear unable to spare sufficient time for the interactive sessions with them and their senior colleagues.

Having initiated the process, top management find that any compelling issue needing their attention or requiring their presence elsewhere – mostly abroad – makes their availability for monthly core group meetings difficult.

Further, it is observed that, the initial novelty and euphoria of experimenting with an important idea and transformational process may wane over a period of time. This again, results in the reduced interest and involvement of the top management.

2. *Core group*: The core group, as noted, plays a very critical role in the process. A small, committed and competent group of functionaries representing the different segments of the organization constitute the core group. However, creating a core group that meets their satisfaction has not always been a straightforward task for the top management.

    First, the limitations applicable to senior management also apply – in varying degrees – to the members of the core group: that is, ensuring the value orientation process is not perceived as the management's 'baby'; being available to attend and participate in core group meetings; and sustaining the momentum of the process at an even and consistent level over a period of time.

    Second, core group members, like other senior functionaries, may feel that participation in *Spandan* meetings and undertaking fieldwork interferes in their regular duties and responsibilities.

    A more daunting task, however, is to create and maintain team spirit among the core group members and to harness the same for the achievement of the stated objective of creating an optimal balance between results and relations.

3. *Integration*: The aim of the value orientation process is *not* to create a spiritual organization but to enable the given organization to achieve its own stated objective(s) more effectively. Hence, the process requires the integration of values (i) with the mission statement, which becomes the anchor; (ii) with other functions of HRD – notably selection, appraisal, training and development, and organizational culture; and (iii) with other managerial functions requiring inter-unit, interdepartmental and intersectional cooperation and working together.

    Understandably, the required integration needs sustained and synchronized efforts at all levels as an on-going and never-ending process. A highly daunting, but challenging and rewarding odyssey!

Spandan Perspectives and Initiatives: A Synoptic View

The book started with an overview (Part I), where the essentials of the Spandan Approach, the Spandan 3D Process and the Spandan Spectrum of Human Values were presented.

Part II discussed the issue of human beings remaking themselves as human beings, deriving strength and inspiration from ancient wisdom and knowledge. How adherence to Transformational Human Values could be the bedrock of the process was emphasized.

Part III looked at the management contribution to remaking an enterprise or organization through human values. The role of the manager as a human being and as a professional, management and groups, management and organizations, management and globalization, and the corresponding Transactional Human Values – personal, professional, group-oriented, organizational and globalization-induced human values respectively – were dealt with. Concurrently, the relevant Spandan approaches were introduced. Experiential learning (Spandan Perspective I) as a key for improving upon interpersonal and work relations was underscored. The manager's role as a *karma yogi* (Spandan Perspective II), a concept emanating from the Indian philosophical treatise the *Bhagavad Gita*, was also outlined. It was suggested that a manager assuming the role of a *karma yogi* is an extension of the management credo of adherence to Transformational Human Values like faith in the basic goodness, innate divinity and intrinsic altruism of human beings.

As part of *Spandan*'s mission to facilitate management evolving a Functionally Humane Organization (FHO), four initiatives for remaking an enterprise and society were introduced, along with their application and the results achieved so far. These initiatives formed Part IV of the book. The first Spandan initiative relates to working towards the synergy of human values between India and the West (Chapter 15). The second deals with Institutional Civic Responsibility to Community through Human Values (ICRC-HVs) (Chapter 16). The third relates to the infusion of family values in management (Chapter 17).

Chapter 18 examined the fourth initiative of identifying efficiency-oriented and happiness-oriented Terminal Human Values. Human beings, in their different roles, at different times and on different occasions, have different objectives. It is postulated, however, that in the ultimate analysis, they gravitate towards two basic objectives: economic well-being and psychic well-being. Material comforts, profits, prosperity, a standard of living are aspects of economic well-being. Happiness, contentment, satisfaction and a standard of life represent psychic well-being. Material comforts and happiness are thus included in the Spandan Spectrum of Human Values as the two Terminal Human Values. It is, however, important to note that these terminal values are mutually exclusive. Indeed, human endeavour aims to strike a balance – an optimal balance at that – between them. Such balancing can be noted in any role a person assumes (Fig 6.1). The need, as a human being, is to find a balance between head and heart; as a professional, between professional attachment and emotional detachment; in an organization, between results and relations; in a society, between economic development and social justice; at the global level, between technology and culture; and at the level of an eco-system, between the use and replenishment of natural resources.

Part IV also considered spirituality and management (Spandan Perspective III) (Chapter 19), advocated as the Spiritual Democracy concept of Swami Vivekananda, for humanizing globalization. The present-day interpretation of spirituality, as going beyond one's own interests and working towards noble and deserving causes, was uncovered with the recognition that such intrinsic altruism may manifest itself in many forms. At the global level, however, Spiritual Democracy is advocated as a means of achieving and maintaining progress with peace as an enduring feature (Chapter 14).

The Spandan 51:49 leadership philosophy (Spandan Perspective IV), built upon the earlier approaches and initiatives, aims at an enduring balance between the task and emotional functions of the leader and the led based upon mutual respect and trust between them.

A synoptic view of the Spandan Approach, its perspectives and initiatives is presented in Table 21.1.

References

Rao, G.P. 1996. *Human Values in Industrial Organizations: Feminine Perspective.* New Delhi: Sage.

——2002. Spandan and the Integral Development of the Human Person: India Insights, Experiences and Experiments. *Journal of Human Values*, 8(1): 67–70.

Table 21.1   A synoptic view of the Spandan Approach, its perspectives and initiatives

	Spandan Perspective/ Initiative	Objective	Chapter(s)
1	Spandan (Heartbeat)	Belief in the innate divinity, faith in the basic goodness and belief in the intrinsic altruism in human beings: the credo of human existence and growth	8
2	Maternalistic management	Empathy of a high order: the willingness and ability of a manager to be sensitive to the needs and aspirations of others *even without being asked*	2
3	Spandan Perspective I: Experiential learning	Introspection by self and feedback from others for the purpose of diagnosing, discovering and strengthening the strength and weakening the weakness of each other	8 to 13
4	Manager as a Professional: Spandan Perspective II: Manager as *karma yogi*	Professional attachment towards completion of the task and emotional detachment towards recognition and rewards. This enables a manager to have equanimity in his or her disposition and to be able to take effective decisions	10
5	Functionally Humane Organizations	An organization with an optimal balance between results and relations, material comforts and happiness, and the head and heart	2
6	Towards a Functionally Humane Organization

Spandan Initiatives:
Synergy of human values between the West and India | To synthesize the Western scientific acumen of intellect of innovation with the Eastern wisdom of love and affection | 15 |
	Institutional Civic Responsibility to Community through Human Values (ICRC-HVs)	An institution's contribution to the community and society to be all-pervasive and independent of the size and objective of the given institution. All stake-holders to be involved in the process as democratic partners	16
	Infusion of Family Values in Management	Emphasis on obedience, loyalty and discipline of a family to be integrated with the functioning of the business such that the family instead of becoming a hindrance becomes a catalyst for organizational transformation	17
	Identifying and optimizing efficiency- (material comforts) and happiness-oriented human values	Terminal value 29: material comforts and 21: happiness or the generic objective of human interaction and activities. The purpose is to evolve an optimal balance between them such that the needed balance between results and relations is accordingly obtained	18
7	Spandan Perspective III: Spiritual Democracy	Humanizing globalization through Spiritual Democracy	19
	Spandan Perspective IV: Spandan 51:49 Leadership philosophy	The combination and culmination of the Spandan Approach, its perspectives and initiatives towards achieving the best from the led on the basis of mutual respect and trust	20
8	Back to Self: Gross Divinity Propensity (GDP)	Effective adherence to the Transformational Human Values enables a person to overcome human frailties, feel nearer to the oneness of the universe as a whole and draw closer to becoming an enlightened, inward-looking and self-contented entity	Epilogue Fig. 3.2

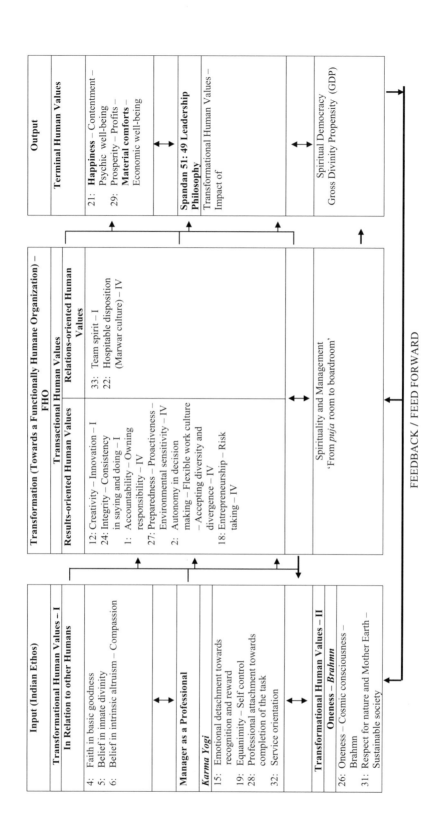

Figure 21.1   Remaking ourselves, enterprise and society: towards a Functionally Humane Organization – revisiting results and relations-oriented human values

Epilogue:
Back to Self: Gross Divinity Propensity (GDP)

Material comforts and happiness as Terminal Human Values in the Spandan Spectrum of Human Values owe their origin to the longing of human beings for, in the ultimate analysis, progress and peace, prosperity and tranquillity, and a standard of living and a standard of life (see Chapters 3, 18 and 21). The aim, therefore, is twofold: first, to work for their enhancement, i.e. increased material comforts and greater happiness; second, to maintain and improve the balance between them.

Human history reveals that individuals, institutions and countries alike accord relatively greater attention to and have relatively greater success attaining material comforts than happiness. Accordingly the measurement of economic development has been given greater emphasis than the measurement of happiness. A further reason for placing lesser emphasis on the measurement of happiness is the fact that happiness, being a psychic phenomenon, is harder to measure. It is laudable, then, that the Government of Bhutan has made remarkable contributions to the development of a Gross National Happiness (GNH) index based upon Buddhist theory as an index of national happiness.

Gross Domestic Product (GDP)

The human desire to know where one stands at a collective level has resulted in the development of, among others, (1) Gross Domestic Product (GDP), conceived in the United States in the 1930s; (2) Human Development Index (HDI), developed by the United Nations in the 1950s; and (3) Human Happiness

Index, developed by Bhutan in early 1970s and being improvised upon in the United Kingdom.

GDP is 'the measure of the market value of all the goods and services produced in the economy' (Kuznets 1934). The UN HDI includes GDP but adds other essentially non-financial criteria like literacy, political freedom etc. The Happiness Index apparently focuses on primarily the psychic dimension of happiness. Each index is an improvement over the other. All three and many other such efforts thus represent the continuing human endeavour to understand one's self at the national level better. It is in this context that the recent suggestion made by France and its President Nicolas Sarkozy that factors like quality of life and the environment should be given greater account is to be viewed.[1] The suggestion assumes greater significance when account is taken of the fact that it emanated from a panel of top economists, chaired by two Nobel Laureate economists, Joseph E. Stiglitz and Amartya Sen, constituted by France to review the adequacy of the current standard of fiscal well-being: GDP.

As can be noted, however, the ultimate in the growth of human beings lies in achieving and maintaining an ever-growing optimal balance between and among the different spheres of their existence. These include the economic, sociological, political, psychological, environmental and spiritual spheres. It is perhaps the last two – environmental, relating to sustainable development, and spiritual, resulting in altruism – that need to be attended to most. Manmohan Singh, an eminent economist and Prime Minister of India, for instance, stated: 'I think the respect for fundamental human rights, the respect for the rule of law, respect for multi-cultural, multi-ethnic, multi-religious rights, I think those have values.'[2] The list of values stated thus is quite comprehensive. What is important is that all of them relate to values between and among human beings. None of these values, for example, talks about the responsibility of human beings towards an environment consisting of other living organisms and the universe.

What is therefore needed is emphasis on a spiritual approach to the environment which over a period of time would result in what is known as Cosmic Consciousness or Universal Oneness. What in other words we need to look for is 'within' ourselves – 'within', beginning from intra self, and moving

---

1   Statement made by President Sarkozy at the unveiling of the Stiglitz Report in Paris on 14 September 2009, as reported in *The Times of India*, 16 September 2009.
2   Statement made by Prime Minister Manmohan Singh in Washington DC on 24 November 2009, as reported in *The Times of India*.

outwards to encompass self, group, community, country, world and ending with the universe. What we need to look for is the divinity, basic goodness and altruism innate to all of us at all these levels. What, accordingly, we need to strive for is the harnessing of these innate divine qualities for the good of ourselves, others and the universe. It is in this sense that the GDP could more appropriately be called Gross Divinity Propensity (GDP).

Figure 3.2 depicts Gross Divinity Propensity from the perspective of *Spandan*.

Gross Divinity Propensity (GDP) is integral to the Spandan Approach since all five Transformational Human Values reflect our grace light, which symbolizes the light of God or a powerful cosmic energy which has the power to change our lives. Hence, when we think of Gross Divinity Propensity (GDP), we have in fact gone back to self!

References

Heard, Gerald. 1963. *The Five Ages of Man*. New York: Julian Press.

Jensen, Michel, C. 2011. The Three Foundations of a Great Life, Great Leadership and a Great Organization. *HBS Working Knowledge (Working Paper)*, 28 July.

Kant, Immanuel. 1998. *Ground Work of the Metaphysics of Morality*, ed. Mary Gregor and Jens Timmermann. Cambridge: Cambridge University Press.

Khilani, Sunil. 2011. The Greatest Mystery. *The Times of India*, 19 December.

Kuznets, Simon. 1934. National Income – 1929–1932, 73rd US Congress, 2nd session, Senate Document No. 124, pp. 5–7.

Stiglitz, Joseph E., Amartya Sen and Jean-Paul Fitoussi. 2010. *Mismeasuring Our Lives: Why GDP Doesn't Add Up*. New York: The New Press.

Tyagi, Atul. 2011. Back to Basics, *The Speaking Tree (The Times of India)*, 28 July.

Index